Wonder and Loss

A Practical Memoir for Writing about Grief

Sam Meekings

BLOOMSBURY ACADEMIC
LONDON • NEW YORK • OXFORD • NEW DELHI • SYDNEY

BLOOMSBURY ACADEMIC
Bloomsbury Publishing Plc, 50 Bedford Square, London, WC1B 3DP, UK
Bloomsbury Publishing Inc, 1359 Broadway, New York, NY 10018, USA
Bloomsbury Publishing Ireland, 29 Earlsfort Terrace, Dublin 2, D02 AY28, Ireland

BLOOMSBURY, BLOOMSBURY ACADEMIC and the Diana logo are trademarks
of Bloomsbury Publishing Plc

First published in Great Britain 2026

Copyright © Sam Meekings, 2026

Sam Meekings has asserted his right under the Copyright, Designs and Patents Act, 1988,
to be identified as Author of this work.

Illustration by Gita Govinda Kowlessur
Leafless tree silhouette isolated on white background © Alamy

All rights reserved. No part of this publication may be: i) reproduced or transmitted in any form, electronic or mechanical, including photocopying, recording or by means of any information storage or retrieval system without prior permission in writing from the publishers; or ii) used or reproduced in any way for the training, development or operation of artificial intelligence (AI) technologies, including generative AI technologies. The rights holders expressly reserve this publication from the text and data mining exception as per Article 4(3) of the Digital Single Market Directive (EU) 2019/790.

Bloomsbury Publishing Plc does not have any control over, or responsibility for, any third-party websites referred to or in this book. All internet addresses given in this book were correct at the time of going to press. The author and publisher regret any inconvenience caused if addresses have changed or sites have ceased to exist, but can accept no responsibility for any such changes.

A catalogue record for this book is available from the British Library.

A catalog record for this book is available from the Library of Congress.

ISBN: HB: 978-1-3505-5076-6
PB: 978-1-3505-5077-3
ePDF: 978-1-3505-5078-0
eBook: 978-1-3505-5079-7

Typeset by Deanta Global Publishing Services, Chennai, India

For product safety related questions contact productsafety@bloomsbury.com.

To find out more about our authors and books visit www.bloomsbury.com
and sign up for our newsletters.

Contents

Introduction 1

Part I **Writing as discovery** 5

1 Beginnings 6

2 Writing into the dark 16

3 Setting myself on fire 27

4 Home/sickness 39

5 Ten ways of thinking about the body 49

Part II **Writing as transformation** 59

6 Palimpsest 60

7 Animal instinct 70

8 Metaphor 80

9 Transformations 90

Midpoint self-assessment 100

Useful resources for support 102

Part III **Writing as renewal** 105

10 Fable and myth 106

11 Personal ecology 115

12 The unknown 126

13 Dreams and the subconscious 135

14 Talking with ghosts 144

Part IV **Writing as magic** 157

15 Pleasures and passions 158

16 Poetic tools 169

17 Summoning 179

18 Endings 191

Conclusion 202

Bibliography 205

Index 207

Wonder and Loss

Introduction

Why wonder?

From a distance there's little to distinguish loss from wonder. Both untether us from logic. Both can nudge us just beyond the limit of our understanding. Grief has a strange, hypnotic quality, like true wonder. Both remind us that the world does not make sense, does not work the way we think it should.

Wonder and loss both offer the possibility of transformation, of seeing the world in a radically new way. We are not the same after loss. Never the same. But nonetheless we find a way forward. We have to – if for no other reason than that we owe it to the people we've lost to keep going, to keep finding joy and meaning and wonder in the world they have left behind.

This book is my journey. A journey of transformation through wonder and loss. A journey of breaking and remaking, of magic and memory and forging a way through the pain.

It is my story, but it is also a guidebook and an invitation. I am inviting you to come with me, to write along with me, to learn to do the same thing: to use writing to forge a way through grief. To both honour and record the wonder-filled memories of the person you are mourning, and to rediscover the person you are and can be.

Why me?

I have been broken apart by grief. My little brother – who I still thought of as *little* at twenty-four, when he was three inches taller and five inches broader and three stone bulkier than me – died suddenly, without warning, from a cardiomyopathy: a swollen heart that we never knew about until it was suddenly too late. I was broken apart by grief. I was two years older, and ever since he was born I'd been tasked with looking out for him. He was my accomplice in made-up games and imaginary battles and dress-up shenanigans and garden adventures, and as the years went by he was my main adversary too as we competed against each other at almost everything and knew exactly how to wind each other up to bursting point. We knew one another as well as we knew ourselves. On his drive home from work at a construction site he pulled over to the side of the road and collapsed in the driving seat. He never regained consciousness. I was broken apart by grief. I'd let him down. And I was remade too, yes, into something I no longer quite recognized.

I knew two things as I moved through loss and tried (and failed, and failed again, and kept failing and kept trying) to process what had happened and to keep going. One, that I wanted to record my journey at the most difficult crossroads I'd faced. I needed to share my grief journey and map out a path through the darkness, a way I might keep living my life without my brother. And two, that I wanted to document how much my brother meant to me, and to preserve my memories of him, while those emotions were fresh and raw and so frighteningly alive to me. I wanted to keep him alive in spirit, to honour, record and remember him.

In other words, this journey is deeply personal. But it is also rooted in research. As well as being an internationally acclaimed novelist and poet, I am a professor of creative writing. For the last decade I have been teaching writing courses while also researching writing and trauma. In one of my most recent research projects, I worked with a neuropsychologist to examine the links between narrative writing and exposure therapy that aids with recovery from deep-rooted trauma. Some of the results were clear: the stories we tell affect our health, our sense of self, our relationship with the world around us. One of the most important things we can do then is to take control of our own stories.

Why now?

We are living in an age where almost everything we can wish for lies no further than our fingertips. All you need to do is type a few details into a generative AI program (for instance, write me a novel in the style of Margaret Atwood about a dystopian society after an ecological disaster; write a frightening story in the style of Stephen King about a dark and haunting mystery) and then you can sit back and read the results. Why bother with the hard work of writing when algorithms can create an eighty-thousand-word novel in the time it takes to make a cup of tea?

Why bother at all anymore?

Because writing is about more than word count. More than plot, or character or setting. Because writing is, at the deepest level, about three fundamental things:

1. It is a way to share the unique and individual way each of us sees the world.
2. It is an act of communion and communication, a joining together, an intimate form of connecting with others.
3. It is a means of reflection, helping us to examine and explore our inner lives.

Writing about your own life, your own journey, means sharing your own personal story and reaching out to others. Both are things that AI, no matter how advanced it grows in the coming years, will never be able to replace. Right now, we need stories of what it means to be human more than ever.

No one can write your story – the story of who you are and the people you have loved – except you. This is your task. Take it seriously, because it is a responsibility for you and you alone. Take it seriously, but also revel in it. Because I hope together we will find the joy and pleasure in writing about even the most difficult experiences.

Why not?

Sharing your story requires honesty, openness and trust. So before we get going, I want to be clear about what this book is not.

This book is not a guide to fiction or craft. I won't list all the rules so beloved of writing textbooks and classes. I won't teach you how to write a story in ten easy steps, or how to structure a novel using the classical three-act framework. We will focus only on writing from real life, and bringing your own experiences to life on the page.

This book is not a guide to getting published. If your sole aim is getting published, I can't help you. I hope you'll become a better writer through this journey, but the goal here is to go on a journey and write through grief.

This book is not an alternative to therapy. I am not a therapist or a psychologist. Despite many easy soundbites, writing on its own is *not* therapy. It can certainly be therapeutic (as I believe this book will show), but I have no intention of making any grand claims or promises. I hope this book helps you to hold tight to the memories of the person you have lost while also moving forward and rediscovering your deepest, truest self – and I believe it will. But deep and persistent trauma requires more than just writing, so if you are struggling and feel you need help, I would urge you to talk to a professional.

Why you?

Because only you can write your story. Because only you can do it justice. Because you have memories and experiences that need to be preserved. Because there is something inside you that needs to be let out.

This book will take you on a journey, a search, a discovery, a path we will forge together. Each chapter is made up of several different sections:

1. My Journey: an account of one step in my own path through loss, diving deep into the world of grief and bereavement.

2. Reflection: a short explanation of the concepts, research and the process behind my own writing.
3. The 'How': writing tips, tools and techniques for writing about particular emotions, settings, memories, experiences and transformations, providing both the theories and ideas behind the writing advice and practical suggestions that you can implement straight away.
4. Prep: a short pre-writing exercise to get you thinking, reflecting or observing in preparation for sustained writing.
5. Write: a detailed and specific prompt that encourages you to write to a specific brief. These tasks include step-by-step guides to start, extend and improve your life writing.
6. Follow Up: a suggestion for how to revise and develop your draft.
7. Read: recommendations for further articles, stories, essays and web resources in case you want to explore the theme and topic of that chapter in even more detail.
8. Try: ideas for activities and actions to build into daily life to focus your writing and thinking process, as well as your engagement with the world around you.

None of the steps are mandatory. You can pick and choose as much as you like. If you only want to read about my own personal journey after my brother's untimely death, then you can just read the first section of every chapter, as they fit together into a larger narrative. Or if you wish to go through the writing prompts without pre-writing or following up, then they will still help you build your process and widen your skillset. In other words, you can do as much or as little as you like: you can tailor your own journey so it fits your own preferences, schedule and writing practice best.

Why wait?

Writing helps us make sense of life, of the strangeness and uniqueness of being in this strange and unique world. So why wait: come with me on this journey, and let's see how writing can help us learn and discover and remake.

Because writing really is a form of wonder, of tapping into the marvellous and strange magic of being in the world, of keeping memories fresh and alive. In this way, writing is empowering. Because it gives us power and control over our experiences and senses. Writing can help us rediscover ourselves.

PART I

Writing as discovery

The first five chapters will focus on ways into writing: how to begin without necessarily knowing exactly where you are going, how to cultivate a writing practice as a form of investigation and discovery, how to build successful beginnings and characters that are true to real life, and how to bring the past back to life.

Chapter 1
Beginnings

My journey

I was wandering through the local supermarket in search of a few odds and ends to cobble dinner together, when I saw my brother. Again. He was leaving one aisle just as I entered it from the opposite end. Though I only caught sight of the back of his head as he turned the corner, I had no doubt at all that it was him. I knew it, deep in the pit of my gut. He had the same red-flecked hair, the same languid and unhurried walk and, as always, the collar of his polo shirt turned up to cover the nape of his neck.

Without a second thought I hurried to try and catch up with him. A pair of doddering trolleys blocked my path at the corner, however, and by the time I'd forced my way between them, my brother was nowhere to be seen.

I considered calling out to him, of course, but I worried that any loud noise might break the spell and so make it impossible for me to find him among the high-stacked shelves. It's easy to set reason aside, but embarrassment isn't quite so easy to do without. I dumped my basket beside the breakfast cereals, abandoning the Merlot and bag of long-grain rice, and began to push past the slower shoppers, desperately searching each lane before rushing on to the next. I was jogging so fast that I almost stumbled and fell into a tall stack of buy-one-get-one-free cola bottles on display at the head of one of the aisles. Several times I ducked back upon myself, and more than once I returned to the dairy aisle for a second look between the stacks of milk and yoghurt.

Soon I was confused about which of the lanes I'd already been down and which I had yet to search. I was panting, my breath coming in ragged, and feeling as though I was trapped in some elaborate labyrinth and might remain lost within it forever. After completing my third or fourth circuit of the main aisles (I was starting to lose count), I decided that Luke had to be in the pasta section. It made perfect sense to me at the time, because for the last few years he had not only eaten pasta with almost every one of his meals but, in order to aid his obsessive desire to bulk up, he had also regularly eaten a large bowl of it as a snack after returning home from work or the gym. He wasn't fussy about it either: this wasn't al dente fresh fusilli, but rather sloppy and limp penne often dressed with nothing more than a quick squirt of ketchup.

Yet when I made my way to the pasta aisle, I discovered that it was completely deserted. I hovered there for a couple of minutes, waiting beside the packets of butterflies, spirals, corkscrews and ribbons.

After a while I started searching again. I turned left at the end of the aisle, then turned back on myself, then stopped. Which way had he gone? People were starting to stare. An old man with gummy jowls giving me the once over. A young mum with bored kids trailing behind her with the scanning gun. Maybe they thought I was drunk, out of my skull or in the middle of some manic breakdown? I didn't have time to worry about that.

Come on Luke, stop pissing about!

I made my way decisively down past the deli counters, but I was sure I'd been down here only minutes ago. The stark glare of the supermarket lights seemed designed to misinform the senses. It was impossible to tell whether it is the middle of the day or the darkest hour of night, and it soon occurred to me that, without either phone or watch, there would be no way of knowing how long I'd spent in pursuit of my brother.

Goosebumps spread across my arms. Soon the supermarket lights gave rise to the impression that the end of time had come and then passed and that this sterile place was all that remained of a forgotten civilization. Rows upon rows of tins and cans did nothing to alleviate the sense that something terrible had befallen the world outside and that the only people left on earth are a few anonymous survivors quarantined within. Even the hesitant and distorted voice crackling over the tannoy – *Jill! Jill to Till Eleven please!* – sounded as though it was, like the first phonograph recordings, the last relic of a distant and unreachable past. Then I was running again, darting past slower shoppers with increased urgency and, more than once, I picked up a packet to scrutinize its expiry date.

You have to calm down, I told myself. Supermarkets are designed to be uncannily similar to one another. That familiarity is an integral part of their design. But why then did it feel as though I was stuck within yet another copy and that the original had long ago been lost among its countless doppelgangers? So many great thinkers throughout the ages have posited that every life has been lived before, and that every conceivable action has already been carried out many times.

Perhaps the world itself is a copy and there are an inconceivable number of other copy-worlds. Perhaps there are more than a million copies, over a billion acts of creation abandoned by dissatisfied gods, a pluriverse of countless universes outside the limits of our vision, and no way to tell which was the first or whether all are duplicates.

What then did that make me? And more importantly, what did it make my brother?

Luke, where the hell are you? I muttered under my breath as I pressed on down the wine and spirits aisle.

By the time I got to the fizzy drinks I was convinced that the supermarket had been designed solely to unravel the loose tangles of my memory. Every shelf taunted me. First there were the fat loaves of bread that, as a child, my brother could not touch without falling sick, forcing Mum to spend hours every day making cornbread and gluten-free spaghetti. Next there were the protein shakes he drank each morning as though he was partaking in sacred communion with the savage and exacting god of bodybuilding.

Finally, there were the fresh bouquets of flowers identical to those that had littered the house and garden ever since the funeral. I was dizzy and out of breath. I grabbed a bottle of water straight from a shelf. I gulped it down. It felt like my first drink in days.

Even though I knew it was ridiculous, I couldn't stop myself. This is what grief does: it rips a hole in the fabric of reality. Once the unimaginable happens, then suddenly anything is possible. The world is unmoored. Yet not for a moment did I even entertain the idea that the man I was chasing might be a figment of my imagination. In fact, I was convinced of quite the opposite – that the past week had been unreal and illusory, and that there was a perfectly logical explanation as to why me and my family had all fallen prey to the ridiculous idea that my brother was dead.

I started off around the next corner, but my heart was no longer in the search. I was simply retracing my steps while my brother remained always a few aisles ahead of me. It didn't help that as I peered down each lane, I encountered the same few faces staring back. But I couldn't give up. I began to head back towards the dairy aisle and it was then, just as I was passing the pharmacy counter – where an old woman in an oversized raincoat was picking through a pile of crumpled prescriptions while the shop assistant toyed with her nails – that I spotted him. He was queuing up at one of the tills, his half-empty basket set down at his feet.

I had to force myself not to run, as most of the shoppers around would almost certainly think I was either sick, wasted or some kind of lunatic, though I couldn't stop myself from increasing my pace.

He turned his head. I began to raise my arm to wave to him.

Luke!

I had to catch his attention. I needed to make him see. But then my rising arm faltered. I stopped mid-wave, my hand held awkwardly in the air. It wasn't him.

The man waiting at the check-out had a boxer's knuckle for a nose and bug-like eyes the colour of wet seaweed. He was nothing like my brother. My arm slumped back at my side. Only now did it occur to me that this man's hair was red, while my brother's hair had lost its fiery colour in his early teenage years and changed to a light brown. The person before me was tall and solid, as my brother had been in his adolescence and early twenties – he was nothing like the bulky colossus my brother turned himself into during the last eighteen months of endless protein shakes and obsessive weight training.

It wasn't him. I had been searching for my brother not as he was the last time I saw him, but as he remained in my memory. It wasn't him.

Of course it wasn't him. He was dead. Dead five days, and still it didn't seem real. It wasn't real. It couldn't be.

I couldn't move. Dead at twenty-four. My baby brother. Luke. It wasn't real. It couldn't be.

I left the supermarket in a hurry, without bothering to look for my abandoned basket or the quickly scribbled shopping list it contained. So often two worlds seem to exist simultaneously, one floating ghostlike and superimposed upon the other, like a spill of oil sloshing on water. Now and then. Fantasy and reality. The ghost in the queue didn't look like Luke at all, yet I wasted close to half an hour attempting to track him down.

And I knew without a doubt that I'd happily do it all over again, if only to keep alive that spark that had burned in me as I dashed from aisle to aisle: that magical idea that perhaps, maybe, *somehow* he might still be here among us.

Reflection

When my brother Luke died – suddenly, without warning, at the age of twenty-four – I didn't just lose one of the most important people in my life. I lost a part of myself.

This isn't just a metaphor. Many social-cognitivist theorists have argued that our identities are dependent on the roles we play throughout life. Think about it. Ask me who I am and I'll probably give you a list. I'm a father, a teacher, a divorcee, a writer, a Brit, an expat, a son, a brother. In each of these titles there lies a simple truth: my identity depends on my relation to others. I am both defined and produced by the people with whom I spend my life. What happens to my identity, then, if one of these roles is taken away from me?

The idea one has of oneself is referred to in psychology as the 'self-concept'. Our self-concept is a multifaceted structure made up of a range of separable elements. Our complex identities depend on both the number of our self-aspects (like the list I made above of different roles, as well as our traits and ambitions) and how independent they are of one another.

According to social cognitive theorists, people with a higher number of separable self-aspects are better protected against the possible depressive effects of difficult experiences such as divorce, job loss or bereavement. In other words, if we have many roles, we are better able to adapt to the ensuing change in identity caused by losing one of those roles.

Loss complicates the self. It changes who we are. I lost my brother and when I did, I lost something of myself. This is why I chose to start writing about my bereavement through the effect it had on me. That afternoon in the supermarket demonstrated what loss had done to me: it had broken my logical way of thinking, made me overthink and unsure of myself. If I was obsessed with finding my (dead) brother among the aisles, it was because I hadn't just lost him – I had lost myself too.

The 'how'

I was adamant that I didn't want to start writing about my brother by describing his funeral. Not because it was a day I do not really want to relive, but rather because it tells you nothing about either me or my brother. In that sense, it felt pointless to describe – after all, you can already picture it all: the priest in black. The pallbearers struggling under the weight of the coffin. The mourners sobbing around the grave. The terrible thoughts that return as the coffin is lowered into the ground or moves behind the curtain. The sky a pathetic fallacy of dark and brooding clouds . . . and so on, with nothing unique or specific about me, my brother or our relationship in there at all.

- Tip:

    Avoid starting where you feel you should. There's a danger in embracing traditional opening scenes: you lose what is specific and individual about your own story. That's also why, if in doubt, I tend to choose an *in medias res* opening: one where we're thrown into the middle of action.

    It keeps readers interested, but perhaps more importantly, throwing all your juggling balls into the air at once gives an impetus and urgency to you as a writer: you need to keep writing to complete the description of the action and also set it in context.

I wanted to show how hard my brother's death had hit me. To show how grief had scrambled my brain, in order to demonstrate the deep effects of this bereavement and how hard I found them to process. The supermarket provided a clear example of this, where all rationality slipped away as I searched:

- Tip:

    Show, don't tell.

    Yes, it's a cliché and you've probably heard it a million times or more, but there's a reason everyone repeats this piece of writing advice: it helps bring stories to life. As Chekhov famously summarized it: 'Don't tell me the moon is shining; show me the glint of light on broken glass.' It would be true to say that I was heartbroken, bereaved, broken into a thousand pieces, gutted, a hole ripped inside of me. But there are no hooks to keep the reader interested with such a list.

By showing the action or running frantically around Tesco, the emotion is brought to life. More, the reader is engaged with that action because they can *visualize* it. Showing rather than telling doesn't mean cutting all the description of emotion and interiority though, but rather to keep reminding yourself to give the reader something they can picture in their head.

Grief knocks you sideways. It unbalances. I was wary at first of writing about my experience at the supermarket, because it's embarrassing. Of course I knew he was dead, even as I hunted lane by lane for a man I thought looked like him. There's something mortifying about admitting how obsessively I stalked a stranger around Tesco. Shameful. Excruciating to admit.

But I knew I had to reveal it nonetheless, not only because it's true, but because it provides a window into my way of thinking a few days after the funeral. I had to open myself up to talk about things I'd usually keep to myself: paranoias, fears, selfishness, anxiety, depression, self-sabotage, all the little bits of myself I normally hide from the world.

- Tip:

    Be vulnerable. There's no way round this one.

    Embrace this discomfort. Be awkward. Be exposed. You will probably feel uncomfortable when writing about your own experiences: that's a sign that you're doing something right. Because there's no other way to get to emotional and personal truths. And truths can be messy, embarrassing, unpleasant.

In terms of this first piece of writing – the first step for me in a bigger project I knew I had to write about my grief journey and my brother's life and death – I knew instantly and without a shred of doubt that I didn't want to start with the sentence: my brother was dead. The writing I wanted to do was about his life, his energy, the profound effect he had on me – so I didn't want to define the project in terms of death.

The word *dead* implies finality. But he isn't gone: he is part of me now, and I have a duty to keep going. To remember and keep those memories alive. This is what I knew I had to do. But a life is a huge, magnificent, sprawling thing.

So where on earth should I start?

In Wonderland, Alice listens as the King advises the White rabbit to 'Begin at the beginning, and go on till you come to the end: then stop'. But of course, it's rarely that simple. Finding a natural starting point for a narrative is tricky. Start with the strongest memory? Or the oldest? Or even the most recent? The first day of his life, or the last? The day after, or the day before? The options are almost limitless. It wouldn't be surprising if you are feeling the same trepidation and uncertainty.

On top of that, beginnings are often fraught with emotion. They can provoke anxiety, especially when we find ourselves staring at a blank page and wracking our brains for the ideal start to our narrative. I felt the same worries and concerns myself: how to translate the raw memories themselves – the magical, emotional, idiosyncratic experiences that spark like fireflies in the synapses of my brain – into the raw, messy, imperfect material of language.

The transition from the ideal to the actual is one that, for me at least, was filled with frustration. I wrote anyway. I wrote shambolic, rambling drafts that were nothing like what I wanted to say. In the next chapter, I'll show you how I dealt with that, and how you can too. But for now, the only important thing is putting pen to paper or fingers to keyboard:

- Tip:

    Begin with yourself. The heart of life writing is the narrator, the person writing, the person sharing, the person reaching out from one mind to another to share something vital. If *you* aren't in that first scene, that first description, then you're stalling for time. You know yourself better than anyone. Start with that and try the prompt below.

Prep

Brainstorm: Write a set of bullet points (or a brainstorm or mind map) listing all the routine activities you do most days. This might include cooking, taking out the rubbish, going to the supermarket, driving to the school gates, commuting to work, running a bath, watering the plants . . . you get the picture. Write as many as you can to warm yourself up before writing (think of this as stretching your muscles before you go for a run).

Write

First, to get the essentials out of the way: find a quiet place, a comfortable space. That sounds obvious, but it's worth saying because it's vital. Make sure you have (a minimum of) fifteen minutes where you know you're not going to be disturbed.

Put your phone somewhere out of reach! I'm not going to remind you of this every time, but I think it's fundamental that you make your writing time separate from the other times you might spend at your desk or curled up on the sofa or sat out in the garden or wherever else you might choose to write. Don't mix this activity with others. There must be no checking emails, for instance. No googling to help you along (any research you need to do for your writing can be done later to help with the revision stages).

This is because I want you to think of writing as something completely separate and distinct from the other tasks and jobs you do in the same area. We want to create a mental space as much as a physical one. Hopefully this way we will begin to carve out a writing routine: the more we write like this, the quicker it will be in the future to get into that writing 'zone'.

Now, with those preliminaries out of the way, let's get to the actual writing:

I want you to write about a familiar routine. Describe an everyday action or occurrence. Something you usually do mindlessly, on automatic pilot. Pick one from the list you made from our brainstorm activity. But before you get started, here's the catch: our goal is to make this commonplace action unfamiliar. Write as though you're describing this action to someone who has never heard of it before – or to an alien visitor baffled by human life.

Writing about the familiar in a way that highlights how weird and unique it really can be is known as defamiliarization. One of its functions is to restore the wonder and strangeness to our lives, especially to actions that can seem dull and commonplace when we have done them many times.

How to defamiliarize an action?

- Zoom in on tiny and specific details that usually go unnoticed. Be alert to colours, shapes, textures. Start small. The biggest truths often lie in the most specific details: focus on the most individual and unique parts of this routine.
- Make your description as individualistic as possible. Write about your role in this action: how do you perform it, how do you feel while you do it?
- Make connections: reach for comparisons, analogies, metaphors.
- Involve your senses: the smells, sounds, sights, feelings that we so often ignore.

Aim to write for at least fifteen minutes.

Now, you may very well be thinking that this doesn't seem to be directly linked to transformational writing, and you'd be right. But as we start out, we need to foster a sense of the world as far more – more various, more strange, more improbable – than we usually assume. If we practice defamiliarizing the routine world, then we'll be better equipped to tackle the world of memory that we want to get just right. We have a long and – let's be honest with each other – potentially torturous and difficult journey ahead.

We need to be well prepared. This foundational work then will feed into how we approach our larger writing project and (as we'll see in the next chapter) help us start on writing into the dark.

Follow up

Put aside that warm-up piece of writing. Leaving it for one day would be the absolute minimum, but a week would be even better when it comes to returning to your work with 'fresh eyes'. This helps us see our own writing with a little more clarity. When you come back to it, I want you to revise it by either cutting or rewriting all the sentences that start with 'I'.

There is a danger, of course, in repeating the same phrasing and sentence structures: it can become predictable and even boring to a reader. But, even more importantly, reworking those sentences that lead off with the first-person pronoun (I went . . . Then I took . . . Later I saw . . .) forces us to consider our own place in the story.

After all, we're going to be writing about ourselves (and our loved ones). Variety will be key, as will maintaining a balance so our writing is personal without becoming solipsistic. Rewrite your description of an everyday routine paying attention to that balance between the world and your place and actions in it.

Read

For a deep dive into the way grief upends logic and breaks rationality, there is perhaps no better book than Joan Didion's *The Year of Magical Thinking* (2006). The book recounts the months following the death of her husband from a heart attack at their dining table. This raw and unflinching look at the effects of loss on the grieving mind stands out because it dramatizes the ways that grief creates uncertainty and a breakdown of the self.

She stresses 'the power of grief to derange the mind' and documents how the magical thinking of the title breaks down the logic of the everyday world – how, for example, the shoes of her dead husband must not be thrown away because he 'would need shoes if he was to return'.[1] The rules of normal life are

---

[1] Joan Didion, *The Year of Magical Thinking* (Glasgow: Harper Perennial, 2006), 37.

suspended as she depicts in razor-sharp detail the long and gruelling journey through the world of bereavement and loss.

Try

Start a scrapbook. It doesn't have to be a literal one: it is much easier, and just as useful, to open a Note on your phone or a folder on Pinterest. We will use it to build a 'mood board' for this project. Any time you come across an object that reminds you of a particular time, a food whose taste awakens a memory, a song that brings back an old conversation – make a note of it. Jot down anything you see (outfits, TV shows, walks, colours, smells, activities, books) that either sparks a memory or conveys a feeling that you want to access. These will come in handy later on.

Chapter 2
Writing into the dark

My journey

Almost directly behind my parents' house lie the Goblin Woods – named by my brother because where the light manages to pick a way through the interlinking weave of branches that make up the dense canopy, shadows are thrown that resemble the twisted forms of imps, spirits and demons. Luke loved the woods. Loved hunting goblins there after school, playing armies or knights or adventurers with such wild enthusiasm that his passions infected me too.

The day before the funeral, the house was busier than ever. My mum fretting about the service, my dad on the phone sorting out last-minute snags. Aunts and uncles turning up to help, neighbours from the village bringing food. To be back in the house where we grew up, where we shared a bunk bed and countless midnight feasts, where we made up riotous pantomimes and waged savage wars against one another, it didn't seem right. Besides, the bustle and restlessness put me on edge, and in those brief moments between tasks a silence settled over all of us that felt impossible to break. I kept stopping by the back windows and staring down towards the start of the woods.

I could hear Luke's voice telling me to hurry up and get a move on.

Before I knew it, I'd pulled on my boots and slipped out of the door before anyone had noticed. The stretch of woods at the back of the garden is tangled and uninviting, and so it was always via the footpath further up the road that we would enter, despite the thickset spray of nettles that had grown up across the path as if to disguise its purpose. I welcomed their sting spreading across my ankles as I made my way in. I was reminded of my brother at about three years of age, listening with an earnest face to our mum's instructions to use the crayons we had been given on the paper placed in front of us and then, as soon as her back was turned, scribbling great looping swirls of green and orange across the pale wallpaper and skirting board. It was as though the nettles too knew they shouldn't but couldn't resist.

Yet despite their best efforts, there was no mistaking the fact that the sting caused by the nettles was only a slight itch and not the throbbing, burning pain it had seemed when I was a child, a pain so insistent that it invariably sent my brother and me searching frantically for dock leaves to rub against the reddening patches of irritated skin.

I hate you, stupid nettles, I heard him shout at them more than once, as though they could hear and ought to be ashamed of themselves.

I was taking this more overgrown route because I needed to retrace the steps we had taken a hundred times before. I had to take the same journey we used to take together, that much I knew. I had to make sure it was still there. Because it was his place, and more than that he always used to say that I never remembered things the way they actually were.

And maybe he was right. Memory warps everything, just as rain warps timber. So I needed to be sure.

The further the path followed the slope down towards the muddy track at the bottom, the closer the trees huddled together. Save for the sound, somewhere in the distance, of deer crunching leaves beneath their tread, the whole woods were so silent that it seemed hard to imagine the trees had ever heard anything louder than a whisper. When we were children even Luke – the loudest, most rebellious among us – would stop running and shouting, if only for the briefest of respites, as soon as the darkness of the woods enveloped us; and we would often be careful to speak to each other in voices low enough to ensure that we were not overheard by the goblins lurking behind the beeches.

I stopped and peered around. No goblins nearby. I wasn't sure anymore what I was looking for. Something, anything, that might be left from back then would have been enough. I knew that the Goblin Woods are home to rabbits, deer and voles; and any number of warblers, pheasants, wood pigeons or finches might be glimpsed among the low-slung branches. Luke made a game out of spotting creatures before I had even noticed the rustle of leaves.

He made up his own names for them though: *look at that wobblybird*, *hey, I've spotted a spear-head-beast*, *oh did you see that tufty-flop?*

I walked on, my eyes alert, but spotting only beech, ash, yew. Maybe they all knew. I stopped at a clearing to catch my breath. Wasn't this stretch of grass the same one we pretended was the long-lost site of the sword in the stone or was it the secret landing site of an invisible alien ship? I couldn't be sure.

Was this what I had been searching for? A place I could still play make-believe. I stood in the centre of the clearing and closed my ears.

These open glades, strewn like bald patches across the bristling hide of the woods, actually mark where trees were felled by the great storm of 1987 – England's worst since 1703. That epic storm of our childhood laid waste to close to 15 million trees. I can just about remember that night in mid-October and the way the windowpanes shook, as though there was someone outside frantically banging to be let in.

I was then a few weeks from my sixth birthday and my brother, sleeping on the top bunk and snoring lightly above my head, would have been about three and three-quarters. The top should have been my privilege as the eldest child, but somehow Luke always got his way. He woke for a minute, peered over at the windows being hammered by that wild gale, then looked down at me.

Turn it off, he said.

It was an order – he bossed everyone around, regardless of age or status – and so there was nothing out of the ordinary in him commanding me to switch off the record-breaking storm.

I was about to point out that unfortunately I didn't have any powers over the weather at all, but he'd already fallen back to sleep. I could hear him snoring once more. He didn't wake again, though the hiss of the wind and the shaking of the trees around the house had me in a state of panic and worry. This wasn't unusual: Luke had the ability to fall into a deep and untroubled sleep seemingly at will, no matter where we were or how much uproar and pandemonium might surround us. Meanwhile I lay still in my bunk for what seemed like a week, trying to summon up the bravery to go to the window to see what was there.

As the night wore on, I began to feel as though the wild wind was calling to me alone, though to this day I haven't been able to work out what it was trying to tell me. I was too cowardly to go to the window and peer out, so instead I stayed awake all night and listened from my blankets while my brother slept. It was always Luke who'd been the brave one.

I kept on through the woods, following the path around a huddle of trees. I was suddenly aware of the frail sunlight falling between the coil and braid of the entwined branches. Shadows multiplied. My thoughts were spinning in odd directions. A copse is a small huddle of trees. A corpse is . . . No. I focused on the woods, on trying to find whatever it was that was calling me back here. I increased my pace. Several times I mistook the call and flutter of birds for familiar voices. I turned at a fork in the path and saw something in my blind spot – I spun back around and caught a glimpse of my brother, his face a trick of the light roaming over the bark of a twisted beech.

I clamped my hand over my mouth to stop myself from crying out. I pushed on, head down and heart hammering in my chest.

As kids we never doubted that the strangest and most wonderful things might be hiding within the forest. Whenever we went to the woods together, my brother would often rush ahead and, when he had reached a suitable distance, he would turn and call back to me, claiming that he had spotted a tiger strutting between the trees, or a huge anaconda slithering among the leaves. By the time I drew level with him, however, he would take great delight in announcing that I was too slow and that the fabulous creatures had long disappeared, no doubt scared away by my clumsy, leaden approach.

I was too late. Always just a little too late.

Luke also used to say that if we got caught in the woods when the sun went down, we would never find our way back out. No matter how much he might have been enjoying the games we were playing, as soon as he saw the sun starting to set he would abandon dens and wigwams half-finished and start racing back towards the path, with me in pursuit. How long now until sunset? I was no longer sure. Only the thinnest arrows of light were able to fight through the thick canopy. Which way did we usually go? All the tracks looked the same.

I was walking faster now, growing ever more confused. Suddenly I was startled by the sound of footsteps out of sync with the echo of my own, and I knew in my heart that I was being chased. But when I drew to a stop the forest returned to silence. I was shaking. Less than half an hour into the walk, I was unable to continue. The mulch that lines the woodland floor seemed like it was no longer made of the familiar mixture of twigs, dead wood, leaves, moss, trampled flowers and other debris stewing down to feed the tangle of roots beneath the ground but was instead the compressed refuse of the past and with each step I took I sank a little deeper.

I wouldn't find anything here but memories and my own worst thoughts. I had to turn back. I swung fast on my heels, so fast I almost lost my balance in the mud. I started back up the track for home.

At that moment there was nothing I wanted more than to be as far away from there as possible.

But still I trudged on, and soon I could see the house again: a home I had not lived in for years. I could leave the woods behind, but the past wouldn't leave me. But something about the little detached house on that little street at the edge of the village didn't look right. There was no sign of the turmoil within. No hint of the everyone inside had been changed – changed utterly – in the last week. It wasn't right at all. What had I possibly hoped to find? I stopped for a minute outside the front door. A minute became two. Three.

I waited for something that would explain everything. Nothing came.

I remembered reading that in ancient Rome there were the most elaborate rituals for funerals. A procession would carry the body to the outskirts of the city, and some of the deceased's family would have worn masks representing their ancestors, whose eternal company the dead would now be joining. The relatives, set apart in black, would have stayed inside for nine days beyond the funeral, never once letting sunlight fall upon their faces. And – perhaps because death is evergreen – the bereaved would have set a solitary cypress branch outside the front of the house in which loss had taken root, letting the shadows of the leaves stretch out like fingertips pressing silently upon the door.

But there were no cypresses outside this house. No black curtains or covered mirrors. No signs at all of what has happened. The house was plain, and I loitered for a long time before the front door as the sun continued to set. There was nothing at all to see, though around me I could feel it teeming. All the past we carry with us.

I took a deep breath and stepped back inside.

Reflection

The great American novelist E. L. Doctorow wrote that 'Writing is like driving at night in the fog. You can only see as far as your headlights, but you can make the whole trip that way'. Sometimes it is more important to start writing – to feed that urge and nurture that spark – than to sit around overplanning or meticulously mapping. I wrote about my experiences on the day before my brother's funeral by following my own headlights, just as I had walked: uncertain of what I might come across or where it might take me.

Don't get me wrong: planning can be vital, particularly in structuring longer projects and setting out story arcs. But for us, setting forth on a personal life writing journey, it is vital to give ourselves over to the possibilities of writing as discovery. Indeed, the romantic myth of a writer waiting until inspiration strikes and sends words flowing through them, like an electric current, is a dangerous and unrealistic one. If you wait for the perfect moment to start writing, then you may end up waiting forever. Don't be afraid of starting without knowing where you are going. It is the act of writing that opens up new possibilities and directions, particularly when we are writing into the past.

Laurel Richardson has suggested that 'writing is a method of inquiry' and can lead us towards results and conclusions that we could not have predicted or planned for. Sometimes we write to find, to locate, to learn something. You don't need to know what that something is before you begin: often it might not emerge until a second or a third draft. Or perhaps it might never become clear – and that's okay too. There's always a risk when we experiment. I had no idea where I was going either when I strode into the woods or when I later started writing about it. I sometimes feel that overthinking is the worst enemy of writing. Don't be afraid of writing into the dark, of starting out with no idea where you might end up.

How then to open up such an inquiry? A beginning is a pathway, a promise, a hint of where we might be heading. The simplest way to proceed is by starting from an inciting incident that sets a chain of events in motion. Physical movement creates momentum and builds tension in a story, both vital ingredients for a narrative, and so I began with fleeing the house. For you, it might be a moment of realization, an email or phone call, an arrival or departure, a last straw, a throwaway comment. This inciting incident should drive your writing forward, and ideally also help you establish narratorial voice, setting and context as you follow its effects.

For my own journey, I realized that the physical activity of searching in the woods had to match the mental activity of hunting through the past for scraps of memory that might help the present make sense. Both then had to be reflected in the restlessness of the writing. I therefore followed my mind wherever it led and found myself weaving between the past and the present. The inclusion of historical asides about the great storm of 1987, facts about local flora and fauna and meandering segues into different childhood memories means that the digressive form of the writing reflects the relentless and wandering search it describes.

Or rather searches, *plural*, since I was searching through my memories for my brother and at the same time searching for who I might possibly be without him.

The 'how'

Writing grief means balancing between depicting the effects of bereavement in the present and dramatizing the memories of the past that haunt those left behind. It can be a tricky balancing act: too much of the present and the reader will get no clear sense of the unique person that is being mourned, while staying too long in the past risks losing some of the dramatic tension. One way to avoid these outcomes is to sprinkle memories, flashbacks and character details like breadcrumbs throughout the pages: we never lose sight of the present, while never being overwhelmed with a huge 'information dump' that pulls us out of the action either.

- Tip:

  Build balance into the way you write. If you notice that you've filled a page with description, then switch to a different narrative mode (such as dialogue, interaction, movement, interior monologue, etc.). If you've spent several pages in the present, try to integrate a short flashback.

  By regularly sprinkling small details about the past or about an important person into your pages, you build intrigue and keep the reader wanting more. In the same way, try not to fall into the trap of being predictable: aim for a variety of sentence lengths and structures; try to start each paragraph in a different way; reach for unfamiliar metaphors and comparisons.

  If you get stuck, switch modes.

Another careful balancing act is required in terms of tone. My brother was silly, energetic, infectiously funny, and yet I was wary of including too many of his jokes and ridiculous sayings in this piece in case they might undercut the pain and tension created by the frantic search. Sustaining mood can be difficult: I wanted to both build suspense with the walk into the woods and give equal weight to the interior world inside me and the exterior world around me.

I made the choice to save a closer depiction of my brother for a later piece, once I had established the effects of grief and loss. This decision proved vital: it is not possible to do or show everything in one go, and I often have to remind myself that I will get to other important sections later.

- Tip:

    Aim for consistency of tone and mood rather than trying to do too much at once. Both mean making explicit choices and sticking to them. Try to identify how formal or informal your writing will be: are you striving for something more poetic or more conversational? Then try to stick to it. Tone can be amplified through long, sprawling sentences that create a meditative atmosphere, or short, curt sentences that come straight to the point.

    Ask questions of yourself as you write, most importantly what do you want to achieve? Do you want to build suspense? Do you want to create an uneasy atmosphere? Or a nostalgic feel? Once you have made this choice, lean into it. For instance, figurative language can intensify emotional moods, while setting should ideally match atmosphere. Reflecting on these will help you work out what effect you want to achieve in each piece you write.

I knew that the walk in the woods would be a good dramatic starting point for delving into childhood memories. There is something about forests that connects them both to childhood (since they are ubiquitous settings for the fairy tales and myths of children's storybooks, from the hiding places of Robin Hood and his gang to Hansel and Gretel being abandoned by their parents in a dark forest, all the way through to the mysterious woodlands of Where the Wild Things Are and the home of the Gruffalo) and gives them an inherent sense of mystery.

They are haunting, numinous places. Time does not move as it should in the woods, and light too travels unpredictably between branches and canopies. The woods are a place of endless fascination for me (as they were too for my brother), and I enjoy writing about them as much as I enjoy walking in them. It can be easy to forget about pleasure when focusing on grief, but there is a joy in describing a landscape I love and spent so much time in. It was important for me to make sure that even when writing about my pain and struggles, I still kept sight of small joys and things that sustained me.

- Tip:

    Play to your strengths. We all have them. I have been writing long enough to know that I can do movement (which serves as a way to instantly engage readers) and scenic description well, and so I leaned into those skills. Few of us can do all styles of writing equally well (this is true across the arts: no one expects Kanye or Eminem to master writing classical symphonies), and so using our strongest attributes can help us create a strong opening and thereby encourage us to keep going.

    If you're not sure what your strengths are, then think of this as an opportunity to cultivate self-awareness about your writing: as you reread your drafts, look for repeated phrasing, images, or narrative modes you frequently utilize. At the end of a writing session, try to think back on what you found easiest to write, and lean into those next time.

I knew this piece of writing was finished when it could stand alone. Though each of these pieces work together to build a bigger picture of my journey through grief, I wanted each one to work as a portrait of an emotion or moment in my journey. By writing to such a short and specific brief, we also have the option to let them stand alone (and submit them for publication in literary journals, magazines, websites, competitions and anthologies) as well as potentially extend them into longer and connected pieces later on.

Work in blocks, rather than trying to cram in too much in one go. Writing about grief can be emotionally exhausting, so be mindful of your emotional limits and the need to take a break from it all.

- Tip:

    Stop writing midway through a scene. If you stop at the end of a scene (or chapter or section) then you'll have a harder time starting up the next time you sit down to write, as you'll be faced with both a blank page and the need to begin a whole new scene.

    If you leave a scene unfinished halfway through, you'll have to finish it as soon as you start your next writing session – the continuation and conclusion of it should be fairly clear in your mind by that point, so it should be easy to get into it. This is likely to warm up your 'writing muscles' and so give you the writing momentum needed to keep going and start the next scene too.

Prep

Listen again to your favourite song or piece of music. Instead of concentrating on the sound, the melody, the lyrics, the flow and surge, try to focus only on how it makes you feel as you listen. Pay attention to the sensations you experience: How does it feel in your body? What does it remind you of, what memories does it open up? What associations spring to mind?

Instead of following each train of thought or memory, try instead to note them, observe them and let them drift by. As writers, it is vital to be keen observers. As life writers, we need then to observe ourselves. Try to carry this observation over into your writing: note where your mind goes, the emotions that bubble up in different situations and places, the memories and associations that spring to mind. The more we pay attention to these, the more we can direct them into our work.

Write

Quick reminder from before: find a quiet, comfortable space where you won't be disturbed. We're working to build a sustainable writing practice. Ideally, we want to create an environment where we'll be able to get into what psychologists call a 'flow state': a mental state when we are completely focused on one task, and where steady alpha wave brain activity allows us to make deeper connections. Some of the best ways to access this flow state are to replicate previous times you've got into this headspace, give yourself time without interruptions and focus on being in the moment.

Once we're prepped and ready to write, let's dive in:

I want you to write about a disruption. A routine that got thrown into disarray. An everyday occurrence that was unexpectedly turned upside down. Zoom in on one particular day (like my afternoon at home, ticking of tasks on the day before my brother's funeral) to show how even the smallest tasks have been cast in a new light.

The literary critic Tzvetan Todorov suggested that all narratives spring from disequilibrium. In other words, interesting stories start when the normal way of life is suddenly disrupted (Hamlet's father dies; Odysseus is called to war; Mr Bingley arrives in the village). This is especially true of the stories we tell about grief. So I want you to describe how your world has been disrupted.

This is, of course, a big task. It is one of the central tasks when writing about loss. So how to write disruption?

- Start with the normal. The ordinary. The everyday. We cannot show disruption or change without first establishing the calm equilibrium that will be broken.
- Think small. It's impossible to show the full effects of grief and loss in one go. So focus here on writing one scene – in other words, one specific day in one specific place. Instead of the rock crashing into the pond, we're focusing on a ripple that skitters out across the surface of the water.
- Observe yourself: record your actions, your movements, your thoughts – the reader wants to see you, so don't hide yourself behind the routine or your surroundings.
- Try to have a variety of sentence lengths and forms, as well as a variety of narrative modes in order to save the scene from becoming predictable.
- Lean into the wonder: disruption can also entail new angle through which we see things. Keep this in mind when you reach for comparisons, analogies, metaphors (but remember that a couple per page is more than enough).
- Stay in the everyday world. Aim to depict how the tiniest of conversation, actions or thoughts has been cast in a new light.
- Make connections: reach for comparisons, analogies, metaphors.

Aim to write for at least twenty minutes.

Grief opens up a crack in everything. This exercise helps us show how these cracks break down our conception of normal. In the immortal words of Leonard Cohen, 'There is a crack, a crack in everything: that's how the light gets in'. Our first step towards remaking is showing the breaks, the shattering, the damage. Don't be afraid to reveal how broken your equilibrium or 'normal' may be. Remember too that we find the universal in the particular.

In other words, it is by zooming into the specific peculiarities and unique aspects of your own life, your individual voice, your personal thoughts, your disrupted day, that you will best connect with the reader, make your point, bring your scene to life, and demonstrate the havoc wreaked by loss.

Follow up

Read back through that scene you've written and find a metaphor that leaps off the page. One that sparks and shines. A cutting comparison, a surprising simile or an unexpected connection. (If you can't find one, look for a place to add a little figurative language: perhaps in the middle of a long passage of description, to add variety and pizzazz, or to help us see the setting or people described in a new light.)

A strong metaphor lodges itself in a reader's mind. So make use of this. Try to find ways to extend that metaphor throughout the rest of the scene: develop it, allude back to it, add to it across the pages. This will help both cohesion and tone. Of course, there is a danger in overdoing it (a little repetition and harkening back goes a long way), but by extending an interesting metaphor or image across a whole piece of writing, you can establish a deeper and more resonant connection with your reader.

Read

The Poetry Foundation is a truly awe-inspiring online resource: a collection of poems as wide-ranging and vast as even the most magical of libraries. Head there for Robert Frost's 'Acquainted with the Night', a stunning sonnet about walking, loneliness and loss written in crisp, direct lines that carry you along on the speaker's journey. You can feel the movement of the walker as you read, as well as all that churns just below the surface.

Try

Take a walk. Whether over hills or into woods, by the sea or in a park, around city streets or through the suburbs, the location isn't important. The key is the rhythm: the steady beat of your feet against the ground. Follow your thoughts as they also start to move. Walking increases the circulation of blood to the brain (as well as to the body) and so helps us better focus our attention and make new connections. So try to compose as you walk. Pay attention to the memories, associations and ideas that emerge as you walk.

Let your mind follow the pace of your thoughts and begin to build sentences in your head: you are likely to find that they match the rhythm of your footsteps. Be aware and receptive to the world around you and try to describe in your head the scenes and people you pass, the sights and sounds and smells you experience. All of this will help feed back into your writing later. Even ten minutes can make a difference!

Chapter 3
Setting myself on fire

My journey

From somewhere down in the deepest slipstreams of sleep, the noise pulled me back to the surface like a fishhook caught through my cheek. The phone ringing. Shrill and insistent.

At first my groggy brain mistook it for my alarm. But it was still dark out. I was working abroad in Beijing: early summer and even the dead of night muggy and slick. I fumbled for the phone. Not even 5 a.m. yet, but two missed calls and it was still ringing.

Mum.

I clicked accept and raised it to my ear.

I don't remember exactly what she said. Or the hours after. I must have packed a bag. Must have booked a flight, called work to explain, made my way to the airport. The memory is a muddle of overlapping moments: a tangle of twine, a cat's cradle gone wrong and almost impossible to unpick. Even at the time it seemed as though there was a part of me that was there and another part that was already far away, watching from a safe distance, as though peering at myself as I went about my own actions through a telescope.

Me but not me.

How did I reach my parents' house on the edges of the South Downs? I have no idea.

The only thing that stayed was that sensation: because every time I lay down in bed that week, I heard that ringing and would jolt awake.

In the middle of the night my hands would grasp for my phone in a mad, scrambling panic. A feeling like something inside of my gut was caught on the end of a corkscrew and was being churned and churned and churned. I couldn't close my eyes without hearing it. The call cutting through the night to tell me that Luke had pulled over by the side of the road on the way home from work, and that by the time the ambulance arrived to take him to hospital it was already too late.

I tried putting my phone on airplane mode, tried leaving it in another room, but that was even worse. Because what if there was an emergency? I needed to be near it at all times. But then what other emergencies could there be anymore? The worst had already happened. And it happened again and again and again, every time I closed my eyes.

I kept thinking of one of Luke's favourite stories as a kid, one we listened to countless times played on a storybook cassette as we lay in our bunk bed at night. In *The Soldier and the Tinderbox*, all it takes is one strike of the flint to turn the world upside down and cause everything to stop making sense. With just one strike of the tinderbox – or one finger clicking the green button and accepting the call – all the rules of normal life are broken. There suddenly appears a dog with eyes the size of teacups. Or a world suddenly broken into pieces.

I couldn't sleep. Couldn't lie down without that ringing echoing around my head. So I drank. I tried to lull myself into a catatonic stupor with cider and wine and gin and anything else at hand. I wasn't picky. I drank till I was shit-faced and drowning in self-pity, until the room was woozy and waltzing around me. Still, I couldn't rest.

It didn't stop even after the funeral. And I couldn't stop either. Many times in those first weeks, eating dinner with my parents, I made excuses to get up from the table – to use the loo or get some water – and snuck to the kitchen to glug down several mouthfuls of wine straight from the open bottle in the fridge. Whenever I heard footsteps, I shoved it back into place and closed the refrigerator door, burning with shame, but it wasn't enough to make me stop.

One evening I crept to the fridge to find the most recent bottle down to the last dregs, and no others on the rack or in the cupboards. For a few minutes I panicked, and then I grabbed my jacket. I needed to get out anyway, I told myself. Needed to get away from the soaking wreaths and bouquets still lying in a neat line at the top of the garden, unmoved since they were set down for the funeral, the petals beginning to wrinkle and curl. Needed a break from the photos on the wall of my brother staring down at me in his spiderman costume, his eyes as big as teacups, as though somehow he'd become trapped behind the glass. And those of myself, grinning away without a care in the world. I had to get out.

I could have gone to meet a friend. My best mate had called. Then other friends, some I hadn't heard from in months. Old colleagues, schoolmates. Inviting me out. Offering sympathy and company. But I shrugged them all off: *thanks for the offer, but it's busy right now with family. Maybe next week?*

I didn't want sympathy. I didn't want to talk about it. I didn't want help. I didn't know what I wanted. Just for that phone to stop ringing behind my eyelids.

I took the train into Chichester, an overpriced market town in the middle of West Sussex where I went to school. I was a quiet kid, studious and thoughtful. But what had that got me?

The thoughts churned and churned.

I didn't want help. I walked up South Street, past shuttered phone stores and newer hipster coffee shops and the little Tesco Express still open. I turned left and kept on past the Cathedral with its great spire rising up to jab through low-skimming clouds, towards the Dolphin and Anchor. As though I was being pulled back by an unstoppable force to the pub where my brother had worked as a bouncer.

Luke stood outside the door, a colossus in a too-tight black suit, his bulging arms folded as he managed the queues that wound down the street on Friday and Saturday nights. More than once he had to be reminded to take off his black sunglasses – *they are pretty bloody pointless*, he was told again and again by exasperated colleagues, *at night*.

Just as the Dolphin and Anchor had changed over the years – from an old coaching inn into an upmarket hotel, and finally now into a public house owned by a national chain that seems intent upon erasing any original features the place possesses in order to make it identical to each of their other outlets across the country – so my brother, by the time he began to work on the door here, had shrugged off many of his former selves. No longer the toddler in my shadow, the little boy convinced he was Spiderman, the obsessive painter, the camouflage-wearing commando, the martial arts devotee, the amateur photographer, nor even the surly and aggressive teen ready to pick a fight with anyone who argued with him, Luke had recast himself as a local hardman, the giant doorman.

It was a role he fleshed out with struts and curses, yet the truth was that no matter how often he went to the gym, no matter how much he bragged that he was nothing like the rest of his family or that reading was only for girls and school for the gullible, it was always impossible to tell how much was performance and how much was for real. Perhaps he would have said the same about me – that I only ever pretended to be thoughtful and reserved. But there was certainly something theatrical about his stock poses and surly gait when he assumed the role of doorman. He often turned cagey when people asked him about where he had grown up and what his parents did, as if he suspected that at any moment someone might see through his act.

I stopped outside the pub, the raucous chatter of voices mixing with the rush of memories.

There were many Friday nights when the two of us would travel into town on the same train, both heading towards the Dolphin and Anchor. Luke would usually be dressed in his black suit and would spend much of the journey casting disparaging looks at my scuffed shoes or the charity-shop shirt I'd chosen to wear. Before he went out, he would spend close to an hour dressing himself in preparation for the part he had to play, and he could never understand how I could bear to go into town to meet my friends, having made so little effort.

If anyone sees us together, he would often tell me, *I'll have to pretend we've never met and I have no idea who you are*. As soon as the train began to draw in to Chichester station, he would go on to say, *If I see any of your friends trying to come in tonight, you know I'm going to turn them away, don't you? They're not getting in when I'm on the door. Bunch of fucking losers. Shouldn't be allowed. No way they'll be allowed in. Not on my watch. Not a fucking chance.*

Nonetheless, he would always let them in without even asking to see their ID. He usually also chatted and joked with them while they were waiting in line on those nights when the pub became so crowded that it was forced to operate a 'one-in one-out' policy. His threats were little more than a well-tested tease. And for all his bluff and bluster, whenever he met one of my friends beyond the Dolphin and Anchor, he would always spare a few minutes to catch up with them – even after I had moved away from home and long left the city behind.

Inside the scuffed floorboards were already a little sticky. Everything whitewashed and faded. A widescreen TV on the wall showing the footie and a quiz machine beeping and pinging by the bar. I ordered a pint of Stella and necked it – the glorious glowing sensation spreading through my senses with each sip equalled by the shame burning beneath. Then I ordered a second pint.

Occasionally, when I hadn't gone to the pub myself, I would come in the car to pick Luke up after work and drive him back home. He usually said little during those late journeys, and perhaps that's why I can still recall with almost perfect clarity the night he turned to me and suddenly began to speak, almost as if to himself, about a fight that he had broken up in the pub. He said that when he was pushing through the throng to get to the brawlers in the centre it was as though everything was happening in slow motion, and each drunken punch took forever to reach its target.

By the time, he continued, *I got to the scene of the altercation, most of the crowd had given up trying to pull the blokes apart. Actually, most people were cheering the brawlers on as they set into each other and went crashing into the tables around them*. Luke shook his head in disbelief as he recounted that one man, himself a muscled strongman whose face had been cut by a broken glass in the fracas, had turned pale when he realized he was bleeding. *For all his hardman mouth, the geezer had looked down at the blood on his hands with eyes as big as teacups.*

It hit me in that moment, staring at the last foamy dregs at the bottom of the glass. Even though I was out of my skull, wrecked on booze and befuddled by grief and sick with sleeplessness, I had a clarity of purpose and a sense that everything had been leading me here. My head hammering with the thought of it.

I don't think I've ever been as certain of something in my life.

I scanned the room and locked onto a pair of blokes at the other end of the bar. Their faces red and their stomachs making their rugby shirts bulge. One had a silver tooth and a buzz cut, the other a thick beard. Both were a good foot taller than me, with arms like tree trunks and necks to match. Perfect.

I started to make my way down the bar. I had to marshal all my strength not to fall forward or give in to the temptation to close my eyes and let the pub spin away around me, but even so I only made it halfway before the men had left the bar with their pints in hand.

But it didn't matter now. Because at last I understood why I was there. I wasn't looking to drink myself senseless. I wasn't looking for Luke either, back in *his* pub I was looking for something else. Something that would cut through the ringing in my head. A reckoning. A way to smash that unstoppable rush of memories into pieces and make it stop.

I spotted a huge guy lumbering out of the bogs and back towards the main line of tables. A brick shithouse, six feet and change to spare, shaved head and shoulders wider than the M25.

And it seemed as I watched this bulky bloke striding through the grotty pub that everything else that week was only a rehearsal for this moment.

I pushed away from the bar at just the right second and went thwacking into his side as he passed.

He span round and stared at me.

'Watch where you're going dickhead', I said.

I saw his teeth set and I braced myself. I felt the seconds slow into centuries, and it seemed as though time might have stopped moving forward, the cogs rusted and refusing to turn any further. I waited for his fist to hit. For the pain I desperately craved.

But nothing came.

I thought that would be enough. It should have been. But maybe my words had been too slurred. Maybe I was still a bit too unsteady on my feet. Because all he did was laugh and shake his head, then stride away towards the tables. As if I was too small, too ridiculous, to bother with.

And that's how I felt. Small. A tiny speck in a vast, indifferent universe that didn't give a damn about me or my little brother. Ridiculous too. A self-pitying, sorry-for-myself clown, so hammered that I was trying to get myself beaten up just so that I'd feel something – anything – that would take my mind off the ringing phone and everything it had told me.

I was an idiot.

I'd like to tell you that I got the next train home. That I spent the rest of the evening with my family, broken and grieving but at least together. Or that I somehow found a way to stop my thoughts prowling in tight circles like a trapped tiger pacing around its cage. But that would be a lie.

I made it out of the Dolphin and Anchor – that much is true – but the walk back to the station took me past The Swan, and I couldn't stop myself. Once I'd worn out my welcome there, I can just about recall stopping into The George and Dragon for last orders, where I heaved my guts up in the bogs while wishing wishing wishing that we'd swapped places and it had been me instead of him, before stumbling out into the night, my bloodshot eyes as big as teacups.

Reflection

In his monograph 'Beyond the Pleasure Principle', Sigmund Freud theorized that human behaviour is driven by two contrasting instincts: the life instinct and the death instinct (often referred to as Eros and Thanatos). Our instinct towards life reflects our biological impulse to survive and reproduce, to preserve and nurture both ourselves and our species. The death drive, on the other hand, can manifest outwards (as anger and aggression towards others) or inwards (in risky, addictive, and dangerous behaviours). In his clinical observations of traumatized soldiers returning home after the First World War, Freud notes that the death drive leads us to revisit and relive our traumas, as well as to repeat compulsive and self-destructive behaviours.

We don't have to agree with all of Freud's ideas to recognize the truth at the heart of that connection between trauma and self-harm. We seek to numb and distract ourselves when the world around us becomes too difficult to bear. From the minute I heard about my brother's death, I began to spiral ever further out of control, into ever more avoidant and addictive behaviours. The French have a term for this: *L'appel du vide* – meaning *the call of the void*. That urge to leap into dark water, to thrust your hand into the fire. And it was this feeling, as much as grief and loss and sadness, that began to bubble up in me after Luke's funeral.

Memoir demands emotional honesty. We cannot hide parts of ourselves; otherwise, we are venturing into fiction rather than revealing our own truths. It was important for me to show the physical and psychological effects of my brother's death on my actions and impulses, and this meant recalling the full range of my self-destructive behaviours.

Recounting them on the page was not easy: in my first draft of this memoir I made no mention of sneaking alcohol from the fridge, not so much because I couldn't bear to recall it, but because I didn't want to reveal those ugly truths to my parents, friends, employer, colleagues and anyone else who might pick up this book. But to leave them out would sanitize what was a messy, distressing and horrible time, and would be to ignore the worst of my own behaviours rather than acknowledging the truth: that grief and trauma drive us to impulses we deeply regret. The truth isn't neat or clean or nice to look at. But it is real.

Avoidant behaviours, distraction strategies, insomnia – all are fairly common physiological responses to bereavement. In this sense, writing about grief means touching those lowest depths. We have to journey inside our sadness to depict it, without trying to hide it, push it down or ignore it. In my attempt to dramatize my own feeling of 'hitting rock bottom', I had to shine a light on my most self-pitying and self-absorbed behaviours and desires after Luke's funeral. If this was difficult, then by the same token it was also beneficial, because revealing the unpleasant truths of my worst days also revealed to me how far I'd come since then.

The 'how'

The dramatic climax of this chapter of the memoir is my short confrontation with the man in the pub. It serves as both the culmination of everything that has gone before (the drinking at home spiralling out of control, the drunk night out, the memories of my brother's role in bar fights) and the point in the narrative where the dramatic stakes are at their highest (will I get beaten up? How bad will it be? What will happen to me?).

I therefore structured my writing around this central point: everything before it functions as rising action (a series of cumulative inciting incidents and gradual building of tension), while everything after is falling action (reflection on how I'd got to this point, and then the slow tapering off into conclusion).

- Tip:

    Try to identify the dramatic climax of the scene, day, topic or chapter you are writing. What is the defining moment or the central idea? Once you've identified this, it will be easier to structure your writing around it, especially by using rising action to increase tension and keep the reader invested in the narrative.

    Rising action means sprinkling breadcrumbs (hints and details that provide context to the story), and showing the challenges and difficulties your narrator is facing. These help build momentum towards the climax: the main focus of that scene or memory.

In order to build to my dramatic climax in the pub, I had to make clear the mental state I was in during the week before and after Luke's funeral. This meant summarizing some key background information that provided the basic context necessary to understand the situation: namely by showing how my drinking and insomnia had spiralled out of control.

Showing my flight back to the UK or depicting the conversations between myself and my parents in the days after the funeral may have been interesting material, but it would have slowed down the narrative and distracted from the main focus of this section. We often have to be single-minded about what we are examining in each chapter or piece of writing.

- Tip:

    Balance between summarizing and dramatizing. It is impossible to bring to life every single moment you have experienced, so it's important to identify which is background (the details that the reader needs to know to provide context for the actions in this scene) and which is central (the actions and interactions that you want to bring to life).

    Yes, I know back in Chapter 1 I mentioned how we should try to 'show, rather than tell', but actually a little bit of telling can help us keep scenes moving without getting us bogged down in background details that may distract the reader from your main focus.

The ringing telephone was something that I could not escape, no matter how hard I tried to numb myself with drink or distract myself. I couldn't outrun it. So I tried in this piece to evoke that feeling of being caught in an inescapable loop. I emphasized this loop with repetition: the word 'ringing' recurs frequently, the motif of 'the eyes as big as teacups' keeps reappearing at unexpected moments and the verb 'churning' keeps reminding readers of that terrible circularity. In other words, I worked to make sure that the form of the writing matched the content.

- Tip:

    Consider how the form of your own writing might be better matched to the topics you are writing about. This means stepping back from your writing and thinking about which theme you want to emphasize in each scene or chapter.

    This will help you decide what changes you might need to make to bring form and content into harmony: perhaps by echoing the beginning of that piece in the final paragraph, or by zooming in on a symbolic image or object, or by using repetition to reinforce mood, to establish rhythm and to emphasize a key idea. But remember, a little goes a long way!

At primary school, I tended to be quiet and shy. It took me time to make friends. I was anxious, an overthinker. Luke, on the other hand, was wild, gregarious, noisy: he attracted people to him. He was also a joker, a prankster, more invested in making people laugh in class than getting the right answer. But I couldn't bear getting questions wrong or being stared at. I've always cared too much about what people think of me, while my brother didn't give a damn.

In writing this chapter, I tried to borrow a little of his fearlessness in showing myself 'warts and all' rather than writing a version of myself that I think might be more likeable or easier to empathize with.

- Tip:

    Try to switch off that inner editor reminding you of all the things people might think when they read your writing. Believe me, I know from experience that this is advice that it's easy to give but often really tricky to put into practice. But we have to work to silence that critical voice inside us, because it stops us getting to the heart of memoir: writing truthfully.

    So write your first draft for your eyes only. Later on, when we get to polishing up our writing in future drafts and edits, we can think about how much we are comfortable revealing to others. In other words, start writing safe in the knowledge that no one will ever see this first draft except you.

Prep

Brainstorm: What are your goals in writing about your own life? Perhaps like me you want to share your unique journey through the deepest wilds of grief or keep something of the person you have lost alive. Perhaps you want to explore who you are through writing about your experiences. Perhaps you have a story burning inside you that needs to be shared. Or perhaps you have a different goal altogether. Jot down what your objectives are: try to note down at least three things you want to show, explore or bring to life in your writing. Try to also consider your reader: What do you want someone reading your writing to feel, understand or reflect on? What themes are guiding your writing? If you can write down three or four, that's a great start. Of course, this plan will evolve as we write, but it's important to be intentional from the beginning. This will help us make sure our writing doesn't veer off in directions that don't fit with our overall goals, and it will also help us be strategic in planning and revising each scene.

Write

Take a deep breath. It's time to dive into writing about your lowest ebb. Rock bottom. The worst of times.

Before we do so, a few caveats. It's going to be difficult. You may feel those same emotions welling up that you felt at the time. If you find yourself triggered, stop. Perhaps this is not something you are ready to write about yet. And that's okay. There's no rush. But at some point, writing through grief means showing how we are knocked off balance, how we suffer and struggle, how our thoughts and actions change. Don't be afraid of showing anger, rage, sadness, self-pity and all those other complex and messy emotions that society teaches us to keep well hidden.

Describing the worst of times – warts and all – takes courage. But it is also rewarding. Revealing your vulnerabilities builds connection with audiences (after all, there is nothing relatable about a perfect narrator who perfectly deals with every challenge thrown their way). Moreover, it allows us to build a dramatic arc for our memoir: by showing the most difficult of times, we have set up the structure for a journey through to recovery and finding a new strength. By showing how we struggled, we establish the stakes of our narrative.

Of course, this may seem daunting. That's normal. Try to embrace your discomfort in order to stay true to the portrait you are creating of yourself:

- A little bit of physical and emotional description goes a long way. Sprinkle in enough details to provide context for the audience, then show who you were through actions.
- Balance internal and external. In other words, aim to build a little internal monologue and reflection into every page, without losing sight of the dialogue, situations and interactions that keep the reader involved in the narrative.
- Avoid generalities. Instead reach for specific details (street names, shops, the specific food you ate or perfume you wore).
- Don't be afraid to show the messy, awkward, embarrassing sides of your actions. Mistakes and uncertainties make us relatable. Embrace the fact that you are real, rather than perfect. Show your complexities and contradictions.
- Let us hear your own voice. We often start writing in our 'best' voice, but try if you can to replicate the natural rhythms of your speaking voice. So say each sentence out loud as you write. Does it sound like how you usually talk?

- Don't forget the senses. All our lived experience is embodied. What did you feel, how did you move, what did you hear or smell or taste or notice? Just because we're writing the ugly truth doesn't mean the writing can't still be wonderful and heart-stopping.

As before, aim to stay in a scene. Don't drift too much from memory to memory or idea to idea. Anchor your experiences in a particular time and place, building your rising action towards one dramatic moment: an interaction, a realization or a discovery. Don't be afraid to delve deep and show the tangle of impulses, motivations and emotions driving your actions.

Follow up

Return to the writing you just completed. Now start a new page in your notebook (or a new document on your computer or tablet), and try to rewrite it with only the essentials remaining. Prune it down to the bare minimum. Challenge yourself – how short, blunt, punchy and to-the-point can you make it? Can you get it down to one page? Five hundred words? What does your writing look like when you've cut away all the unnecessary and distracting material?

This exercise isn't designed to create a stronger draft – on the contrary, your stripped-down version is likely to be missing a lot of the dramatic details, descriptions and momentum that keep a narrative going. What it will do, however, is reveal to you the heart of your story: the central themes and ideas that are most important to you. Understanding what these are will not only help with emphasis and revision later on but can serve as a guide into your next piece of writing as you develop those essential themes and key ideas.

Read

For a work that explores the depths to which grief might drive us, and its far-reaching effects, I recommend *H is for Hawk* by Helen MacDonald (2014), a mesmerizing memoir about how the author turned away from society after the death of her father and found solace in the natural world through training a goshawk. A beautiful book that explores the ways we engage with the world around us radically differently after loss.

Try

Next time you're out in public, try a bit of strategic people watching. When you're at a coffee shop, sat in a waiting room or in the queue for the supermarket checkout, resist the urge to scroll through your phone. Instead, try to pay attention to the people around you (try to do this subtly!). How do they hold their bodies? How do they move? Easily and confidently, or slowly and carefully? What about their clothing, their hair, their size and shape? What tics and mannerisms can you see? What do all these tell you about their character? Can you hear them? What are their voices like? Their accents and dialects, the quirks of their speech, the words they choose? All of this is great practice for description. A little bit of keen observation while out and about can help us the next time we want to bring people's personality to life through their physicality and the way they speak.

Chapter 4
Home/sickness

My journey

Grief is sneaky. Like the most stubborn of weeds, it finds its way through every crack. Sometimes I'd be working on my computer and hear my phone ping or the sound of a car turning onto our road, and I'd nod to myself and think that must be Luke, and it would take a moment before the penny dropped. Something in me refused to believe he wasn't somewhere close by. After all, he couldn't possibly have gone far. At any second I expected him to come strolling nonchalantly into the kitchen and order whoever was in there to make him some food.

I mean, this was a guy who'd lived his whole life within half an hour's drive of home. In the last decade, he'd left West Sussex only a handful of times. Mostly with the Middleton Hockey Club, going on tours that took the team across France and Spain as well as to the Netherlands. Yet for all the photos I saw, and all the obscene tales I heard of drunken dares and riotous pranks on these trips, for some reason I found it hard to imagine Luke outside the small locus within which he spent almost every day of his twenty-four years.

It made sense that he only travelled with the hockey club. They were the only people who could persuade him to do anything. Hockey meant everything to him. On the pitch – and celebrating in the clubhouse afterwards – were some of the only times I saw that mask slip, and that air of nonchalance and disinterest with which he inoculated himself against the world disappear to be replaced with pure joy and celebration.

He'd practiced not caring for a long time. This last year had seen him attempt to start his own business managing and hiring out a posse of bouncers and doormen, a short-lived venture whose lack of success he found deeply frustrating, but whenever you asked him about it he'd simply shrug off any questions. *Yeah, whatever*. If he pretended hard enough not to give a shit about anything, then he'd be immune to the humiliation of failure and self-doubt. It was an act he'd carefully honed since he was first diagnosed as dyslexic and later perfected when he started secondary school.

In fact, as soon as he finished primary school he began to change. Perhaps it was the formal diagnosis of his dyslexia itself that was the catalyst. All of a sudden he found himself in a straitjacket that no amount of struggling or fantastic contortions could shake loose. More even than his fiery red hair, this new tag marked him out and set him apart.

Overnight, he changed from a curious, outspoken and imaginative child keen to try and understand everything around him to a boy whom successive school reports characterized as anarchic and uncontrollable, deflecting each task with an obscene joke, flippant remark or wild prank. The only place he really seemed to feel at home was on the hockey pitch. He played for Middleton Hockey Club for the best part of ten years, amassing close to a thousand goals according to his teammates at the funeral.

It wasn't that Luke was a different person once he put on the shirt, shorts, long thick socks and studded boots, but that he somehow seemed to inhabit himself more fully on the hockey pitch. He was blunt remade as sharp, sharp as a sliver of broken grass. Sprinting across the Astroturf towards the goal, he possessed a grace and refined agility that puzzled and amazed anyone who had only seen him sitting slouched and morose in the classroom or had witnessed any of his blundering attempts at riding a bicycle, trying to cook or even catching a ball in the park. During hockey matches he was quick and alert, unexpectedly dextrous and cunning, and he revelled in it: showing off with dummy passes and half-twirls as he dodged effortlessly past the defenders determined to stop him.

Almost every week he attempted seemingly impossible shots at the heavily guarded goal, playing as if he was convinced that the outcome of any game depended only upon his confidence and self-belief.

There was something both uplifting and melancholy about watching him play. As soon as a game got going it appeared as though his mind and body were working in perfect tandem, with no gap between thought and movement, and no room left for even the slightest doubt. Normally he must have felt that his body was out of sync with his brain and unable to keep up, since I'd seen him dent countless tennis rackets and golf clubs by angrily throwing them to the ground when they would not do what he wanted them to.

Hell, he'd thrown a few tennis rackets at me! And many times, I saw him grow enraged when his dyslexia prevented him from translating his thoughts and stories into words on the page, or from getting to the end of even the simplest book. And that is why seeing him shrug off his frustrations and give in to instinct and intuition was both elating and upsetting, for once the weekend game finished and he got back home, thoughts of school on Monday morning dredged up all his resentments and disappointments, and it wasn't long before he had returned to his usual sullen, clumsy and surly state.

In the clubhouse, the world must have made sense to him. As soon as he was wearing his number and clutching his stick, everything was reduced to winning or losing. For a few hours, nothing else mattered, and that other life no longer existed – the one where random luck and chance often ruled, where everything was perplexing and threatening, and where the future promised only the possibility of further humiliation. It must have been exhilarating to go from being the boy who came last in every test during the week to being the club's star forward, bearing the hopes and dreams of all his teammates.

It seems likely that some of my brother's happiest times were on the pitch and in the clubhouse bar afterwards, because in the aftermath of those games when he was lauded as the saviour of the hockey team, he must have believed that anything was possible. Yet he was always the first person to say that *nothing lasts*. Even in the midst of celebrating, he would tell his teammates that they should enjoy it for now because things would probably be different next week – it was as though he had accepted that it was his fate to never be allowed to hold on to any of the glory or success that occasionally passed through his fingers.

Nothing lasts, but everything persists.

He never, of course, went away to university, but instead worked in a gym within walking distance from our parents' house. Even when he was living with his girlfriend in a small ex-council house in Lavant, working all day on the building site and half the night as a doorman in Chichester, he still frequently found the time to drive the 15 miles back home so that Mum could cook him dinner and he could kip for half an hour on the old, battered sofa in the living room. He was intimate with the area and took a great amount of pleasure in the fact that everyone who visited the local pubs and clubs knew his name.

When he talked of friends and relatives who had left the area and started again in new cities – including myself – he usually shook his head with a certain weariness. He felt we had failed some kind of test and, furthermore, our endeavours were ridiculous. How could someone hope to find happiness and contentment in somewhere strange and new if they couldn't find it in that intricate spiderweb of friends, family and memories we call 'home'?

I wanted to go home. But home didn't exist anymore. Because home was the place where my brother would be snoozing on the sofa or urging Mum to make him some pasta *and maybe a nice cup of tea while you're at it*. . . . Home was where we'd shared bunk beds and made forts. Home was the place where I knew I'd always find him.

And I know he felt the same. He knew where he wanted to be, and even as a kid he couldn't bear to travel too far from home. I remember our first trip across the channel, when he was five or six. We were walking back to our campsite after lunch in a neighbouring village, following a route that led down a dry, dusty road flanked on one side by a line of lanky sunflowers, their sullen faces peering down from over a pale stone wall.

All the local cottages had their windows shuttered and the roads were deserted save for a few shepherds and their flocks slumped in the shade; we didn't realize, though, until we were already halfway down the path and sweating furiously, that this was because everyone in this part of rural France was sensibly hiding from the midday heat.

The sun was blanching the road and a sandy-backed lizard scuttling across my foot when I stopped to draw breath. I remember Luke dragging his feet at the back, something we rarely saw him do as he usually delighted in taking the lead, rushing ahead every so often to make sure the path was safe for the rest of us. On this occasion, though, he was groggy from the heat and as we walked he asked again and again how much longer it would be until we got back to the campsite. Every so often he would kick up small clouds of dirt that, instead of falling back to earth, hung in the air around us.

We turned a corner and ahead I saw the burning air trembling above the path, the trees beyond it warped and contorted in the searing afternoon sun. For a second, I felt terrified, since it was as if the very fabric of the air was so flimsy and slight that at any moment it might rip apart and leave us staring into a gaping black hole, into which everything around us might suddenly be dragged.

It was then that Luke began to scream. At first I thought he had also seen the quivering heat lines distorting the track before us and was reliving the paralysing fear he had felt the first time we visited a fairground and wandered together amid the hall of mirrors – he had glanced into one of the panes of convex glass and thought that by some malevolent carnival magic the whole world had suddenly been transformed. My second thought was that once we rounded the corner he had seen how far the path wound down between fields and hedgerows before it sank into the valley where our campsite and our toys were waiting, and at the thought of walking that much further through the blazing sun something within him had snapped.

When we were finally able to decipher the words, he was babbling between sobs and sniffles; however, we recognized a familiar childish refrain, bawled over and over: *I want to go home*.

I want to go home. I understand that longing now more than ever. All I want is to go back home too.

He simply wouldn't move, and so we stood still for ages, the minutes made endless by the heat and the baleful urgency of his wails. At seven or eight years old, even I could see that his refusal to budge from the spot where he had set down in the middle of the dusty country track was completely at odds with his repeated desire to be taken back home – though I was careful not to point this out in front of him. I knew better than that. Eventually, my parents calmed him down with the promise of sweets and ice cream and he was coaxed up onto my dad's shoulders. Even then he continued to assert that he wanted to be taken back to England: to his own home, his own boglins, his own cats, his own beanbag.

He didn't cry again, though he remained withdrawn and restless for the rest of the day. We tried to distract him with Frisbee games, then with a trip to the small river beside the campsite where we tried to catch minnows and other tiny fish in our wispy nets, but nothing worked. He abandoned each activity after only a few minutes, only to reiterate his longing to be taken back across the channel. My parents repeatedly assured him that we would be leaving France the next evening, but it was clear he didn't believe them. He suspected that they were making this up simply to placate him and cover up the fact that we would never return home.

I have not witnessed such profound homesickness since. My brother acted that day as though his desire to go back home had taken the form of a physical ache that grew more unbearable with each step he took. He seemed somehow bound to this small part of the south coast, and that is why it is impossible, even now, for me to imagine him somewhere else.

Reflection

Homesickness is a form of dislocation, founded in a sense that who we are and where we live are somehow deeply intertwined. In some sense, then, it springs not from memory but from the body, and is not only the wicked cousin of nostalgia, but also a sibling of vertigo: that dizzying sensation whereby the body seems suddenly at the mercy of its surroundings.

Homesickness is also intertwined with grief: because home is made up of memories and people just as much as (if not more than) it is made of bricks and mortar. For me, it is one of those emotions central to bereavement. I've never had much time for the idea that grief has five stages – denial, anger, bargaining, depression and acceptance – because for one thing each person's journey is different, but also because the list seems woefully short. Where is profound homesickness? Where is panic, where guilt, where vertigo on the schedule? Nostalgia too, for that is the emotion that most often knocked me sideways in the weeks after the funeral.

Looking back with the warped perspective of hindsight, it is peculiar to think that the word 'nostalgia' itself was coined in the seventeenth century by the physician Johannes Hofer to describe the feeling of extreme homesickness suffered by Swiss mercenaries gone to war far from their homelands. Perhaps, then, I had inherited Luke's homesickness, but instead of yearning for that little house and familiar bunk bed where a host of boglins and toy guns and nunchucks and leather jackets were ready and waiting, I yearned for the past. Hofer suggested that the Swiss were particularly susceptible to nostalgia because when they left the Alps and descended to fight in the wars of the European plains, the change in atmosphere caused blood to rush from the heart to the brain. The nostalgic can be noted, Hofer went on, by his melancholy air, and by the general wasting away of his person.

There is no logical way to explain why certain images travel effortlessly from the short-term memory to the dull and murky depths of the long-term memory while others, just as vital and worthy of memorial, are lost somewhere along the way and cannot be reclaimed. But I can't help but think that we hold onto memories that remind us of home, that help us build up a picture of a tiny place that stays unchanged inside our hearts. During the heartbreak of loss, I came to understand that this place inside our hearts can be a source of strength: because home is something you carry with you, and in this way can never be truly lost.

The 'how'

The brutal truth: there is no way to write about grief without confronting the inevitable need to describe the person you have lost. As I gathered my notes and jotted my memories before writing this chapter, I started to worry that conjuring my brother's happiest times (and most frustrating failures) on the page would be too much for me. Too triggering. Too heart-breaking. Too hard. In fact, I found the opposite to be true: writing about Luke on the hockey field felt exhilarating, energizing, even pleasurable. To remember him doing the things he loved best seemed right.

- Tip:

    Show character through action. Description of appearance, clothes, personality, tics, traits, hobbies, likes, and all the rest of our ragtag bag of character-building tricks can be great. But they give us only a photograph: something static.

    Instead try to think of the page as your camera lens as you show us your best home-movie – show us how someone looks in their element, when they are most fully themselves. How would they want to be remembered?

The idea of home was my anchor for this chapter. It allowed me to explore different facets of my brother's character and life from one specific angle. This kept me focused and kept my writing from sprawling off in too many different directions. By setting myself a research question to answer (why did Luke never like to venture far from home?), I ensured that the writing I did was thematically connected and that I didn't try to do too much (something I'm often guilty of in my writing).

- Tip:

    Stay on task. Set yourself an explicit question that you seek to answer through your writing. This will not only get you writing faster and help you organize ideas and memories according to topic and theme – but will also allow you to build hooks into your writing that will keep your reader engaged as they seek to find the answers to this question too.

The idea of home was also important as it sustained me during writing. The memories of that childhood room we shared – the bunk beds, the boglins, the cassette player, the bookshelf – became a safe space that I began to think of every time I needed to relax or recentre myself (because writing about loss is realistically going to bring up difficult emotions). As I continued writing, I returned often to that place, to calm myself when I felt rushes of emotion and anxiety that threatened to derail me, but also to prepare myself to return to the past at the start of many writing sessions.

- Tip:

    Build your own internal safe space. Make sure you're in a quiet, relaxing environment (sometimes calming music or sounds can be useful), then close your eyes and try to visualize a safe and calming place that only you are in. Like mine, it can be somewhere from the past. Or it can be imaginary.

    Try to use all of your senses to picture your safe space: go through each sense one-by-one. Try to think of it as a welcoming space: one that needs your presence to be complete. Pay attention to the warm and relaxing physical sensations in your body while you are in this space. Enjoy the calm and return to it any time you need to.

Having a guiding topic allowed me to move smoothly and easily between different ideas and different times in Luke's life. His successes on the hockey pitch and tours abroad, our childhood holidays, his resistance to moving far from where we grew up were all linked by concept rather than setting or time period, and so it was important for me to re-establish that theme and anchor the reader in that connecting idea before making each movement to a new scene or memory.

- Tip:

    Pay attention to transitions. You can use disruption or digression to move into a new setting, a new reflection, or a flashback, but you need to do so smoothly. Sudden jumps are disorientating for a reader. Like me, you can first sum up or remind before moving in a new direction, or you can use contrast or character, action and dialogue to signal a change.

Be wary of boring and predictable transitions (the next day . . . on the other hand . . . in addition), and instead try to let the action of the scene or the ideas you are exploring show the link to new memories or reflections.

Prep

We're going to warm up by doing a quick character sketch. Surprise twist: I mean this literally. Yes, I actually want you to draw yourself in your notebook or on a spare scrap of paper. Don't worry if you're the worst artist in the world (like me!), our goal here is to jot down ideas quickly. So sketch a stick figure. That's you. What do people see when they meet you? You can add to the drawing, or annotate it with notes, doodles, thought bubbles and text. Spend just three minutes scribbling down what you think people notice when they see you.

Write

Now that we've sketched what we think people pay attention to when they first meet us, we've probably been reminded that first impressions can be misleading, and that appearance barely scratches the surface of who we really are. Identity is at the heart of memoir, and so a focus on all aspects of character is fundamental.

I want you to turn your gaze away from yourself and onto the person you've lost. There's no getting around the brutal truth here: this will be hard. It will involve calling up memories and emotions that are difficult and sad. If you get overwhelmed during this task – or even at the very thought of it – then stop. Wait. There's no rush, and we can come back to it later. But when we do get to it, you'll hopefully find the same thing I did: that the act of remembering and preserving something of the unique spirit of the person you miss is also deeply rewarding.

Characters come to life on the page through action – behaviours, traits, interactions, dialogues – and so I want you to write one scene where your person showed who they really were. Try to confine it to a single time and place where a conversation or action revealed something vital about their true character. In other words, let the reader see their full self. Remember them – and preserve them on the page – as they really were in all their complexity.

How might we show character in action without falling into listing or eulogizing?

- Give a hint at backstory and background (how we got to this moment, what you already know about this person) without letting it pull us away from the scene. Stay in the one time and place with only minimal asides or digressions.
- A little visual detail goes a long way. There's no need to describe every item of clothing they were wearing, for instance. Instead, pick one that might reveal something about their personality: shy or extroverted, slipping into the background or wanting to stand out.
- Focus instead on mannerisms, movements, presence. How did they act around others? What habits, tics or traits did they have? By focusing on physicality and sprinkling in a few of these details, the character will begin to stand out on the page.
- Character is relational. So show how they acted around others. Around you.
- Think about how they spoke. The little quirks of speech, the phrases they often used, their own unique turn of phrase. Were they earnest, sarcastic, gently spoken, rough and ready?
- Perfect people don't exist. So don't be afraid to show (or hint at) their flaws, imperfections, attitudes, niggles, annoyances: all the things that make a character portrait authentic.

It will be tempting to drift. To make connections to other things that happened before or after, to follow your train of thought to other days and other memories. Resist that urge.

Stay on task, and if you feel yourself wobbling, then remember: our goal in this writing is not to mourn them, but to celebrate them – to show who they were in the world and what made them startlingly, unforgettably unique.

Follow up

Read your scene back and zoom in on the interactions. Look at the dialogue: Have you done enough to make each person speaking sound distinct from one another? We all have different speech patterns, different dialects and different vocabularies, and dialogue is the perfect place to show some of these distinctions.

The reader wants to hear what people sound like, so try to make sure you're showing enough of this. Then check through each quote to make sure it sounds like the person, paying attention to the kind of words they might use and the way they agree with or challenge others. If this is tricky, then try to think about people in TV shows or in books that they sound like.

As you read back and revise, remember that all dialogue should have a function in a scene. If the dialogue doesn't reveal something about character or relationship or the wider world they inhabit, then it's almost certainly not necessary and can be summarized. Real speech is messy, and so it's better to convey the heart of the message rather than try to accurately report back a conversation word for word.

See if you can identify the emotion behind each line of dialogue: if not, try to rewrite it to bring this out. Be wary of repetition. Cut the ums and ahs. Use dialogue to show what makes people stand out. A little sprinkling of accent, dialect and dialogue tags (she said/he said) goes a long way.

Read

The root of the word memoir comes from the Latin *memoria*, which I'm sure will not surprise you at all to learn means 'memory or remembrance'. Writing memoir means diving into memory as a primary source, and so I recommend Tansel Ali's short video on YouTube titled 'Powerful Recall Strategy (How To Remember & Retain Better)', which provides a few tips for focusing our minds on calling up details from the past.

Try

Dig out some old mementoes: photographs (yes, the old-fashioned printed kind if possible), old diaries, schoolbooks, souvenirs from holidays, the kinds of things you might not have taken out of a loft or attic or old shoebox in donkey's years. Pick one item at random, and spend a little time sitting with it. How does it feel in your hands? What memories does it nudge awake? What emotions do you feel sparking through it? Make an inventory of these old 'props' that can be used both to feature in your writing to add authenticity and detail to your descriptions of the past and that can be set on your desk or writing space to get you into the right frame of mind when writing about your memories.

Chapter 5

Ten ways of thinking about the body

My journey

1. The body is memento mori

Your body is a reminder. A history of trauma, a language written in scars, a map of everything you have endured. But I don't need a reminder that he's not here, that his body is gone, his ashes scattered. I feel it in every bone.

Another way to look at it:

Crack an egg. Out slops the albumen, slick as snot, with the sun-bright yolk jiggling on top. Shards of speckled shell litter the tabletop. And the world lets you stay stunned for a second or two, and then tells you: put it back together again. Come on, come on. You're offered every tool you might need: soldering iron, superglue, screwdriver, needle and thread, microscope, grips and pliers. But you can't scoop up the gooey white without it slithering between your fingers, and there's no hope in hell of getting it all back into the broken shell. But the world says: get on with it.

2. The body is a battleground

As teenagers we would constantly pass comments on each other: I would call him ginger and scrawny, he would call me fat and greasy. I would call his friends 'chavs' and he would call mine 'gay'. I would call him 'stupid' and he would call me 'weak'. In short, we taunted each other without mercy or respite. We did it all so that we could briefly lord it over the other, taking infinite pleasure in those few seconds of put-downs until one of us would reach breaking point and lash out. He knew exactly what I hated about myself, all the little secrets I tried so best to hide, all the things in my heart and personality and appearance and social life I was ashamed of and wished I could change. And I knew the same about him.

We seemed to spend half our time in one another's minds.

And I am surprised to find that, despite the years, something of all this still burns within me. The love I feel for him is held in perfect balance against the hatred I nurture. Yes, I hate him, with a hatred that throbs like a raw wound. I hate him because he is gone, because this is bloody typical of him. It is just the kind of thoughtless, selfish and reckless thing only he would do: to piss off and leave us all to clean up the mess he has left behind. I can feel that anger and hatred throb in my head and grind in my teeth, in my tightening jaw and clenching fists, until I have to splash icy cold water onto my face to calm myself down.

3. The body is capital

Everything has a price. Here are the costs of saying goodbye to my brother: flowers, £168 (lilies with bobbing heads, carnations, dark chrysanthemums); crematorium fee, £1,100; doctor's fee for cremation certificate, £164; celebrant's fee for officiating the service, £150; funeral director's fee, £2,530 (preparation and transportation of the body; hearse; light oak veneer coffin, and four strong pallbearers in black to help us carry it); a scattering urn made from recycled paper, £85; wine and spirits for the wake, £400. Adjust for inflation.

4. The body is a site of desire

For his tenth birthday Luke begged for a black leather jacket. Every day for a month he pleaded with my parents to buy him one. Every mealtime, without fail, the conversation would be turned to the leather jacket. *Think how good I'll look in it*. *Think how impressed everyone who sees me will be. I'll clean my room every day, and never tease anyone again.* Pause. Silence. Then: *If you don't get me one I'll wait until everyone's asleep and then throw ice-cold water on the lot of you!* In the end, Mum and Dad had no choice but to give in. The one he chose was a tough, hardy biker jacket, black as octopus ink and with an oil-slick sheen and a musky animal smell.

Whenever I catch the scent of new leather these days, I see him prancing up and down the living room, flexing and snarling as though it had made him suddenly more animal than man. He wore it all the time, and it became difficult to take him anywhere since he couldn't pass a mirror without stopping in his tracks to admire himself, either nodding his head approvingly or else raising an imaginary gun towards the assailant he saw in the reflection, the enemy who might or might not have been just a figment of his imagination.

5. The body is a clock

I sat at my desk and attempted to total up my brother's allotted time. I estimated that his life amounted to only 8,923 days. Of these I could account for perhaps two or three hundred at best, though admittedly most of these are woefully incomplete and full of holes. I tried to add to this deranged arithmetic the new experiences he never got a chance to try, the places he never visited, the hours wasted on sleep, the lost opportunities and even the percentage of his life the two of us spent fighting, arguing or simply ignoring each other. Soon I was standing at the edge of an arithmetical abyss, with nothing below but an infinity of lunatic calculations. Life and death and numbers, numbers, numbers and nothing adds up.

6. The body is a pose

Machismo is a role people play, and he played it better than most. The strut and the grizzly poses. The weight training and the bulging suits he wore as a bouncer. The leather jacket and the disdain for anything poncy (like writing books). He had two girlfriends throughout his life – and by a strange accident of chance and caprice, both had the same name.

Becca and Becky. And in the months after the funeral, I so desperately wanted to ask them: *in those last years of frantic bodybuilding, how much of that boasting and bravado was a mask? How often did he let his guard slip, and let his feelings out? Did he know he didn't have to put on an act all the time? Or was it the case that the mask became indistinguishable from his skin?* But, of course, I could never find a way to ask a question like that.

7. The body is a receptacle for pleasure

Up in his bedroom, teenage Luke would often play his favourite songs so loudly that he made the floor shudder. Though he usually stuck with one of the latest West Coast hip hop releases, his taste ranged from reggae through to metal, the only common theme being that the songs he played at maximum volume had to be either raging vehemently against the world or else telling everyone in it to go to hell.

Extra points were awarded for the number of expletives a song contained. His music came pounding out while he bench-pressed in the small corner of his bedroom that had been converted into a mini-gym, or practised throwing darts with such violence that he often found it impossible to pull them out from where they had stuck deep in the dartboard or surrounding wall. None of this would have mattered that much, were it not for the fact that once he found a tune he liked he would play it on repeat, listening to the same track again and again, sometimes for hours. When this happened, the rest of us would have to resort to earplugs or rival music to prevent ourselves from being driven mad.

Just as we found his habit of playing the same few songs again and again to be a form of torture, so Luke would often grow enraged when he heard any melody that was placid or calm, as if he could not quite fathom why anyone would listen to music to relax rather than to rouse or stir them. Among the CDs of his that I came across after the funeral were *The Last Meal*, *Fuck It*, *Lucky*

Star, *Deeper Shades of Euphoria*, *Back to the Old Skool*, *A Grand Don't Come for Free*, *Confessions*, *Born Again*, *Death Row Greatest Hits*, *Rhythm & Gangsta*, *Shock Value*, *The Big Dawg* and *Execute*. Anything with a bucketload of attitude and swagger.

As I searched through his bags and boxes, these titles reminded me that his idea of a great song was one that had a relentless fist-thumping beat, wall-shaking bass, and lyrics that were either brag or slam. I cannot confirm this impression, though, since I had no intention of listening to any of them. Indeed, the first batch I found filled me with such anger that I decided to smash them to smithereens.

At first, I tried to snap a few between my hands, but it proved almost impossible. Next, I stamped on a handful as hard as I could, but CDs turned out to be remarkably resilient and so I had to take a rolling pin from the kitchen to break them into pieces. It was slow and methodical work, and by the end I felt ridiculous, not least because I had to find the dustpan and brush to sweep away the destruction before my parents saw it.

Once again, I felt like Luke had deliberately tried to make me look stupid.

8.   The body is taboo

Sometimes in the morning, I wake up wanting to scream at the top of my lungs: *My brother died. MY LITTLE BROTHER IS DEAD.* I'm not interested in trading euphemisms or shrouding the worst of it in silence, and the last thing I want is to turn away from the heart-mangling truth of it. Give me a chance and I'll holler it from the rooftops so the whole wide world below knows. *My brother died and I don't know what to do.*

Shame is something we are taught. The body betrays us. We shit, we sneeze, we burp, we hock and spit, we piss, we bleed. Copiously, endlessly, exhaustingly. But that's nothing. Worse still, we cry. We leak salty water. And that's far more shameful. Better to hold it in, and let your pain scald your insides. I want to scream a blood-curdling, ear-splitting scream. But I'm all screamed out by now. So instead I get up. Sling my feet into my slippers. Go and fill up the kettle.

9.   The body is a fluke of biology

At school Luke turned nonchalance into an art form and made it clear that he couldn't care less about books or learning or *any of that nerd stuff*. But once out in the world he threw himself into life: working at construction sites in the morning, then hitting the gym to build muscle and size straight after, then to town to work as a bouncer some evenings and working odd jobs all weekend to save up for his own place. He had too many plans and ambitions to keep still. Luke was so certain that he was gonna be successful – a champion bodybuilder, a self-made millionaire – that he'd already started bragging about his achievements long before he'd made them. He was going to make it.

And he almost did it. But for the quirks of his DNA that made him prone to cardiomyopathy, that hidden defect that made his heart swell and thicken and stretch and that none of us knew about until it was much too late. He didn't know, couldn't have known, that no matter how hard he schemed and worked, his whole trajectory was already mapped out for him, set in motion by nothing more than a few random mutations of his genes.

10. The body is a vessel

I've heard it so many times: that the body is just a bottle holding the bubbling essence of who you really are. And even if the bottle gets smashed or shattered the soul swimming inside cannot be harmed. I kept picturing my brother lying in the hospital mortuary, his eyes closed and his skin cold, and I had to tell myself again and again: that isn't him, that isn't him, that isn't him. The real Luke is already far away. But the problem is, I know exactly what he'd say: *You don't seriously believe that steaming pile of bullshit, do you? Pull the other one!* I can hear his laugh echoing around the dusty corners of my skull. He had little time for sentiment, for grand philosophies or the beliefs of 'bible-bashers', as he called them.

So, instead, I cling to the idea that the soul isn't something spilling out from the broken bottle and wafting up into the clouds. Maybe the soul is the part of ourselves we give to the world. The part that does not belong to you, that you cannot take with you when you go. And so I see my brother in every room I enter, in every object I hold close and in every person whose life he touched. His soul is the part of him that lives on in me.

Reflection

There are really no rules in memoir beyond sharing our truth. How we approach that is up to us. Of course, a blank canvas can be an incredibly daunting thing, and so it is tempting to fall back on familiar patterns of storytelling, such as the chronological account of our lives: childhood – adulthood – loss – coping with loss. Or, alternatively, following the Todorovian narrative model: normality – catastrophe – adaptation. But if each of our lives is unique, then shouldn't each of our stories be unique?

There are as many ways to tell a story as there are people on the planet. You could choose to tell yours as a letter to the person you've lost, as a collection of recipes, as a series of postcards, as an index of facts and data about that person, as an annotated map of all the places you visited together, as a list of all their favourite songs (or movies or books or snacks). You could write backwards, starting in the present and moving back through the past, or you could write alternating chapters that show two different timelines moving along until they meet. You could write a memoir in a series of Tweets, or as a script in the form of a dialogue with the person you are grieving.

The possibilities are almost endless.

My brother was unlike anyone I've ever met. Obstinate, stubborn, funny, difficult, odd. So why should a book about him be regular, formal, predictable in its structure and form? In this chapter, I wanted to embrace the multiplicity of how he was, and to show many different angles to our relationship.

None of us is one-dimensional, and none of our relationships are straightforward and predictable. No, we are all of us complex and often contradictory, and our interactions are intricate spiderwebs. If you want to dive in and unpick those webs, you can't be afraid of getting messy. Give yourself permission to experiment, to try out different structures or forms and see what fits: be guided by those unique quirks of personality.

My brother was obsessive about his body, particularly in the last years of his life. It loomed large, larger than life. His body was also the thing that let him down, that caused his sudden death. I couldn't ignore that (though for a long time I tried as hard as I could to not think about his body in the mortuary or to remember the more spiteful side of our interactions), and I soon realized that it made for the most obvious lens through which to examine our relationship. I can't tell you what angle would best suit your own writing, but I can tell you that it has to come organically: it has to grow out of your own interests and obsessions and quirks (or indeed those of the person you are grieving).

You'll know it when you find it.

The 'how'

Our body is our greatest resource. And yet so often our mind gets in the way. We overthink, get caught up in distractions, tend towards analysing when we should be feeling. How can we rectify this? By practicing embodied writing.

Embodied writing means letting the body lead the way: recording the tiny and subtle ways that our physical self and all our senses respond to stimuli and experiences. It seeks to share every nuance of what it is like to experience the world through our bodies, especially through creating a resonance with the reader so they might feel what you felt. How might we give embodied writing a shot? According to Dr Rosemarie Anderson, embodied writing follows a few key rules, such as:

- Tip:

    Focus on physicality in your writing. Try to depict an entire scene from the point of view of how you experienced it in your body. This means avoiding reflection on what happened, cutting out any time jumps (flashbacks or flashforwards), refraining from analysis and steering clear of any description of setting or character elements that you did not feel or experience directly in the body.

Good writing involves the reader in the reading. Writing is strengthened, then, when it is relatable in some way. I knew that most people have experience of arguing and fighting with siblings, so I focused on that aspect of my relationship with my brother to draw in the reader.

- Tip:

    Draw on common experiences. What are situations common to all humans? What are emotional states we've all felt? What are places and circumstances that make us all uncomfortable?

    Focus on the emotions and experiences that your reader will likely share, in order to build sympathetic resonance, so that each page of your writing is reminding your reader what it feels like to feel like *this*.

Our brains are constantly whirring, juggling multiple ideas at the same time. By breaking this chapter into smaller sections, I forced myself to slow down and tackle each individual idea in the space and detail I felt it deserved. Don't be afraid of slowing down. Of lingering, of zooming in, of focusing attention. There is no rush. Take your time to say what matters to you.

- Tip:

    Write from the inside out. In other words, try to ignore the continual mental chatter of the brain and write from your feelings, your memories, your guiding ideas. Don't let competing ideas distract you or lead you to rush into the next thought, reflection, memory or scene.

    You can help achieve this by balancing in your writing between internal and external data: in other words, between what you felt and what you witnessed. Try to spend a roughly equal amount of time on both and this will bring your writing into focus.

When I describe a scene, my first impulse is always to focus on the appearances of people, plants, buildings, streets and rooms: the colours, sizes, shapes, tricks of light and the movements, objects, tiny details that stick out. I'm a visual thinker, and I often go straight for how things look to help create a picture in the reader's mind. But writing from the body means balancing between the five senses and trying to have them in harmony.

For this reason, I made an effort to zoom in on the songs my brother loved to play and the visceral sensations of anger in the jaw, the head, the fists, for instance, to develop the physical effect of my writing.

- Tip:

    Don't rely on just visual imagery. Try to utilize all of the five senses. If you're not sure where to begin, consider all the different ways our bodies experience the world (such as our kinaesthetic, proprioceptive, visceral or intra-psychic reactions).

    Pay attention to how our bodies relate to and interact with environments and other beings around us, and try to describe these as you write.

Prep

Brainstorm: describe your favourite outfit. That dress or shirt you save for special occasions. The one you wore on a date or to a job interview. Set a timer for two minutes and jot down the colour, the texture, the shape, the effect. How does it feel when you wear it, and how do *you* feel: How does it transform you? Try to note down as many specific details as possible as well as memories it evokes.

Write

Memories are not just stored in some dusty old corner of our minds. They live in the body. So now that we've discussed embodied writing, I want you to write a map of your body.

This shouldn't be simply a physical description. Everyone has a pink tongue: what is interesting are the tastes you remember most vividly (the perfect knickerbocker glory you were given as a treat after coming second in the sack race at sports day in Year Two). Our bodies are time machines, and so I want you to think of the scars, traumas, pleasures and experiences that are held inside your body or written on your skin.

Be selective rather than trying to be comprehensive. I picked just ten ways of thinking about the body to focus on the role my brother's physical presence played in his life (and in his death), while in truth there are countless other ways of conceptualizing the body that I did not address. In the same way, there is no way to record all the memories and experiences connected to your own body.

Being thorough would also be draining and reductive: not everyone has a memory that springs to mind when they look at their little toe on their left foot. So instead, aim to explore those sensations, situations and recollections that spring straight to mind when you cast your gaze over that part of the body.

Start at the soles of your feet (I'm already thinking of the luscious sensation of sun-warmed sand beneath them, and of the shock of pain and cursing that spills from stepping on a misplaced Lego) and work your way up. Listen to your body as you move; follow the tangents and reminders. Move slowly up until, at last, you have reached your head and are considering your hair and its role in your life story.

As you construct your map, try to:

- Stay focused. Cut any backstory, explanation, reflection or analysis. We're aiming for short vignettes: brief, evocative descriptions or episodes before we move to the next area.
- Use the mapping of the body as an anchor. In other words, don't worry about transitions, connections, segues and circling back. Write each memory and then keep moving, rather than stopping to figure out how to fit things together.
- Try to match both image and cadence with the mood of the memory each area evokes: the giddy, sprawling rush of wild emotions that comes from the manic run to the ice cream van on a sunny half-term afternoon to get your hands on a Mr Whippy! Or the short, slow, laboured staccato from the time you twisted your ankle and the world slowed around you.
- Write from your emotional centre rather than from your analytical brain. Focus on feelings: What parts have you hurt before? What parts have helped you? What part of your body were you most self-conscious about in your teenage years? What parts have changed the most over time?
- Let your body guide your writing and tell its stories.

Aim to write for at least twenty minutes: longer if you can.

Practicing embodied writing will hopefully open up new possibilities for you to draw on when you write, as well as generating several possible memories and scenes you can later return to and develop.

Follow up

Take the writing you've just done and, if it's in a notebook or journal, photocopy those pages. Or, if you wrote on a tablet or laptop, print them out. Then use a pair of scissors to cut up each individual sentence and shuffle them into a pile. Then draw from the pile at random and see what happens when you build new paragraphs in this way. They may seem a little strange (and occasionally nonsensical), but don't let that put you off. We're not going to rewrite all our work like this. Instead, I want you to see what new ideas appear from these unpredictable and incongruous pairings, what new possibilities are opened up by these chance creations.

Do they give you new thoughts about how to connect ideas, or how to structure your writing a little differently? Make a note of them to help in your next writing session.

Read

For a thought-provoking poem that explores grief from an unexpected angle, check out Laure-Anne Bosselaar's 'Stillbirth', a moving meditation on loss that uses the image of a train at a station to paint a visceral picture of the slow and gradual process of bereavement.

Try

Embodied writing reminds us that sometimes we have to make an effort to shut off the critical and analytical part of our brains and instead dive into the physical, emotional and visceral world of our senses. In the same way, at a certain point, as a writer, it is absolutely vital to step out of your own head. There is a limit to how much we can reread and revise our own writing without getting lost in it. What we need, therefore, are readers who can help us confirm what works and what still needs tweaking. I therefore urge you to join a writing group to start sharing your work with others.

A quick search on Google or X or Meetup ought to reveal some writing groups in your area (and if you live in a really remote area and there aren't any, then you can join one online). Sharing your work can be daunting, especially when you're writing such personal material, but it can make all the difference. My hands were shaking the whole time I read the 'My Journey' section of this chapter to other people, and they were still shaking for a long time afterwards. But it really helped me clarify what I was trying to do, and to see which parts got a reaction and which bits fell flat. Just by reading your work aloud and discussing it with others, you are likely to get a clearer sense of what is successful and what isn't quite coming alive, as well as new ideas on how to develop your work. Be brave and give it a shot!

PART II

Writing as transformation

The chapters in this section will focus on transformations, from imagining to writing new versions of ourselves. Each of the chapters – on digging deeper into our thinking about place and belonging, on metaphors that guide us, on our inner natures and on writing transformations – aims to guide readers on how to use writing to foster resilience and access emotional truths.

Chapter 6
Palimpsest

My journey

I waited until everyone was out then took the car and drove east: before long I joined the slipstream of traffic moving steadily along the coast, following the rows of jagged cliffs that rise above the water for many miles, looking like huge teeth sticking out from some ancient giant's jawbone. Soon I turned from the dual carriageway onto the thinner road that leads to the sea, an almost unbroken line to Eastbourne, where my brother was born twenty-four years ago. This was no spur of the moment decision. I had been planning it for weeks since the funeral, itching for a chance when I could go alone.

Because I was being drawn back – back to the ancient pier and promenade where as children we had walked almost every morning, back to the grey terrace where we once lived. The past has its own peculiar gravity.

The wind was a low hiss by the time I reached the seafront. Thick grey clouds were being summoned up from the blurred line where sea met sky. I left the car in a small car park close to the beach and started walking into town, passing a long line of hotels and guesthouses, their whitewashed façades rising imperiously over the beach: Bay Lodge, Ivydene, East Beach, Sea View, Atlanta. Despite the discount signs in the windows and the new coats of paint, it looked as though many of them were unchanged since the time they first opened their doors to gentlefolk escaping the heat and noise of the city, back when the cool and invigorating sea air was thought to cure any ailment. Any ailment but grief.

I kept on past lonely postcard stands set beside empty Punch and Judy kiosks and stalls selling plastic buckets and spades, wind-spinners, rubber rings, inflatable dinghies and tooth-chipping sticks of rock. Eastbourne is a town that has not quite managed to shake off the archaic connotations of the Edwardian seaside holiday, and my mind was soon filled with images of red-faced men wearing straw boaters and daring ladies dressed in cumbersome, knee-length bathing costumes. How is it possible that we are able to feel nostalgic for something that we ourselves have never experienced?

The signs and posters on the shopfronts dotted along the shore bore testament to a time when families would save for many months for their annual holiday at the seaside: donkey rides, penny arcades, deck chairs for hire, paper cones of freshly picked cockles, pink candy floss, a funfair with dodgems, the camera obscura at the end of the pier. Unable to afford the luxurious guest houses on the promenade, most of these families would have made their way through the maze of terraces to the bed and breakfasts peppered around the old playing parks.

And it was here, in the backstreets, that my brother was born.

He was a winter baby, born on 20 January – a day of frosty winds and high, storm-harried tides. It was the dog-eared year of 1984, less than two months before the start of the Miners' Strike. He was a small, colicky baby, brought home to a small, draughty terrace whose windows thumped against their panes every time the wind stirred. Of the first year he lived with us all I can remember is that he cried and cried and cried.

As I walked on along the seafront, I tried to remember when I was last in Eastbourne. It must have been more than a decade before: the last trip I could recall was when my brother and I had been taken by our grandfather to play in the penny slot machines on the pier and attempt to enlarge his already impressive collection of copper coins. The sickly smell emanating from the numerous deep-fat fryers being used to cook ring-doughnuts on the boardwalk hung about the arcade, and there was a dense red carpet that whispered beneath our feet as we wandered between the machines.

On special occasions we would head out from the arcade towards the end of the pier, making our way past the poster shops, glassblowers, fish and chip outlets and tattoo parlours to take a ride on the clunky ghost train that stood beside the entrance to a nightclub. The door to the club was always padlocked shut when we passed by in the middle of the afternoon, and this made it more mysterious than the ghost train itself, especially after Luke hazarded a guess that locked inside were the demons and phantoms that had grown too dreadful to be let loose within the ride next door.

At the entrance to the pier, the sound of children fighting mixed with the shrill calls of the seagulls hovering in wait for a passerby to drop a chip or ice cream. I couldn't bring myself to step into the bright and swirling lights of the arcade. The place still left a bitter taste in my mouth because those childhood outings to the pier had too often ended with me feeling cheated. I used to hold on to my share of the coins as tightly as I could, studying the machines carefully to try and work out how long a penny might take to fall to the first level, while also looking to see which of the miniature mountains of coins wavering on the ledge looked most precarious. Once I had made my choice, I would take out one coin at a time and attempt to feed it in at the optimum moment, praying that it would push as many other coppers as possible over the precipice below.

Given the care with which I worked, it was all the more galling to see that though Luke took handfuls of coins out of his pot at a time and shoved them as quickly as he could into any slot within his reach, he was frequently rewarded with an avalanche of pennies. I could only conclude that he was somehow blessed, a judgement that now appeared ridiculous, not least because looking back upon his life, the one constant appeared to be his perpetual battle against that strange thing we call luck.

I closed my eyes and could see him there, watching all his winnings come clinking and jangling from the bottom of the penny machine. He wore a self-satisfied grin that he didn't bother to hide, while his eyes were dancing with mischief – the same expression he pulled every time he won at bowling, crazy golf or tennis, determined always to milk his hard-won success to the max. On those occasions he would be almost unable to contain himself, glowing with boastful pride and braying that it was not luck at all that had helped him but *skill alone*. Yet we all knew – but didn't dare say to his face – that the opposite was true.

Aside from the skills he later developed at hockey, Luke was incomparably clumsy and cack-handed at every game he tried. He was always too rash and impatient to master the basics of any new sport and was easily goaded into a blind fury that only made him still more inept.

Perhaps because Luke's victories occurred so infrequently, no one ever interrupted his bragging, and so usually he'd strut around like a peacock, recounting in epic detail every one of the moves that had led to his triumph. He had the worst short-term memory of anyone I knew – taking off his shoes and then spending hours searching for them, or later in life getting in the car and, halfway through the journey, finding himself unable to recall where he was supposed to be heading – but somehow he could recount perfectly every single one of the times he had beaten me at any game, from table tennis through to monopoly.

Since luck seemed to him so vital and yet so fleeting, he did all he could to recreate those circumstances when he had felt its touch. If he had once won a game of tennis while wearing a black headband, he would then put on the same headband every time he played. He amassed a whole army of talismans, small items that he had invested with meaning in an attempt to ensure that good fortune did not desert him: lucky penny, lucky socks, lucky teddy bear, lucky this, lucky that, lucky anything. And just in case this was not enough, whenever we started a new game he would set out a long list of detailed specifications about not being watched while he was playing, or the order in which we all had to take our turns.

There was always a lucky way of doing things. And an unlucky one, of course.

I turned from the pier and started to make my way deeper into the town, still hoping I'd soon recognize my surroundings and so be led by memory back to the place where we used to live. Even though we'd only lived there for two or three years when I was small, it loomed large in my imagination: a cramped terrace where Dad kept his bike in the front hall in order to ride to work each morning; where you had to wiggle the television aerial for hours to pick up a signal; where the yellowing carpets matched the yellowing wallpapers and where a bus stop could be seen from the front window so that we might run out just in the nick of time to get a lift into town.

I took a left onto a narrow street that appeared to be made up almost exclusively of pubs, betting shops, bingo clubs and pool halls. After a few hundred yards I turned another corner and found myself on a wider road where most of the houses were hiding behind tall and weathered hedges. Over the rooftops ahead of me I could see the thickly wooded hills that for centuries have looked down upon Eastbourne. Dark clouds hovered precariously over the range. I pushed on, walking down another road of high-backed houses, making my way further from the beach and drawing closer and closer to the hills rising up in front of me, all the while searching still for that small, terraced house.

I worked hard to focus my mind on our time there, only to find my memories starting to feel fuzzy and impossible to trust. When I tried to conjure up the day my brother was brought home from the hospital and entered my life for the first time, a picture appeared in my mind of the tiny, wrinkled child being carried through the door. He was not dressed in baby-grows and warm blankets to ward off the last of the winter chill but instead wrapped in old sheets of newspaper, just like the greasy portions of fish and chips for sale upon the pier and all along the seafront. Was this my imagination or something stranger?

The sky was now almost completely dark, with the silhouettes of the trees at the very top of the hills ahead hoarding what little was left of the light. I pulled my jacket tight against the wind. On any other day I might have taken the worsening weather as a sign that I was being warned off, that the gathering clouds were cautioning me to return to the car and leave the past unstirred. But I kept on walking, determined to prove, both to myself and to my brother, that our Eastbourne, the Eastbourne of our childhood, had not been lost.

I wandered past endless terraces, all the while clinging to a memory of the small bedroom where my parents first set down that little alien, still blotchy and red with creases. I remember that Luke had screamed, without pause or respite, every night for the first month of his life. At first I found it frightening and upsetting that my own mum and dad could have brought something so wild and untamed into our house, and when the little savage began to cry I did my best to stay as far away as I could. But I couldn't temper my curiosity and would sometimes creep in to peer at the boy between the wooden bars of his crib.

When I finally summoned enough courage to reach out to him, I discovered that if I placed my hand on his round, wheezing stomach, the tears would suddenly stop and his tiny blue eyes would blink open and stare at me as though it was I who had suddenly appeared from some distant planet. Every time, with this simple touch I could make him stop crying. I felt as though I had acquired a kind of magic power.

The shore was far behind me now, but the smell of it still carried through the streets and hung about the alleys leading down between the houses. I studied each building in turn, but I could find none that jogged my memory. Instead, the more I tried to call back our time in Eastbourne the more confused I became, for the fragments that remained of the years we spent there rushed back without order or sense.

Time seemed to flow in fits and starts back then – some days we would go into the garden in the morning only to look up the next moment and find the sun sinking behind the house. When we were four or five, I remember Luke frequently warning me not to even peek at the wooden clock in the kitchen, in case we would suddenly find it was dinnertime and so would have to give up our game. He believed that if we didn't look at it then it would not dare move ahead. Even when we took felt-tips and drew watches on our wrists, we made sure that the hands were always set to nine or ten in the morning so that the day would not be able to rush away and escape us. Time was unpredictable and every clock a potential enemy.

A light sting of rain began to whip across my face. The rain grew harder as I hurried around the next corner. It was soon blurring the yellow glow of the streetlights, and I was lost. Completely and utterly lost. I tried desperately to remember the way we used to walk to the shops, or even the way I'd come; but once darkness falls the streets of a town change shape and turn in upon themselves. I would not find the house now, not in the dark and the sudden downpour. Perhaps I never would.

I'd been foolish to think that going back would be so easy. The past is a place you can revisit every night but never really touch, and so soon I found myself running through the driving rain, coat pulled up high around my face, trying to find my way back to the car.

Reflection

In one of the most famous passages in twentieth-century literature, Marcel Proust described how after experiencing a familiar taste, that of madeleine biscuits dipped in a cup of boiled lime-blossom, suddenly 'the old grey house upon the street, where her room was, rose up like a stage set . . . and with the house the town, from morning to night and in all weathers, the square where I used to be sent before lunch, the streets along which I used to run errands, the country roads we took'. A whole universe of detailed memory is vividly conjured up from the depths of memory by the stimulation of a single sense.

But it is not only sensory details – the reminders prompted by seeing an old photograph, hearing a song you used to love, catching the scent of the same perfume a loved one used to wear – that provoke intense memories. Place also has the power to awaken the past. In fact, I would go even further and suggest that place *contains* the past. Memory is not only internal but also external, captured in the rooms, houses, restaurants, offices and cities we have lingered in, and waiting to be reclaimed.

For me, location is a form of palimpsest, in which different 'layers' of time co-exist and might, therefore, be accessed at any particular moment. The act of revisiting is not only a form of research for the memoir writer then – it is also a form of summoning.

Place can therefore function as a kind of archive. In many of my previous chapters, it is a specific location that dictates the action. When I wrote about the woods I used to play in with my brother, or the pubs where he used to work as a bouncer, the past came alive through stepping into those places. The same was true of returning to Eastbourne, the town where Luke was born. In short, place has a kind of agency all its own, with the spirit of the place, or 'genius loci', having the power to drive the narrative.

I wanted to show how place functions as a kind of palimpsest in which different pasts – both public and private – all overlap. I therefore sought to balance between descriptions of Eastbourne (both in the present of my journey through it and in its history as conjured by its landmarks and topography) and my family history there.

My journey in this chapter weaves between the present and the past to show that just because things occur concurrently does not mean their relationship is any more significant than any other two events. I wanted to highlight how meaning and emotion could be spurred in my grieving mind by any locations or ideas that provided a point of connection with my brother's life. In other words, I used these points of contact between different historical eras to show how the present is composed of splinters of the past.

The 'how'

Most memoirs are, in many senses, collages: collections of memories, places, experiences, people and minutiae. One key issue in life writing, then, is how to connect these disparate elements (which in all likelihood stretch across many decades and different settings) together into a coherent and accessible narrative.

In order not to end up with writing that is chaotic and all over the place, then, it is important to write purposefully: to identify what you are aiming to do in each scene or chapter. This will help you stay on track and keep the reader with you.

- Tip:

  Make sure you have an anchor. For me, the search for the old house where we used to live 'anchors' this chapter in the present. This allows me to explore different tangents and ideas (from the history of seaside towns through to the role of luck in my brother's life and my first memories of him as a newborn) without losing the reader.

  The anchor should be a moment or action in the present of the text, and you should keep coming back to it every few pages so that readers don't get confused. That way you can explore flashbacks, ideas, memories and reflections without losing focus and momentum.

Linking different time periods together can be tricky. Realistically, we have two choices. One, if you want to explore a specific past memory or experience, then commit to it and give it the space it deserves to do it justice. In other words, devote a whole chapter to it. Two, if you want to explore a memory from the vantage point of the present, you'll need to integrate the past into your scene. The easiest way to do this is through a flashback.

- Tip:

  Keep flashbacks focused. There's no need to provide a lot of backstory or preamble for flashback. Dive into the heart of the memory and show us only what matters. You still need to ground the experience in reality by including setting and character description, and including crisp and specific details, but these details should be sprinkled throughout the scene rather than being listed in long paragraphs or 'info dumps'.

  Finally, keep flashback to the point and remember to use transitional words and phrases signpost the return to the anchor in the present.

My scene was driven forwards by my desire to return to the first house we both lived in, the place where Luke was born, our shared origin. It ended, however, with anti-climax and disappointment. I didn't find the house we grew up in – either that day or any day since. But that didn't matter as much as the search for it.

- Tip:

  You don't have to have a neat ending that ties everything perfectly together. Fiction demands a cliff-hanger, a twist, a neat resolution –

but we are writing real life. Not everything works out perfectly. Failure, frustration and unfulfilled expectations are inescapable in our daily lives. Don't be afraid to show that. Embrace things going wrong: it will make your writing all the more relatable.

I wanted to show how the past overlaps with the present, and to do this I needed to bring Eastbourne to life, with its mixture of newer arcades and pubs and old-fashioned pier and rundown seaside guesthouses. I did this by accumulating precise and specific details, such as the exact items sold at the seaside stalls and the names of the guesthouses, to bring the setting to life.

- Tip:

    Use parataxis or hypotaxis to build up layers of imagery. Parataxis means to list, particularly by cutting out co-ordinating conjunctions and 'normal' grammar patterns in order to create a long, flowing, stream-of-consciousness style inventory of details.

    Hypotaxis, on the other hand, means using many short dependant clauses, linked by commas, to slowly build up a layered portrait of a person, place or thing. Try these out, but remember that one or two of these go a long way!

Prep

Look through old photographs. Maybe you've got some stored on a phone or in the cloud, but it's more likely that this will involve digging into family photo albums. Your aim is to find a picture that evokes a place: a family holiday, an old house or flat, a school or school trip, a party, a wedding or any other specific location.

Think of this as a precursor to diving into more formal research. Then jot down a minimum of ten bullet points about the background details you can spot in it (colours, objects, geographic or topographic details, people and their clothing and expressions, buildings and architecture). These will be useful later as utilizing some of these details will help in bringing flashbacks and recollective passages to life.

Write

One of the dangers of writing about grief and loss is that we end up spending a huge amount of time in our own heads. This can be draining for both the writer and readers. So for this piece of writing, I want you to focus on the external world and describe an object with a special personal relevance for you.

If you can find the object right now, grab it and put it in front of you while you write. A photo of it would also work. If you don't have either, then close your eyes and spend a minute visualizing it before you start:

- Begin with a description. Approach the object as though you have never seen it before. Try to describe it as though you are an alien who has never encountered such an item before, and tell us what makes it unique. Engage as many of the five senses as possible, particularly touch: What does it feel like? Think of the weight, the texture, the feel on your skin.
- Avoid listing. There's nothing more boring than a long catalogue of adjectives ('the tall, round, red, faded post box'). Instead show how your object looks from different angles, when the light catches it.
- Segue into the history of this object. How old is it? When did you get it? Did it have a life before you? Where is it from? Stick to the facts for now.
- Use these facts to move into reflections: What makes this object special to you? What emotions does it stir in you? What role has it played in your life story? What memories are stored within it?
- Let the flashback emerge from the object (like the genie wafting from the lamp). In other words, let the object stay centre stage and have the scene in the past revolve around it.
- Return to the present. Use the object as an 'anchor' and tell us what it means to you now. What emotions are bound up in this object? How often do you usually take it out or use it or look at it?
- Finally, write towards the future: Do you still have it or is it lost? Where do you keep it? What are your plans for it?

Aim to write for at least twenty minutes.

This exercise helps follow a pattern: moving from the present to the past, then re-orienting the narrative in the present before looking ahead. It is a simple structure, but an effective one for both peeling back the 'layers' of personal history and for anchoring a narrative in the present while also allowing for flashback and reflection. It also opens the door to thinking of other ways of writing about our own lives without always having to put our own thoughts, feelings and presence centre stage. Try to continue using this variety of narrative modes next time you write.

Follow up

Read back through the writing you just did and identify the places where you move from one time period to another (for instance, where the flashback begins, and later where you move back into the present). Are these smooth segues? Or do they feel formulaic ('in the same way . . .' or 'that reminded me of the time . . .') or a little forced?

Could you utilize repetition or juxtaposition to pivot towards a new idea or memory instead? Can you shake up the transitional phrases you're using and reach for some fresh ones? See if you can rewrite each linking sentence to test whether this is the smoothest way of moving the narrative to a new time period.

Read

For a deeper dive into writing that peels back the layers of history that lurk beneath the surface in different places, check out W. G. Sebald's *The Rings of Saturn*, which is both an account of a walking holiday across the Suffolk coast and a haunting and hypnotic meditation on history and memory.

Try

We can't write about what we can't remember. Studies have shown that working memory is improved by taking part in any of the following activities for as little as five minutes per day: meditating, code-breaking games, learning a new language or learning to play an instrument, mindfulness exercises and even painting. Pick one from the list and give it a go to keep your memory sharp.

Chapter 7
Animal instinct

My journey

When I first entered primary school, each of the students in my class was asked the same question: What do you want to be when you grow up? I was a shy child (and I'm a shy adult, though over the years I've grown much better at masking that shyness with well-rehearsed lines and predictable responses) and almost everything made me anxious. The only person I really felt comfortable talking with was my little brother.

So I really struggled with that simple task. What to be when I grew up? I listened as the other kids gave their answers: astronaut; striker for Tottenham Hotspur; ballet dancer; train driver. When it came to be my turn, I gave the only answer that honesty demanded: I wanted to be a dog.

This was no sudden whim. I'd given it careful thought. Running wildly through the woods, chasing shadows, hunting imaginary foes in the garden and the bushes, following my nose towards adventure. It sounded perfect. I'd be a dog. Because the human world is hard.

I'd put my hand up to give an answer in class and when I was picked by the teacher to speak, I'd open my mouth, but no words would come. I'd want to join in the football games at break time but feel too worried that I'd trip and fall on my face. Friendly kids would come to say hi to me and I'd find myself red-faced and sweaty and not sure what to say.

Luke would tease me mercilessly for my shyness. When I put on weight as a teen he made fun of me every day. I was fat, lardy, gross. A nerd, a suck-up, a teacher's pet. A billy-no-mates, a pussy, a waste of space. *It was clear*, he told me. *I was a joke*. And I gave it back to him as good as I got, because that's what brothers do: they say all the things that no one else would dare. And now I have no one left to be so brutally honest with me.

If I wanted to be a dog, then Luke would have chosen to be a cat. Not just because he was contrary and had to pick the opposite side to me in everything, but also because he always seemed to have a special relationship with felines. I was never a huge fan: there has always been something about cats that unsettles me. They have a sleek and haughty coldness that can make me shudder and, as a child, I dreaded the gifts of maimed and bloody baby birds, dead field mice clammy and warm, or voles still twitching in agony that our pet cats would bring to the doorstep each morning. I didn't mind sharing my home with them, but I never spent as much time trying to stroke them or tempt them into games as my brother did.

He treated them as though they understood each word he said, and he alone was in tune with their every animal whim. Like familiars, they came when Luke called, and often sat outside his bedroom door waiting patiently when he was not at home. At the time it didn't seem strange to me that each of the successive cats we kept as pets chose to sleep in Luke's room, at the end of his bed or curled up on his chair, while a number of them even took to following him around the house, staying so close beside him that it was possible to believe they had become knotted to his trouser leg.

We got through a few cats as kids. A fat tabby who disappeared after we moved house from Eastbourne to near Chichester. A small Siamese with a milky-white coat and dabs of brown upon the tips of her ears and the pads of her feet who became the first of our cats to be killed on the busy road beyond. A black and white ragdoll named Frodo who we lost to a tumour grown rigid and stiff within his stomach. A dark shorthair with zebra markings, superior and sly, who was the second of our cats to be killed on the road outside our house.

And finally, Mog, the only one who lived out her natural life with us, though I suspect this was only because she was too lazy to ever muster up the energy to force her podgy bulk through the cat flap in the back door.

Other families might have given up on the idea of keeping cats after the first two or three attempts. But somehow each new cat tragedy only made Luke more determined than ever to keep on stubbornly investing his time and love in these capricious creatures. Sometimes they were the only ones who took his side. Sometimes they were the only mammals in the house he felt like talking to. He alone among us treated them not as mere pets but as intimate allies, and he alone could describe in detail the distinct characteristics and preferences of each one.

In the day they were partners in most of his ragtag plans and schemes, and in the evening boy and cat often collapsed together in one great heap. Almost every one of the cats we had was deeply loyal to him. His legendary temper and his dictatorial approach to games of make-believe meant there were many afternoons when he would alienate even his closest friends and so be forced to play alone, and it was then that he would enlist a cat as brother-in-arms. Occasionally I even thought I saw him engaged in conversation with them.

I remember him once stating proudly that he was close to learning how to interpret every glance and movement – from the attentive way they preened their whiskers, through to the diverse ways in which they would flick and roll their tails as if tracing upon his leg a secret alphabet.

Sometimes I even felt a little jealous of the cats. Even during his unruly teenage years, when my brother was with them, he appeared to shrug off some of his usual belligerence and hostility. They alone were allowed to enter his private den, and they alone were invited to find a place in his world of weights and weapons. Luke would argue passionately that they were the most intelligent of animals, hunters so fierce and quick that they could catch their own shadows should they ever wish. Indeed, should anyone dare suggest that they were stupider than dogs, he would become enraged.

No matter how much affinity he had for cats, however, they weren't his favourite of all the animals. In fact, if I'd asked him what animal he'd choose to be, I have no doubt he'd probably pick a snake instead. Because he loved reptiles, yes, but more specifically because he knew how much I hated them. After all, that's why he'd begged our parents to let him get one when he was ten years old. At first, I thought he was just trying to wind me up or freak me out. But he wouldn't let it go. For weeks he harassed Mum and Dad from morning to night with endless requests for a pet snake until he eventually wore them down and they gave in.

I remain convinced that his sole reason for choosing such a pet was that he knew they were the only creatures I'm afraid of. He certainly succeeded in keeping me far from his bedroom for the year and a half it lived in there.

My phobia wasn't helped by the fact that Luke contrived to let his snake escape from its slim glass tank as often as he could. I have never felt more petrified than the time we were taking it back from the shop and it somehow managed to get loose in the car. For ten long minutes, I did not know whether it might suddenly appear slithering up my leg or whether it might drop unexpectedly from behind my seat and wriggle down the back of my T-shirt. For a long time afterwards, I couldn't shake off the conviction that something horrifying might be about to occur at any second.

His snake was never given a name. It was always simply The Snake, as if it were the only one of its kind left upon the earth. The Snake lived with us for about eighteen months, though I remember little else about it, no doubt because of my studied avoidance of my brother's room. I'm not even sure what type of snake it was (adder? grass snake? corn snake? ball python?). Though it often featured in my dreams I rarely got close enough to get a good look at it. All I can recall is that it resembled a short braid of frazzled rubber, with green scales and pinprick eyes that I never once saw blink.

Looking back, I feel as though the time my brother got the snake marked the point where our lives diverged. Never again would our interests and preoccupations overlap as they had when the two of us were young and did almost everything together.

Our lives raced off in different directions. He forgot about snakes, and over time he became obsessed with making himself into a different kind of beast altogether: something hulking and bear-like. In the eighteen months before his death, he worked out with astonishing intensity. He'd suddenly decided that everything about his life was too slight. He wanted weight, size, heft. He wanted to fill the whole room with himself.

Every day he followed a zealous bodybuilding routine, driving straight from the building site where he worked to the bodybuilding site we call a gym, stopping only briefly on the way to wolf down a huge plate of pasta. Then, about six months into this intense new regime, he denounced as inadequate his daily schedule of protein shakes and assorted vitamins and supplements and his diet of raw eggs, bunches of bananas and piles of bland carbohydrates. What he needed was anabolic steroids. These he began to procure from a contact at the gym.

What role did the drugs play in his death? Even the coroner admitted that it was impossible to say. Did they help push his heart past its limit, exacerbating the genetic mutation none of us knew about until it was much too late? Or did they keep him going, giving him the extra strength to carry on while his buried disease grew worse and worse? The only thing that is certain is that Luke was careful to keep his secret well-guarded, and only a few of his closest friends knew about the drugs he took each week.

But that didn't stop many more from correctly guessing what he had been doing. It's far from usual to gain more than three stone in little more than a year. His chest turned into a huge barrel of strained muscle, his biceps threatened to rip every T-shirt he stretched over his head and his neck became a bulging tree trunk knotted with swollen veins. He was growing into a huge grizzly bear. Somehow, though, we – his family – neither asked whether drug use played a role in his sudden metamorphosis nor even suspected it.

I cannot help wondering whether this blindness was accidental or whether we willed ourselves not to see what he was doing to himself.

Did Luke think only in terms of size, of the effect his great hulking presence produced, of the looks people stole at him, of the comments they whispered? Did he think the larger he grew the more threatening his appearance might become until no one in the whole world would dare to challenge him? Did he ever believe he had achieved his goal? Or did he dream of growing even bigger, of outgrowing everyone else in the local gyms until he was the undisputed colossus of the south coast?

Though it is impossible to second-guess the strange mechanics of his interior life, I am certain that his mind returned to his obsession again and again throughout his final weeks. None of us had ever seen him as focused and determined as he was over the idea that he might remake his body completely. The project consumed him: the harder he trained, the more fanatical he became.

For the best part of two years, he was absolutely relentless in his bodybuilding, in his singular project of slowly transforming himself into something new.

I have no idea what drove him to such extremes. But then perhaps none of us can pinpoint with certainty where our longings are born from, nor where our dreams might lead us. So maybe he wasn't like a cat or a snake or even a bear at all. Maybe Luke was more like a giant panda or a dodo, creatures whose inner nature has somehow driven them towards destruction. Pandas were once carnivorous and, equipped with great speed and ferocity, were able to hunt down any number of smaller mammals on which to feed.

Yet, for some unknowable reason, they have long since evolved into herbivores who survive almost solely on bamboo, though their stomachs and digestive systems remain those of meat-eaters. This means they are condemned to spend more than half their waking hours eating and, in order to conserve the meagre nutrition gained from their new diet, spend most of their lives in a slothful and sleepy state. This strange and gradual adaptation means that the few thousand wild pandas still living in the mountainous forests of Sichuan Province are now facing extinction. It is as if something deep within the species is urging the pandas towards annihilation.

But Luke wouldn't have had time for such philosophizing. He'd have mocked me for being pretentious, for overthinking everything.

An animal? I'm not like any bloody animal, he'd have said. *I'm me. And there's nothing else like me on this stupid planet, and that's a fact.*

Reflection

It's impossible to write a good memoir without opening up and being vulnerable. I wrote about my debilitating shyness and my fear of snakes in this chapter because these are unavoidable parts of who I am. Writing about ourselves is also good for us.

A study by Baikie and Wilhelm back in 2005 found that journaling every day about your feelings and experiences can improve your mood, enhance your sense of well-being, reduce feelings of depression (especially before stressful events like exams), help with the processing of trauma and even improve memory. Why might this be? Because by writing about your experiences, your thoughts, your life, and your emotions, you are taking control of your own story.

That's not always an easy thing. In all honesty, I don't often feel like I'm in control of my story at all. I might be the main character in my life, but half the time the obstacles getting in my way were ones I'd created. I've self-sabotaged before. I've talked myself out of applying for jobs or going on dates because of that little voice in my head telling me it'll all only end in failure and regret. I've often felt like I'm my own worst enemy.

But that narrative is dangerous. I learned that I had to stop telling myself *why bother*. To stop saying I was my own worst enemy. Because the things we tell ourselves have a profound effect. In another study, back in 2008, researchers at Emory University in Atlanta, Georgia, made students more or less confident about their physical strength by randomly telling half of the participants that they were stronger, and the other half that they were weaker.

They picked these students completely at random, regardless of how strong they really might be, their gender, their weight, their size and their gym or sport experience. Then they gave them a handgrip to squeeze to measure strength. The results were astounding: the group who had been told they were stronger held the grip for 30 per cent longer than the group who had been told they were weaker. The group who had been told they were stronger also felt less pain and discomfort in their hands.

This shows that the stories we tell ourselves affect our brain, and our brains affect our bodies. We're able to do more if we're told we're feeling good. We feel less pain if we're told we're doing well. There's a clear danger in telling negative stories about ourselves.

So, tell yourself you are stronger. Even if you don't believe it now. Even if you think it's ridiculous to talk to yourself and say: *I'm strong, I'm confident, I'm going to succeed*. Van Gogh once said, 'If you hear a voice within you say you cannot paint, then by all means paint and that voice will be silenced'. In other words, don't let that negative voice be in charge of telling the stories of your life. Cultivate a positive way of talking about yourself, of thinking about yourself. It really will make a difference.

The 'how'

Writing about our most primal characters and instincts, I was drawn to animals and the roles they played in mine and Luke's lives. This also allowed me to develop a juxtaposition between my own character (shy, anxious, dreaming of being a dog) and my brother's (more wild, mercurial and cat-like). To do this I had to first carefully map out the overlaps between distinct ideas and 'animal' natures in order to move smoothly between different characteristics and memories.

- Tip:

    Use story beats. A beat is the smallest action within a scene that marks a shift in tone. They can mark a turning point in a narrative or a switch to a different time period, incidents or actions/reactions, or moments of realization.

Try to make sure you have beats every couple of pages to keep the narrative moving. Don't get stuck too long in one moment and look for natural turning points that will drive the narrative forwards.

I knew I also wanted to 'zoom out' from my brother's unique and peculiar habits and characteristics to reflect on those inexplicable self-destructive impulses that sometimes drive us close to disaster.

- Tip:

    Think of yourself as a camera operator. In other words, consider what kind of shot each paragraph requires. I needed to zoom in on my brother's daily workouts and the changes in his body to show his dramatic transformation, so I wrote all those paragraphs in close up. I then zoomed out for the following paragraph to discuss a broader, more general idea.

    However, best to stick to one type of 'shot' for each paragraph, otherwise the reader can get dizzy from all the zooming in and out.

Balancing between small, specific, intimate details and more reflective ideas was important for me in building this chapter. It was equally important to not let the momentum of the narrative sag or come spluttering to a halt. If you flick back, you'll see I therefore tried to balance between different lengths of sentences and paragraphs to avoid falling into a predictable or routine pattern.

- Tip:

    Vary pace to keep readers engaged. One pitfall of writing about grief is that interiority can be like quicksand: once we get sucked in, it can be a struggle to pull ourselves out again.

    You can vary pace by switching between longer descriptive or reflective paragraphs and shorter ones that focus on action, events, interaction. Break up long, slow sections of description or emotion with dialogue or changes of direction.

My memoir gives my own theories and suppositions on my brother's actions and thoughts. It is, of course, his life as seen by me. It was therefore important for me to give Luke the last word in the chapter, and make sure his own unique perspective and voice didn't get erased by my own.

- Tip:

    Use dialogue to show character. Try to capture the specific phrases that person might say. The slang they use, the particular tics and idiosyncrasies of their speech. Consider confidence, mannerisms, in-jokes, little digs: all the things that stop us sounding like robots.

A little sprinkling of authentic dialogue goes a long way to building a picture of a unique individual.

Prep

Have you ever asked that silly question – if you were an animal, what would you be? For our warm up, I want you to take it a step further. Pick an animal that you feel best represents your character, personality and/or traits. Note down some of those particular reasons and overlaps. Then dive into some online research: aim to find and note down five weird or unusual facts or bits of information about the animal you have chosen. This will help sharpen the comparison and potentially even prompt some new ideas.

Write

Some of the most fascinating medieval books are the bestiaries created by monks and scribes many centuries ago. These books of beasts contain both real and fantastical creatures, a mixture of facts and myths and moral lessons. They are deeply weird and wonderful. We're going to create our chapter for a book of beasts: I want you to explore the links between animals and the people you love.

Why animals? Because it's an unusual angle, so it should get you thinking about your memories in a different way. Approaching character from a different perspective can help open up new paths and possibilities for our writing. It's important to be able to surprise ourselves sometimes. Explore the memories and ideas that are summoned by this wacky comparison.

- Start with habits, traits and characteristics. What is it that reminds you of a certain animal in this person's behaviour?
- Dig a little deeper: What specific events or interactions are called to memory by this comparison? Don't tell us about them. Instead, bring the memory to life by showing us a scene. Describe and depict a conversation, action or event.
- When we talk about our animal natures, we're often describing instinct and impulse. What about this person's actions and behaviours was impulsive or unusual? What set them apart from the crowd?

- These kinds of comparisons can be funny and ridiculous. Don't be afraid to lean into the humour and use a little hyperbole and exaggeration to amplify the comedy.
- Consider what impact this person had on the people around them. What was their affect? How did they interact with others?
- Don't forget about physicality: movement, mannerisms and of course those defining physical features.
- There's no getting around it: humans are weird creatures. Embrace the strangeness of this piece of writing. Swerve away from the normal and predictable, and instead follow the freaky and the quirky.

Try to write for at least twenty minutes. Try not to get caught up on tying everything together and writing a polished character study. Instead, aim to generate new material: approach your subject from this strange angle and see what sticks. There will be plenty of time to build it into a cohesive and focused narrative later.

Follow up

Return to the writing you just completed. Read through it and focus on what you have revealed about yourself and others. With each bit of information, ask yourself: Have I been completely honest here? Have I opened up and told the truth, or have I summarized, abbreviated, sugar-coated or omitted something important?

Memoir means opening up and sharing things that are difficult to write. Are there any places where you could add more information, where you could reveal more uneasy truths, where you could be open about difficult emotions, where you could share things you now regret? Seek out those places in your draft where you might dive a little deeper into the unpleasant or the shameful. These are what make us fully human.

Don't be afraid of adding more vulnerability and raw, brutal truths to your writing. Think of these as opportunities to make your writing real and to make it soar.

Read

I explored the affect of the stories we tell in our heads in more detail in my 2022 TEDx talk titled 'Changing the Story', which you can easily find on YouTube. In the talk, I explained some tips and strategies that can help us learn to thrive in adversity by rethinking the language we use and the stories we tell about ourselves in our heads.

Try

I want you to do a little more writing. Take your notebook and your laptop and write about something that happened in the past that still bothers you today. How did it make you feel? Angry, hurt, sad, broken? Add as many details as you can. Then find a comfortable space and lie on your back. Breathe deeply, focusing on taking full breaths in and letting them out again. Once you feel comfortable and relaxed, focus on the memory you just wrote about.

Try to picture the emotion of that experience as an iron ball on the end of a shackle, just like prisoners used to wear hundreds of years ago. This is what you have been dragging around with you, day in and day out. Imagine stepping out of the shackle and leaving the ball and chain behind. Leave the emotions with them. You do not need them anymore. Isn't it much easier to move freely without them holding you back? Now keep breathing. Try to relax the muscles in your body, starting from your head and moving slowly down to your toes.

This is a simple meditation, but hopefully one that will leave you feeling lighter and less bothered by that memory from the past. Studies have shown that meditation can reduce stress hormones by calming the sympathetic nervous system, so give this a try. Don't get frustrated if this one doesn't work for you – there are other types that might suit you better. The key here is making a focused effort to leave the things we don't need behind us instead of struggling on with those weights tied to our legs.

Chapter 8
Metaphor

My journey

heart

noun /ha:t/

courage, determination or hope

Everything comes back to the heart. More has been written about this fragile organ than any other part of our anatomy. It has been characterized as reckless and mercurial, the source of love, locked in battle with the more sober and restrained head.

While the brain formulates careful plans, the heart gives sway to whims and passions. It is the enemy of restraint and rationalism, the furnace in which our desires are fired. If that was true, then Luke was guided more by his heart than his head. His gobby cheek got him into countless detentions as a teenager and countless more fights on boozy nights out once he was a little bit older. On dares and sudden whims, he climbed up onto the roofs of houses he and his friends were walking by, only to find he wasn't quite sure how to get back down. He was more often guided by what would make his mates laugh than any thought of what might be logical or sensible.

The heart is not rational. And perhaps it was because he followed his passions so fully and indiscriminately that it swelled up so much: for when his heart was removed, it was found to be close to three times the normal size.

The post-mortem recorded that the walls and ventricles of the organ were so swollen that it was only with the most arduous labour that blood could be pumped through. His heart struggled, every day, until it could not go on. It was too big. So says the report.

At first, I felt relieved that I was getting close to understanding what had happened to him. But as I read on, I grew confused. I read the same sentence again and again: *Histological examination of the left ventricular myocardium revealed widespread myocyte hypertrophy with replacement fibrosis as well as an element of myocyte disarray.*

The words meant little to me, even after a day and a night with a dictionary stolen from a hospital. What, I wondered, did such words have to do with Luke? They were words that, no matter how many times I returned to my stolen book, refused to make sense. I couldn't bring myself to believe that the statement was about my brother – it might as well be describing the orbit of a planet I have never seen, in a universe far beyond my own.

The heart is a fist of muscle. But is that all it is? A collection of ventricles, veins, valves, arteries, vessels, muscles, nodes and tendons? What about the rest? Everything else hidden within – his dreams and passions, his quirks and idiosyncrasies?

The report told me nothing of why the illness settled on him and not another – like *me*. It wouldn't tell me why he in particular had been chosen. It didn't hint at where the condition had appeared from, or how long he might have borne within him such a fatal secret. It didn't say how he might have felt, or how the disease changed him as time went on.

I knew that he had in fact been in the hospital twice in the eighteen months before his death – once to fix a hernia developed after overworking himself at the gym, and once to fit a cast where the bones in his wrist had been fractured by an iron pole. But it seemed clear that he didn't speak about what else might be wrong with him, nor to admit he might not be as invincible as he often boasted.

The Romans suggested that the heart is the place in which our best memories and thoughts are stored. A kind of safety deposit box, a strongbox for secrets. Luke kept his locked up tight.

And all those secrets must have weighed him down. In fact, the only fact that makes sense to me from the autopsy notes is that his heart weighed 886 grams. The same weight as a bag of rice. Or a small watermelon. The weight is important.

The weight of his lumbering heart. It is important not only because it must have weighed heavily inside him for many months until the day that it finally gave in, but also because it is by such criteria that lives were once measured.

Because the heart holds onto all your regrets. The ancient Egyptians, preparing the body for mummification, would lay out the corpse and, after making an incision across the abdomen and cleansing it with wine both within and without, would remove the lungs, liver, intestines and stomach. Even the brain would be removed, courtesy of hooked rods inserted through the nostrils, after which time the body could be coated with resin and bound tightly in strips of linen. The only organ left in place was the heart. This was for good reason: the soul could not travel on into the next world without it.

At the very beginning of the journey into the underworld this most vital organ would be weighed, it being well known that all a person's sins and mistakes were written within the heart. Greed, malice, hatred, envy; all these were thought to make it grow fat and swollen. So on a great pair of scales the heart was to be weighed against a feather that stood for truth and fairness. If the scales did not balance perfectly, the heart was cast aside to be devoured by a terrifying creature with the body of a lion and the head of a crocodile.

When this happened, the soul of the deceased would be trapped forever somewhere between death and life. Only those with the lightest of hearts were allowed to continue their passage on towards the next world.

The heart is a cage, and without it maybe Luke is free. After all, it had only slowed his steps, until finally stopping him altogether. He had a literally heavy heart. Did he sense what he was lugging around with him in those last months? Surely, he must have felt it, the immense weight inside him like a stone, a cast-iron padlock, a dumbbell. Every night in the months after his death when I woke with my heart racing, I thought instantly of him, and wondered whether its inevitable thumping ever terrified him, or whether by the time he realized what was happening inside him it was already too late.

Did he try to ignore it, to forget about that feeling inside him?

The heart remembers.

The word *record*, to note something down and store it for the future, is derived from the Latin *cor*, meaning heart. When we commit something to memory, we say we learn it by heart, and it was once believed that our heart records our longings, our ambitions, our regrets. It is not difficult, then, to see how a heart can grow heavy. He always had so many schemes and wild ambitions. In the twelve months before he collapsed, Luke had sought to set up a doorman business, doubled his training at the gym to put on even more muscle in the hope of becoming a competitive lifter, bought a rundown wreck of a collapsing house on the cheap that he planned to do up and flip for a profit and started a new relationship.

He'd barely managed to start any of these plans. No wonder his heart was weighed down. And now so is mine.

Because the heart is a book, and according to the early church fathers this is the place in which our thoughts, our works and our sins are inscribed. Did Luke carry with him the weight of any regrets, or doubts or mistakes? What actually did he regret? My few guesses were feeble at best. Did he regret doing so badly in school? I wasn't sure. He had certainly been glad to see the back of the place, though in the last few years he had worked hard at college courses to gain several advanced construction and design qualifications of which he was certainly proud. Perhaps, though, he regretted his inability to control his temper.

I thought of the fights he and I often had in our teenage years, and of his legendary fits and rages that would cause everyone within earshot to scatter and flee. Yet those were long in the past. In his final months he hadn't warred with anyone. Not even me.

The heart is a mystery.

The more I thought about the things that might have weighed heavy on his heart, the more I began to think about how little I knew of the person my brother had become at the time of his death. As kids we were inseparable. He used to follow me around when he was little, so much so that I would get annoyed at how much of my shadow he always seemed to steal. We made up games and stories for afternoons on end, putting on little plays with all our teddies as actors, each one of us knowing exactly what the other would say.

And then as we got older there were the mad competitions and the desperate attempt to best each other: who could build the tallest Lego tower or find the fattest conker in the park or run quickest to the end of the street and back or spin a penny the longest or leap highest from the swings and many others even more ridiculous besides. Our days revolved around each other. But after reading the post-mortem report, I couldn't shake off the thought that I had lost my brother some years before he died.

I remembered the double in the supermarket, who looked not like my brother did in his last couple of years, but as he had been close to four years before. That made me feel even worse. His heart was too big; mine, it seems, was too small.

The heart is China, is glass, is something that can crack and splinter into pieces. How had we drifted so far apart? Was it my fault? As teenagers we had gone out of our way to avoid each other. Any time the two of us were in the same room some war or other would break out; at least once a week we shouted or screamed at each other or even came to blows. But those belligerent days had long been left behind and, in recent years, peace had broken out and we had laughed and joked as though the warring years had never happened.

If we often put off meeting up for that drink or getting together for a meal, it was only because we were both sure that the other wouldn't mind and that there would be plenty of time for all that in the future.

The heart is a ticking clock, a metronome. But there isn't any time left. Not now. Not only have I lost that future, but I also began to worry that over time my memories of our shared past would grow increasingly hazy and that each day I might lose a little more of him. Yet at the same time I felt as though I couldn't break away from him, and exactly two months after the funeral, just as I thought I might be coming back to myself, I began to be gripped by a strange feeling. Almost every night, as soon as I closed my eyes, I was overcome with the sensation that he was still there, lying as ever in the bunk bed above me.

If I listened closely, I could sometimes hear him snoring or muttering in his sleep. Occasionally I was even able to suspend disbelief enough to believe that at any moment he might swing his head down and suggest a midnight picnic or ask me to tell him a story about the land of bogey-brained monsters we might find if we were to venture through the secret tunnel at the back of the cupboard. Sometimes I even got as far as opening my mouth to reply.

The heart is a tiny treasure chest where we bank our ghosts. And here was one of mine, creeping out each time I turned off the lights. He can only have been three or four when we shared a bunk bed. We were living in a cramped terrace then, a house where the pipes gurgled and babbled all night. My brother and I had a raggedy stuffed toy that served as a doorstop so that our room wouldn't be completely given over to darkness. We also had a cassette player which told us fairy tales as we drifted towards sleep, and I can still remember the first time that I managed to force myself to stay awake (by repeatedly pinching my arm) until the story came to an end and the tape clicked off.

Silence.

For once.

Complete silence.

Or, not quite. Because once the story finished all I could hear was his snoring, as clear and as close as my own heartbeat.

Reflection

Around 2,500 years ago, Aristotle noted that metaphors played a vital role in speeches, theatre and poetry, but were not of much use when trying to express fundamental truths. More recently, linguists and cognitive scientists have shown that Aristotle was woefully mistaken. We don't just use metaphors to 'talk fancy' and write pretty poems. Cognitive research has proved that we *think* by using metaphors: they are crucial to how we understand and navigate the world.

We make sense of ideas and concepts always in terms of other ideas and concepts. Metaphors shape our reasoning and mould every aspect of our lives.

In other words, metaphors are the *beating heart* of thought and expression. (I couldn't resist throwing in another.) The common metaphors we use every day therefore reveal much about how we conceptualize the world around us. They also often leap and recur from language to language. For instance, in Mandarin, 心 (*xīn*) means heart. In Chinese, you would describe someone newly in love as 心醉 (*xīn zuì*), meaning heart drunk. Our dreams and ambitions are our 心病 (*xīn bìng*), namely our heart's longing. And the Chinese use exactly the same metaphor in Mandarin that we do in English: 心碎 (*xīn suì*), meaning heartbreak. Metaphors affect how we construct reality and communicate at a fundamental level. They are therefore some of the best concepts for us writers to dive into, explore, experiment with and tease apart.

The poet Tristan Tzara created the cut-up technique – where a text is cut into smaller pieces and then rearranged at random to create surprising new meanings – in order to both create original and unique metaphors and imagery, and to demonstrate the power of unusual or unexpected connections and juxtapositions.

The same technique has been famously used by William Burroughs and David Bowie, among others, and lies at the heart of all the sets of fridge magnet poetry ever sold; more importantly, it reminds us that new combinations of images and ideas – literally, new metaphors – can not only startle and inspire us, but can actually make us think in different ways. Some research even suggests that new ideas and metaphors forge new neural pathways in the brain.

The unusual quirks of language – the metaphors, the clichés, the idioms – also play a key role in stimulating creativity. Homonyms (would/wood, pear/pair, meat/meet, buy/bye) generate not only puns and dad jokes, but also the misunderstandings that provide the foundation for the plot of a farce, for instance. Meanwhile, idioms reveal much about the environment, setting, culture, character: the Swedish, for instance, say *Det är ingen ko på isen* instead of 'there's no need to worry'. The literal meaning is: *there's no cow on the ice*. Doesn't it make a wonderful kind of sense?

Figurative imagery isn't just a literary technique. For my brother, in the end, everything depended on his heart and how it broke, and so by pushing the metaphor of the heart as far as I could, I discovered new ways to look back at his life and our relationship. The raw building blocks of creativity, metaphors are also transformative: they help us make new connections, forge original and unique ideas, and approach the world in new ways.

The 'how'

Writers are often divided into two groups: *planners*, who outline and prepare each stage of their work before they start writing; and *pantsers*, so-called because they fly by the seat of their pants and figure out where they are going as they write. In actuality most of us find ourselves somewhere in the middle: overplanning can kill spontaneity and sudden flashes of inspiration that pull us in new directions, while lack of preparation can lead to our writing fizzling out and losing momentum after the first few pages.

For my practice, I find it most useful to begin with a specific question or theme, and then see where this takes me. This chapter's memoir, however, I approached as if I were writing a poem: by letting an image guide the writing, and by returning to that same motif of the heart again and again to bind the ideas together.

- Tip:

    Utilize repetition. We're so often told that repetition is cacophonous and lazy. But when used properly, it can pull readers into the rhythm of your writing. Think of songs and the choruses that you can't help singing along to. Or think of spells, where repetition takes on an incantatory power.

    This doesn't mean you should use the exact same words in the same order each time, but rather that referring back to ideas and images can lead them to build a cumulative power.

The heart beats like a drum. Time is an ocean. There are plenty more fish in the sea. The problem with many metaphors is that it doesn't take long for them to turn into cliché. Since my brother's heart was the thing that killed him, I couldn't avoid it, and yet I knew I risked wading deep into cliché with a number of the images I drew on. The trick, then, is to put a new spin on them. Think of those common clichés I just listed: What if we gave them a bit of a remix? The heart beats like an ocean. Time is a fish out of water. Now we're starting to create something new and surprising.

- Tip:

    Subvert cliché. Instead of avoiding them completely, play with your reader's familiarity with them. Scramble them, rewrite them, modernize them, crack them open.

    If that doesn't work, replace them with an image of your own creation that can do the same job but with your own individual imprint (after all, there are plenty of socks on the washing line).

A strong image sticks in the mind and makes the reader do a kind of mental double take. I was pleased with the image of 'a fist of muscle' because the word fist contains so many connotations (anger, violence, squeezing or being squeezed) that we do not normally associate with the heart.

- Tip:

    Use juxtaposition and unusual connotations to create startling imagery. Don't be afraid to get a little weird. Throw together contrasting nouns. Combine words that usually don't play together. Mix-up sense categories.

    Place words with positive and negative connotations side by side. Match action-oriented verbs with abstract nouns. In other words, throw in anything you can think of and see what sticks.

Part of my goal in returning again and again to the image of the heart was to replicate the way the grieving mind works: it stalks round and round in circles, like a tiger in a cage, going back to the same thoughts and ideas. In grief we get stuck. Our thoughts spiral. Yet the dangers here are obvious: the narrative too keeps going round and round in circles too. How then to break the cycle?

- Tip:

   Write towards resolution. When I'm structuring my writing, I try to think of each scene or chapter as similar to a joke. If a rambling anecdote goes on too long, the listeners will start to get restless and lose interest. In other words, it has to get to a punchline.

   What will be revealed, uncovered or learned here? What is the emotional beat you want to end on? Try to identify that, and then make sure each paragraph carries you closer to that point.

Prep

Make a list: try and write down as many types of writing as you can think of. I'll get you started: memoirs (obviously), Facebook posts, online recipes, work emails, shopping lists and so on. Keep adding to it. Aim for at least twenty. This will help warm up our writing brain but also give us some options for the writing task below.

Write

We don't talk about form much in prose writing. Poets understand that a haiku works better at depicting a short, elliptical image or moment, while a more detailed reflection on the giddy excitement of the start of a new relationship might be better suited to a sonnet. Ideally, form should match content and help emphasize theme and subject matter. Yet so often we think about the form of prose only in terms of paragraph shape and chronology.

Structuring my memoir in this chapter as an exploration of a single word, just as you might find in an encyclopaedia, forced my writing into different directions. That's why we're going to practice writing in a different form. Specifically, we're going to write a hermit crab essay.

Hermit crabs live inside shells that they find around them. They borrow their homes. And this is exactly what a hermit crab essay does: it borrows the form of another type of text. Hermit crab essays have been written in the form of letters, shopping lists, how-to guides, recipes, WhatsApp exchanges, diary entries, Twitter threads, star charts, questionnaires, job applications, obituaries, crossword puzzles and many more besides. They force us to think and to write in different (and often unexpected) ways and remind us that sometimes the message is the medium.

- Start by brainstorming some forms that appeal to you: greeting cards, resumes, brochures and so on.
- Select one of these forms that corresponds to the theme or topic you want to write about. For instance, if you want to explore love and compatibility, you might choose to write in the form of profiles from dating apps. Experiment and get your hands dirty: try out writing the first line of a few different forms and see which one pulls you in and makes you want to keep going.
- Be alert to the requirements of the form: What key information is communicated by this form? What is its usual length? How is it structured? How does it look on the page?
- Read through some examples of this form 'in the wild' and don't be afraid to borrow some of the specific terminology and vocabulary frequently used in it. You will need to modify your usual voice and tone to fit the requirements of this type of text.
- Pick out experiences from your life that relate in some way to this form, and see how you can make them fit. Experimentation and play are vital here.
- Don't worry about where it's leading. It might be a disaster. It might fail. It might lead somewhere surprising. Trust your subconscious and try not to overthink it.
- Have fun. This should be pleasurable, like diving into a dressing-up box as a child.

The French writer Jacques Jouet argues that when we work with new or unusual structures, 'the constraint is the problem; the text the solution'. See what solutions you might create by trying something new.

Follow up

Go back to your hermit crab essay. Hold it at a distance from your eyes (or move a metre or two back from the computer screen). Now scan it. The first thing we notice, often subconsciously, is how writing 'looks' on the page. How does this look? Is there a lot of white space? Are you writing in very short paragraphs or long and sprawling ones? What punctuation leaps out: Are you overdoing the commas and long, compound sentences? Are there lots of parenthesis or dashes to lead us into segues and digressions? Are you overusing semicolons or ellipsis? Do you have lots of rhetorical questions? Or is your writing only really using full stops? By paying attention only to how your writing looks on the page, you'll begin to spot your 'tells': the sentence structures, punctuation tricks and moves you fall back on a little too often. And if we can identify what we do too much (or indeed too little), then we can work to redress the balance and add more variety to the shape and structure of our writing.

Read

A great example of a hermit crab essay in the wild, so to speak, is Brenda Miller's 'We Regret to Inform You': a memoir about failures and regrets told via (recreated) letters received by the writer throughout her life. Look at how Miller uses this unusual form to build up a cumulative portrait of endurance. It was published online in the *Sun Magazine* (Issue 455) and is easy to find with a quick search on Google.

Try

Step outside your comfort zone. Read a genre or a form you don't usually turn to – some modern poetry, perhaps, or a philosophy book? Go to a gallery or a museum you haven't ever checked out before. Listen to a type of music you'd normally avoid. The more we step outside our regular routine and surprise ourselves, the more fuel we give that creative side of the brain that makes unusual connections and encourages new ways of thinking.

Chapter 9
Transformations

My journey

There was a brief period, between the ages of five and six, when Luke believed there might be a magic word that could alter the very fabric of reality. He'd spend whole afternoons after school in the bedroom we shared whispering different combinations, from *abracadabra* to *alakazam* to *bibbidi-bobbidi-boo* to *open sesame*, then leaving a pause after each one, just in case a genie might fizzle up from the floorboards to do his bidding, and occasionally looking down at his fingers to see if they had perhaps turned invisible.

I should have found the whole thing hilarious. He looked ridiculous, his face scrunched up in concentration as he invented ever more incomprehensible gobbledygook, long strings of nonsense syllables and weird noises, sometimes even shaking his arms above his head to magnify their power. It goes without saying that none of them worked. But I was enrapt. His certainty was infectious, and I couldn't shake the feeling that perhaps he was right: all we had to do was find the right secret incantation and we'd suddenly sprout wings or turn day into night or summon up an impossible door in the floor that might lead down to the kingdom of the goblins.

Because Luke was crazy about goblins. We watched *Labyrinth* on repeat, Luke whooping with glee whenever goblins scuttled across the screen. Every time we went for dog walks into the stretches of woods behind our house, he'd somehow spot the shadows of goblins darting behind every other tree. And at bedtime, he was captivated by *The Princess and the Goblin*, George MacDonald's classic Victorian fairy tale, and asked to hear it again and again.

I searched for our copy in the boxes of relics and mementoes from our childhood in my parents' attic not long after the funeral but couldn't find it anywhere. Perhaps the book itself has been spirited to the kingdom of the goblins.

I could still recall a few details of the adventures of the young princess and the son of a local miner as they attempt to thwart the wicked plans of a race of goblins that dwell in murky caverns and winding tunnels beneath the mountain. In particular, I remember that in the area around the mines the sound of goblin hammers and pickaxes could be heard pounding away throughout the night and that, though the goblins had strong, sinewy bodies, they had weak and tender feet without any toes on the end. I remember also that, at bedtime, after our mum gave into Luke's repeated requests and read from *The Princess and the Goblin*, so many of the images seeped into my dreams; I would often wake in the night certain that I had recently been wandering through underground caves in search of treasure.

Luke often told me that in the night he had seen a hidden trapdoor suddenly appear in the floor or in the corner of the ceiling, and out had poured an army of goblins, sneaking through our room and on through the window into the street. All this he watched with his eyes half-closed.

He would always deny that this was a dream and would often spend half the morning searching for traces of the trapdoor, even going so far as to root through all the cupboards, haphazardly throwing out the clothes within so that he might find the hidden passageway he was sure was located somewhere in our house.

We had to be careful, he said, or they might be back the next night and bring more of their companions with them.

I was more worried about the goblin I *had* seen. Because when he was four or five, my brother had a goblin inside him. It appeared whenever he wished to do something he knew he was not supposed to and, after the requisite mischief had been done, it would disappear as quickly as it had arrived. Luke didn't attempt any secrecy, though, and actually went out of his way to announce his imminent transformation, shouting that *Bebe is coming! Bebe is coming!*

I am not sure how he had alighted upon the name 'Bebe' for the creature he became, but those short, repeated syllables seemed to perfectly suit the manic and frenzied character that ran wild about the house. Although I was two years older, 'Bebe' attempted to bite me a number of times and broke many of my toys. Bebe, it seemed, had no concern over what punishment might follow his devilry. He would stamp on train sets, throw out the contents of cupboards and drawers and attempt to wrench every limb from every teddy bear, all while shrieking at the top of his voice – and the more annoyed and enraged I got at his wild behaviour, the louder he shrieked in pleasure.

Whenever I mentioned Bebe to my parents in the months after the funeral, however, I was amazed to find that they had no recollection of him at all. One night, after a few glasses of wine, we were sharing memories – keeping Luke alive in our thoughts and in our lives – but when I started reminiscing, they looked at me as if I'd told them the sky was upside down. They remembered the boglins that littered his room, but not Bebe. Boglins, I should explain, were rubber puppets with grotesque, distorted faces that looked as though they had been left to shrivel up, like raisins, in the sun.

To be honest, they were little more than a giant misshapen head; their eyes and mouths could be moved by thrusting a hand into the pit of the creature's skull, and their sole purpose seemed to be to allow the owner to frighten sensitive siblings. Luke kept them lined up in their cages against his bedroom wall, their wrinkled faces twisted into permanent grins, their boggle eyes glowing green in the dark.

My mind kept returning to Bebe though – was I remembering right? My parents swore they had no memory of him and all, and there were no other witnesses. So perhaps I am just imagining Bebe. Or perhaps he was summoned only a handful of times, tried out on a couple of rainy days and then abandoned forever. Or perhaps he simply kept his mischief well hidden from our parents, his power dependent on his being a secret.

If it was a secret, then it is one that is now trusted to me alone.

I have become Bebe's sole keeper and custodian, and though once I would have recoiled at the sight of him I am now glad to have him beside me. Bebe has grown less querulous with age – though also a little ragged and world-weary, with the first few white hairs starting to show. Maybe our minds are little more than dumps or junkyards, and in the weeks and months following the funeral, I felt as if my own memory might as well have been a mess of pruned branches, bags of cut grass, mattresses pierced by unloosed springs, broken crockery, outdated globes, collapsed shelves, brass beds given over to rust, piles of flies living like kings amid the stink and more junk arriving by the hour to be compressed, compacted, composted or buried deep beneath the rest. How strange then to find, amid all the scrap, something antique, something precious that only I know about.

Whether this makes me more of a curator or rag-and-bone man, I am not sure. But even now all it takes is for me to hear the word *goblin* and I am five again and witnessing another of my brother's whirligig meltdowns.

What seems strange to me, looking back, is that it took so little for Luke to transform into his goblin. One time he was building a tower of Lego, and he set a brick wrong and accidentally sent the whole structure crashing to the ground, and that was it: he began to turn. Another time in the midst of a childish argument – the kind we had every other day – I called him slow and stupid, and in less than a minute he was hollering *Bebe is coming! Bebe is coming*! Maybe he was right all along. All it takes is the right (or wrong) word for the world to be upended.

Because there were words he didn't like said too. He wouldn't tolerate anyone saying he was dumb, and he didn't like being told what to do. He hated anyone suggesting he might lose a game of hockey or a round of Monopoly, because he was a fierce believer in the power of the jinx. And if you said the word 'goblin' after dark, then he was adamant that one might find a way into the house through a crack beneath the door or jimmy a window open to sneak inside. He seemed to believe that as long as we said nothing, as long as we kept our secrets and worries unspoken, they would never become real – but the moment someone says something out loud, it will find a way to come true.

I pride myself on being rational, and Luke pranked me so much growing up that I am fairly certain my gullibility has by now all run dry. I'm not superstitious, and I'm convinced that most things have a logical explanation. But nonetheless, over time I've come to think that maybe Luke was right all along.

I remember the first time a girl told me *I love you*: nothing seemed quite the same after. Suddenly so many things seemed possible that before I'd never considered. I remember too, years later, a time I said *I love you* only for it to be met with awkward silence. The world seemed to shrink and contract, to become smaller, sadder, less worth living in. Three small words, and so much power.

I never told Luke how much I loved him, though. Never said how much he meant to me. Such small words but so hard to say out loud. I had a million or more chances, but I never thought to put it into words. He would have mocked me mercilessly, anyway, pointed and laughed and made me feel foolish for saying such humiliating and *gay* things. Though that's a poor excuse, and no comfort to me at all.

So let me say it now:

Luke, I loved you. Loved your laugh and your silliness and your sense of adventure and your bossiness and your passion and your funny stories, and even loved the way you fought me and wouldn't back down and your stubbornness and your mean acts of revenge and your little goblin too.

I love you still.

I say it now, even much too late, because I have come to understand at last what my brother always believed: that words really can transform the world. There are simple spells all around us, hidden inside tiny phrases that half the time we ignore. I say it now because these are the only magic words I know, the ones that make real what otherwise might remain only as fantasy and wishful thinking.

Reflection

The great British poet and critic Fiona Sampson noted that 'to write is to articulate and develop the thinking self'. Writing can help us process events, help us respond to challenges and help us (re)define who we are. This can be particularly important when we are dealing with grief. Trauma and bereavement can lead to a separation from the self (without my brother, for instance, I no longer knew who I was), which in turn can sometimes lead us to disconnect from others and view the world in a more closed way.

How can anyone else understand what I'm going through, some of us ask. Or, *I don't want to bring my friends or loved ones down with my misery.*

This creates a vicious cycle: because when we cut ourselves off from the people we care about and the things we enjoy, we end up becoming further alienated from ourselves. This is where writing can help.

Let's be clear: there are also dangers. If I had started writing about Luke's obsession with magic words and his freakish collection of boglins while my grief was still white-hot and scalding, I have no doubt that I would have triggered many emotions that I was in no fit state to control. There is a risk of re-traumatizing ourselves if we are not yet ready to process what we've been through. A simple test, then, is to see whether looking back leads to spiralling thoughts and emotions, or whether – despite the pain of grief – the memory awakens some pleasure.

I was wary about revealing Luke's little secrets – like Bebe – that were mine and mine alone. Yet by describing those childish outbursts and passions, I found myself chuckling away at my laptop. This gave me the courage to admit the things I'd never told him, and writing that down also committed me to telling others I care about how I feel. The writing, in other words, wasn't just about looking back: it also helped me envision a path forwards.

This shouldn't be too surprising. Research on grief has shown that the act of revisiting the story of bereavement in all its painful details (Stroebe and Schut, 1999), or writing down (Wagner, Knaevelsrud, and Maercker, 2006) that story to encourage different ways of thinking about the loss, has a demonstrably positive effect on the bereaved (i.e. one that surpasses control conditions). In other words, it is the writing that makes the difference, rather than the form. For myself, when I write about my brother, I feel the link between us sustained. Writing about Luke is a way of bringing that love I feel for him to life.

The 'how'

Even before I started writing about my brother's fascination with magic words, I knew where this chapter would end. After all, in many ways all of my writing in this book is an attempt to redress one of my biggest regrets, and to say the things to and about Luke that I was never able to say when he was alive. I had a destination, in other words, and geared my writing towards reaching that point.

- Tip:

    Select an ending that directly connects with the theme, topic or idea you are writing about, and keep it in your mind as you write. You might know you want to end on a final symbolic image; on an ambiguous note; on a revelation; with one of your 'characters' having the final word; with a circular return to the beginning; or with a reflection.

Whichever you pick, consider how you might get there: you can judge the paragraphs you then write in terms of whether they get you closer to that climax and whether they fit with the tone and atmosphere you need to build for that climax to resonate as strongly as possible with the reader.

It can be tempting when writing to feel that we always need to be building drama and racing towards the next denouncement or climactic revelation. But this can sometimes lead to rushing, and stops us from fully immersing the reader in our world. I could have written out my metaphor comparing my brain to a junkyard and then moved to the next idea, and the reader would have understood perfectly what I was getting at.

By unpacking that metaphor, by diving in and writing out nine unique and specific images, I slowed the scene down and forced the reader to not just understand, but to also *feel* what this metaphor meant in practice to me. I was bogged down, so I made a choice to bog the reader down too. Don't be afraid to take your reader with you.

- Tip:

    Utilize the power of lists and deep dives. The gradual accumulation of crisp, specific detail can help immerse the reader in the world you are creating. They can help in grounding your scene in a recognizable setting, or in opening up an idea you want to illustrate or explore.

    We often stop our lists at three balanced examples, but this is a reminder to sometimes go all in and use everything you have!

My brother's childhood transformation from a funny and silly playmate into a raging, tantrum-consumed 'goblin' would not have been interesting if it didn't mark such an extreme contrast. It would have been dramatic to open this chapter with a description of one of Luke's meltdowns, but that wouldn't have fully shown what exactly changed. Juxtaposition is a crucial tool in writing, but all too often writers focus on the change without enough set-up to establish the dramatic stakes and what has been transformed.

- Tip:

    Don't skimp on the build up. Writing about loss means establishing what has been lost. Writing only the aftermath, in other words, gives us only half the story.

In the same way, the power of a transformation or disruption depends on setting up the world before it was so radically altered. This doesn't have to be an exact 50/50 balance, but be mindful of tipping the scales too far in one direction.

As a teenager, it was possible to make friends with someone new through one simple question: Who's your favourite band? The question was often unnecessary anyway, given that most of us would be wearing a tour T-shirt emblazoned with artwork from the latest album by Blur, Pulp, Kula Shaker or any of those long-mourned Britpop acts. My point is that the things we love are not incidental: they are integral to our identity. Even as a little child, Luke was a collector of freakish toys and boglins. His favourite movie and book were crucial to his character, to who he was.

- Tip:

    Sprinkle in the things you or your 'characters' love. Our passions, collections, obsessions and hobbies are what make us interesting.

    Welcome the reader into your world by describing favourite books, songs, foods and places: suffuse your writing with the little joys that are peculiar and unique to the people you're describing (including yourself).

Prep

Our life is full of tiny transformations: some tiny and some wildly dramatic. As a warm-up, I want you to draw a rough timeline of your life so far. Mark down key life events and the big memories that stand out. Then go along that line carefully and try to identify turning points and transformations.

For instance, I've noted down the large transformation of starting secondary school (which I think transforms most of us!), of travelling abroad on my own, of my first day in an office job and also some of the smaller transformations like the first time I said the words I love you, when I grew my hair longer than my shoulders and when I started to really believe I could be a writer. Try to balance between the large and obvious transformations and the smaller, more subtle times you (or the world around you) have changed.

Write

Memoir is of course focused on the past – and how it impacts the present. But what if we were to move the goalposts just a little? For this writing session, I want you to travel into the future. Specifically, I'd like you to write a description of what your life will look like five years from now.

How exactly is this memoir, you might ask? Surely writing the future is purely speculative. An educated guess at best. But we've already seen that the tools of fiction (thinking about how we 'construct' character on the page, writing dialogue that captures the spirit of what happened even if it isn't an exact recreation, reaching for details and images that have symbolic power) are integral to life writing.

This exercise will help us flex those imaginative muscles and develop those skills that help make scenes all the more vivid and intense. More importantly, visualizing a positive future can be beneficial in building resilience and in aiding personal transformations.

First things first, it has to be positive. That's not to say that you have to imagine yourself as a multi-millionaire living on your own private tropical island without a care in the world. It also has to be realistic: to be grounded in experience. But it is important to make an effort to turn down the volume on that inner critic that may be whispering to you about worst-case scenarios and downward spirals and everything getting worse.

Let's start instead from the position that things will get better and the things you do today and tomorrow will result in positive outcomes. Let's focus on our inner strengths and our values and explore where these might lead us.

What I want you to describe is a typical day in your life, five years from now.

- Start with when (and of course where) you wake up in the morning.

- Don't be tempted to rush through the day and head straight to where you work and so on. Instead, take your time and explore each step of the morning.

- Try to engage all of your senses. Tell us how the bed you wake up in feels. The colour of the duvet or the curtains. The sounds coming from the window – birdsong? An ocean breeze? The bustle of a busy city starting its day? What do you smell – food cooking, coffee brewing, plants and trees outside?

- But don't forget to describe yourself as well: What do you see in the bathroom mirror when you brush your teeth? How do you look? What outfit do you pick to suit this new phase in your life?

- Root each sentence in the present tense. So no 'I will . . .' phrases. Stick to 'I am . . .' as though you are walking through this future scenario right now.

- Focus on actions, rather than thoughts. One way to do this is to keep your writing full of a variety of verbs that take us from one action to the next.

- Think about the people you interact with as well as your own actions: family, friends, colleagues and so on.
- What are the things that bring you joy in this daily routine? Stay on those positives.
- Try to zoom in on different aspects of your future: How do you picture your life physically, mentally, spiritually, socially, financially and professionally?

Write for twenty minutes, or until you've reached the end of that day you are describing. Then be proud of yourself: imagining a better future is one of the first steps to transformation and building resilience.

Follow up

Grab a pen and a notepad and then read back through the writing you have just finished. As you go through your description of the future, I want you to make notes on what might be needed to achieve each of the goals (if you envision doing a different job, what skills or training might be useful that you could research and start to learn now? If you want to finish writing your memoir, how will you continue to build time for writing and writing groups into your schedule?). Once you've made these notes, translate them into action plans: write down *three* concrete actions that you can start this week that could help bring your vision of the future a little closer.

Read

One of the leading experts on trauma, Dr Gabor Maté explains in a YouTube video entitled 'The Childhood Lie That's Ruining All Of Our Lives' how childhood traumas can influence our behaviours and the ways we react to the world around us. In this fascinating video discussion, Maté outlines how to recognize actions that might be trauma-driven and how authenticity can help us heal old traumas. Well worth a watch!

Try

Recent research published in the *Annual Review of Psychology* suggests that giving ourselves frequent positive affirmations can improve our health, our focus and our relationships. Affirmations are a type of self-talk where we make an effort to give credit to ourselves. They're a way of counteracting the negative and critical voice in our heads. So I want you to try to integrate positive affirmations into your day.

First, think about what you want to develop. This could be your focus, your confidence, your resilience or even your regular writing practice! Now try and think of some positive words and phrases that describe things you already do well in this area. The next bit is easy, though it can feel super awkward: repeat them every day. You can do this in whatever way feels most comfortable to you: you could say them to yourself in front of the mirror before you start your day, or you could scribble them on post-it notes you can put above your laptop or carry around in your bag. The key thing is to be consistent and build new positive thinking patterns by reaffirming these positives each day: use language that makes you feel good, and don't be afraid to modify and adapt them as the weeks go by.

You may feel a bit silly saying or writing these affirmations about how wonderful you are at first, but really, what have you got to lose?

Midpoint self-assessment

Well done: you've made it halfway through your writing journey!

This is a good time to take stock. We've written together about our most difficult times, and also about the joys of the past. We've looked at our animal, instinctual sides, and looked at possibilities for transformations. We've built a consistent writing practice, and that's a solid foundation for all the work we still have to do as we venture further along this path together. But before we stride on ahead, it's important to stop and reflect.

Because let's be honest: writing about grief is often draining. It can be pleasurable – but it can also be hard work. It requires emotional labour. So I want you to answer the following questions carefully:

1. Were there any times when writing about the past triggered emotions that completely overpowered you?
2. Were there any times when you felt you'd unearthed something through writing (a memory, an emotion, a realization) that was too difficult for you to process?
3. Do you ever feel as though you are not in control while doing these writing tasks?

If you answered 'Yes' to any of those questions, then it is probably a good idea to pause here at this point. You may not be as ready as you think to continue writing through grief. You may want to consider taking a little more time to grieve and to process your bereavement, or perhaps even talk to a therapist or professional. Please look at the useful resources on the following page – they are likely to be helpful. It can be a bad idea to dive into writing when all your feelings and thoughts are still raw, since you may risk re-traumatizing yourself. So slip a bookmark in here, and come back and start writing again only once you're ready.

If you answered 'No' to those questions, then you're ready to keep going. It's good to keep checking in with yourself, however. So before we leap into the next chapter, I'd like you to quickly reread the literary and artistic goals you wrote in Chapter 3. Do these still accurately reflect where you want your writing to take you? Have the results of the writing exercises in the last few chapters reflected these goals? Do you need to update your objectives in light of your recent writing? Or do you need to consider how you can more closely align your writing with your overarching plans? Now is a good time to see if you're still following the same track you mapped out near the start of this book, or if you need to do a little bit of course correction.

It's vital to occasionally step back and look at the big picture. After all, it's never too late to do a bit of tweaking. Once you're happy that everything is moving in the right direction, then let's keep going!

Useful resources for support

The Samaritans is a twenty-four-hour helpline that offers support every day of the year for anyone in distress, including those who are feeling suicidal, and can be reached at 08457 90 90 90 or via www.samaritans.org

The Good Grief Trust is the UK's largest bereavement support network, with a choice of more than a thousand charities and tailored local and national support services under one umbrella: www.thegoodgrieftrust.org

Ataloss is another charity that focuses exclusively on bereavement and loss, and has a huge amount of resources that offer self-help for grieving individuals and guides to well-being: www.ataloss.org

Cruse Bereavement Care provides one-to-one and other support to the bereaved, as well as running a support helpline – find your local branch number at www.cruse.org.uk

The mental health charity **Mind** offers peer support and self-care advice for bereavement on its website: www.mind.org.uk

Child Bereavement UK works with families and children affected by a death and also produces excellent resources that can be used by those who are bereaved: www.childbereavementuk.org

Sue Ryder Online Bereavement Community is a place to share experiences, get things off your chest, ask questions and chat with people who understand what you are going through: https://community.sueryder.org/

TCF (formerly The Compassionate Friends) charity offers support by telephone, or at local groups and meetings, for anyone affected by the death of a child (irrespective of the age of the child at the time of death): www.tcf.org.uk

The British Association of Counselling & Psychotherapy is the accrediting body for counsellors in the UK and includes a directory of professional counsellors via the 'Find a Counsellor' section at www.bacp.co.uk

PART III

Writing as renewal

The chapters in this section will help foster different ways of thinking about writing and our place in the world: the myths we make and the way we manifest our journeys, our relationships and interactions with the natural world around us, the internal dreamworld that we might summon into the daylight and how to write into the unknown.

Chapter 10
Fable and myth

My journey

Before there is an ocean, there is a sea. And before there is a sea, there is a river, a winding watercourse that twists and turns like a snake, its back ridged and knotted with the flex of its current. And where it turns a sudden corner in the midst of a wooded valley, a sliver of sunlight gets snagged between the branches that dip down towards the drift.

There it stays, tangled and fluttering in the stream, until a man out fishing one Saturday morning catches that same bolt of sunlight on his hook and reels it in. Then he tosses it into the bucket beside him. In the bucket that little fire writhes and burns, sparks and blazes, and while the fisherman has his back turned it grows into a newborn baby with a shock of fiery red hair, as burning bright as pure sunlight. Before the fisherman gets a chance to spin around, the little baby with red hair has clambered out and wandered off into the woods.

A born adventurer, he lives there for who-knows-how-long, raised by owls and wolves and badgers and does, a wild child learning wild ways from secretive beasts. He becomes a boy who prefers to eat with his hands, who loves nothing more than mud and mess, and, because of how that spark of him was first trapped and brought to earth, for the rest of his blazing life he avoids the ocean and lakes and rivers and even puddles on the pavement after a whole week of rain. Restless and curious, he wanders further and further until, at the edge of the woods, he spots a house with lights on late into the night.

He waits until the last one is switched off and then sneaks inside – finds a little bed in the corner of a room beside a sleeping child, then curls up and makes himself at home.

He becomes part of the family overnight, and no one speaks of the wild place from where he came, though there are times when his brother peers at him as though trying to fathom what kind of creature he truly is. After all, it is clear he is something different: that eye-watering scorch of red hair, that spray of freckles like the map of some impossible constellation scattered across his face. The boy knows it too, every time he glances in the mirror: he was made for something different than other creatures.

Otherwise the two of them are inseparable: brothers bound by oaths and imagination, united in inventing as many elaborate games and role-plays as they can squeeze into each day. His early years brim over with blissful adventure: drawing, building, snooping, inventing, exploring, all side-by-side with his brother.

Like the sun from which this blaze of fire came, others follow him everywhere, drawn by his energy and warmth and light. And like the sun, he burns furiously all day, running and drawing and even gabbling at such a furious speed that as soon as night falls he collapses into bed so worn out that he always falls asleep within seconds.

It is only when it is time to start school, forced into grey trousers and a forest-green jumper, that he begins to get a sense that not everything in this world is sunny. It starts as a small suspicion, like an itch he cannot quite reach to scratch. But no one else says a thing, so he tries to ignore it. Yet it niggles and prickles at him, day by day, that little doubt that spreads like a rash until it becomes a cold and terrible certainty: something is not right at all.

Soon it is impossible to ignore. The world is not quite the exciting paradise he'd imagined. Oh no. He soon works out what has happened. The planet has fallen under the control of a savage race far worse than demons with splinter-sharp teeth, far worse than the mischievous goblins who live in the hollows of trees and in abandoned rabbit warrens, far worse even than the violent giants who used to stomp across the earth crushing houses beneath their footsteps and feasting on human flesh. No, this time it is much worse: a thousand times, a million times, a gazillion times worse. For now, the world is under the horrible and sick enchantment of *teachers*: a truly vile kind of creature in a league of evil all their own.

Teachers: the very word makes him shudder.

He watches with horror as they try to make him and his friends conform and act sensibly in class instead of running riot and having fun. He recoils as they force him to try to read instead of daydream and create new and inventive games. But the letters seem to rearrange themselves every time he looks at a page. It is clearly some trick, designed to quench his spirit and dampen his imagination, like pouring water over a firecracker.

He decides in that very first year at school: he will not let them bend or break him. He will resist.

What bothers him is that no one else seems to have realized. But of course – they have been brainwashed and put under this strange and putrid spell. Nonetheless he tries to save them all before it is too late and they too have been transformed into mindless drones. He urges, he argues, he pleads. But no one takes him seriously. Even his brother, the one person who ought to believe him no matter what, does not take him seriously. Something in him hardens.

He fights back. He becomes a master of distraction and diversion. He learns that jokes can be weapons. That a well-placed comment can land like a bomb and undermine almost anyone. That pranks and practical jokes can sometimes be a teacher's kryptonite. He becomes evasive. And when all of that does not work, he lets his mind drift elsewhere as the classes roll by, convinced that it is only a matter of time before everyone realizes what he'd been trying to tell them for so long.

He waits. And waits. And waits a little more. Growing more impatient, more frustrated, until the frustration crystallizes into anger. Most of us accept the hardships we are offered without question. But not him. He continues to seethe and rage against a brainwashed world, and for a moment it looks as though the anger bubbling inside him will reach a boiling point and he will burst into flames and be consumed, burning himself down until nothing is left but cinders and ash – but then he makes another discovery.

This one, however, is not so terrible.

For he finds that he has a power. Sketching on a sheet of paper one afternoon, something strange happens. His doodle of a butterfly, a wonky thing with lipstick-red splotches dotted across its wings, starts to shake and rustle. He leans back from the page, eyes wide. It twitches and fidgets, flaps those splotchy wings, then peels itself from the paper and flutters across the room. He follows it, giggling with glee, even as it slips through the open window and out into the garden.

Back at the table, he grabs his pencils and a fresh sheet. He starts drawing: carefully, exactingly, his fingers slow and ever so precise. Minutes melt into hours. Until he has traced out the perfect tabby cat with whirlpool eyes and bristling whiskers: it wrinkles its nose, poises, ready and alert, then leaps from the page and struts across the table. He whoops and cheers. The cat purrs with delight.

He continues to battle against the spell that has enslaved everyone around him and made them yearn to be normal, to conform, to get good grades and do whatever the teacher says. But now he has something else to sustain him. The only times he ever stays still are when he is drawing or painting. He sits happily for hours on end with his paints or pens, while his brother eyes him enviously, jealous of his skills and of his powers. He doesn't look up. His brother is already brainwashed to do exactly what teachers ask. It is too late now.

He conjures up poisonous tree frogs resplendent in shocks of sharp colour that go hopping around the garden and then off towards the duck pond in the village green. In a fit of anger at another day berated in class for not doing his homework properly, he sketches a knot of dark clouds that rumble and bellow and burst from the pages to fill the sky with thunder and storm. He draws a snake because he knows his brother fears it, and when it slithers free he keeps it in his room to mark out a space free from the evil enchantment that seems to be growing more powerful everywhere else around him.

One year he draws a leather jacket and nunchucks and so transforms himself into the image of a rebel, a miniature terminator with the black shades and frantically gelled quiff to match. Another year he sketches a hockey stick and a team shirt with yellow stripes, and within days he becomes the star player of the hockey team. Yet another year he sketches bulging muscles, and overnight they grow until he has become a bruiser, a bouncer, a brawny giant. He stalks round town fearless and proud. And that helps, for a while: the hockey trophies, the friends, the movies, the hardman reputation. Years go by, and he almost learns to push that itch to the back of his mind. But somehow it always returns. The enchantment is unbreakable, no matter what he draws: the world is still against him, under the spell of an evil conformity.

Then one night it comes to him. If this universe is trapped by this terrible magic, then perhaps all he needs is to find another. One without schools, or books, or exams or pressure. One where people are free to follow their imagination. Even though the hour is late and he hasn't drawn a thing in years, he hunts down a pencil and tears a scrap of paper from a notebook. Then he begins to scrawl:

It starts as a rough squiggle of overlapping lines. A swirl. A scribble. The pencil going round and round. A dark circle. It grows and grows. An hour passes. Another hour. Finally he sits back and looks at it.

All is black. Not a single corner of white left on the page. A black hole. A portal.

He knows what he must do. He was made for something different than other creatures. It is time. He takes a deep breath.

Then he dives in.

Reflection

In his book *The Hero with a Thousand Faces*, Joseph Campbell suggested that throughout history, different societies and storytellers have returned, again and again, to the same fundamental story. Campbell called this the 'monomyth', a structure that is repeated in fables, poems and religious stories across the ages, always following the same pattern: a hero is forced to leave his comfortable and ordinary home behind and venture out to overcome some obstacle or difficulty. He faces challenges that almost defeat and destroy him, but eventually succeeds against all odds, and is finally rewarded for his perseverance.

This structure is familiar to us from ancient epic poems like *The Odyssey* and *Beowulf*, religious texts like *A Pilgrim's Progress*, Marvel movies and a large swathe of detective novels, as well as so many Netflix dramas that it would take another chapter just to list the title of each one. In other words, throughout history, we have dramatized our struggles to help make sense of the difficulties we face, and to foster hope. All myths help us process and understand the complex realities of the world we live in, and this 'monomyth' is no different. I therefore decided to experiment with my own 'monomyth' in order to try and see my brother's story from another angle.

Myths and fables are some of the first stories we are exposed to. Goldilocks, Little Red Riding Hood, Hansel and Gretel, King Arthur and Merlin, The Lion, The Witch and the Wardrobe . . . they all tap into our sense of both the wonder and the danger that surrounds us, and they all have something to teach us. By rewriting my brother's life as a fable, I allowed myself to do all the things he loved most as a child: to play, to experiment, to invent, to imagine and to tap into that vein of magic and wonder that runs through our lives. In other words, I set myself free from having to write factually, and instead I did what myths do best: I focused solely on the emotional truth. What resulted was a brand new way of thinking about, and empathizing with, my brother.

The 'how'

One thing that the 'monomyth' reveals is that many societies across the ages share a roughly similar definition of what a story actually is: namely, a series of events that involve facing challenges and overcoming obstacles. Even today, one of the defining characteristics of a narrative is that the protagonist goes through some kind of journey and is changed in the process – that's precisely what is meant by the term 'character arc'. With that in mind, this is a good point to step back from your writing and think about the bigger picture: How much do you want to cover in your memoir writing? Where might be a natural place to stop? In other words, what challenges or obstacles need to be overcome to find narrative resolution?

- Tip:

    Write your ending. Once I'm around halfway through a project, I skip to the end and write the last paragraph of that story. This helps remind me where I'm heading, which keeps my writing on track as I go forward.

    Don't worry about this ending being perfect: in all likelihood it'll change completely later on. But that doesn't actually matter at this point. What is useful is having a destination that you can work towards.

Fable and myth rely on the magical, the fantastical, the uncanny. Reality is always stranger and more wonderful than it seems. To maximize this sense of the unexpected, I wrote in the present tense. This created a sense that anything could happen at any moment.

- Tip:

    Write a scene in the present tense. Just because we're writing about the past, it doesn't mean to have to be bound by convention. Remember, on the page, the past is immediate and alive.

    The present tense is immersive, and lets the reader experience the narrative turns in real time. When you write in a different tense, you may find it easier to access the sights, sounds and feelings of that time. You may even take yourself by surprise!

Myths are often about discovery and adventuring into the unknown. Like all old stories, they rely on surprise and shock to keep the audience gripped. For my fable, I wanted to capture some of Luke's curious and adventurous spirit. I therefore tried to make my sentences match that breathless rush of excitement with which he embraced the world around him as a child.

- Tip:

    Use run-ons to build urgency. We're always told to be careful of joining multiple clauses together without the proper conjunctions or punctuation, but sometimes it pays to throw the grammar rulebook out of the window.

    Linking together short, sharp sentences with commas or simply 'and' will speed up the pace and help you gain momentum as you build towards a climax, reveal, or new turn in your narrative. However, be careful not to do this too often or your readers will get exhausted!

One of the dangers of memoir is that we can sometimes get stuck in a single point of view. I don't know about you, but at times I get fed up writing about myself and my own perspective – and if I feel like that as the writer, then I can be sure that readers will feel the same way. Writing a fable gave me the chance to slip into the background as a minor character and explore telling a story from another point of view.

- Tip:

    Switch gears to stop getting stuck. In other words, when you feel you might be slipping into the same patterns (structuring scenes in the same way, falling back on familiar descriptions, repeating character details), shake things up.

Write from a different perspective, or structure a scene backwards, or write an entire chapter in dialogue and text messages, or jump forward in time. It never hurts to step back every so often and make sure your writing isn't in danger of becoming too predictable.

Prep

To warm up, I want you to do three minutes of free writing. Remember, keep your pen on the paper (or your fingers on the keyboard) at all times, and write without letting your inner editor get in the way. The goal is quantity, not quality, so write down anything at all that leaps into your mind. We're going to make a list: all the unexpected or surprising things that have ever happened to you. Try to jot down as many as you can. Ready? Set. Go!

Write

In his startling modernist poem, *The Love Song of J. Alfred Prufrock*, T. S. Eliot writes 'No! I am not Prince Hamlet, nor was meant to be; / Am an attendant lord, one that will do / To swell a progress, start a scene or two', as the narrator resigns himself to a life lived mainly in the background of other people's dramas. Most of us believe ourselves to be the star of our own lives – the main character, the protagonist, the Hamlet. So what would a memoir look like when we relegated ourselves to secondary characters in other people's stories?

I'm sure you've already guessed that I want you to write your own fable. But to nudge you even further outside your comfort zone, and to get us really experimenting, I want you to go one step further: make yourself the 'villain' or the antagonist of this particular story.

There's a danger in memoir of prioritizing one viewpoint above all others. This writing exercise will help us decentre our own perspective and help us practice seeing and thinking through other's eyes. It may feel unsettling at first, but stepping out of your comfort zone like this is bound to make you recognize some of the subconscious assumptions and expectations that usually govern your writing:

- Every fable needs a hero. Focus on the person whose experiences and story you think you can show in a new light.
- Embrace the tropes and clichés. Don't be afraid of diving in with a 'Once upon a time . . .' as long as you make it your own.

- Let the traditional structure guide you. Follow the regular format of a fable: introduce the 'hero', then show us the obstacles in their way. Use that conflict to build to a climax, then end with a resolution. Of course, feel free to change any of these – but if you ditch all of them, then it won't be a fable anymore!
- Fables are supposed to be fun. Use humour. Keep it relatively light. Entertain the reader.
- Keep moving. Fables are driven by action and events.
- Sprinkle in a little magic and wonder. Don't be afraid of hyperbole or a little bit of the impossible.
- Don't lost sight of the central journey: stick close to your protagonist and show us how they overcame a 'mythic' struggle.

More than anything else, the goal here is to experiment, play, have fun and try things you wouldn't usually consider in a memoir.

Aim to write at least three pages (even if you have to spread this over a couple of writing sessions).

Follow up

Return to the writing you just completed and focus on those first couple of sentences – otherwise known as the 'hook'. This is the place where we should be aiming to grab the reader's attention. Does your opening set up the tone and atmosphere you want for this narrative? Is it specific, or is it a little generic? Does it set up any questions for the curious reader that will make them want to keep reading to find the answers to? Does it surprise in some way, or is it predictable? Try to rewrite these first two sentences – change the order, the images, the descriptions or even the action itself – until you have created something that you feel grabs the reader by the lapels straight away and drags them kicking and screaming into the page.

Read

If this chapter has given you a taste for fables from a different perspective, consider diving into one of the recent retellings of ancient myths. One I'd recommend is *Love in Colour* by Bolu Babalola, a collection of vivid and magical retellings about characters whose lives are complicated by the whims of the gods.

Try

Sometimes we can spend so much time rewriting, editing and revising that we no longer feel sure whether we've improved a draft or made it worse! That's why many writers turn to a reader they can trust to give them a bit of honest feedback as they go along. Consider finding an 'alpha reader' to read your work-in-progress and to discuss your goals and objectives with. This could be a trusted friend or family member, it could be someone in your writing group or it could be someone you've never met. If you have no idea who to ask to be your alpha reader, look through the *r/writing* forum on Reddit or search through the *#writingcommunity* on X for advice and sites to match writers together. Finding someone who will give you unfiltered feedback is a great way to help you find out what is working in your draft and what needs a little more polishing.

Chapter 11
Personal ecology

My journey

It was a cloudless day when we gathered in Fittleworth to scatter my brother's ashes, with the sun reeling low in the sky and burning upon the back of my neck. I kept my head down as I followed the dark track of trampled leaves through the slopes and inclines of what Luke had named the Bracken Woods on account of the incalculable amount of coarse ferns that cover the slopes. From the car park we had to scramble up a sharp ridge amid a scattering of silver birches leaning towards the drop, some slanted at such a dramatic angle that it seemed a miracle they didn't tumble backwards down the hillside when we rested against them to draw breath.

Halfway to the trig point we passed a few lolloping dogs and their owners striding close behind and, though each of us was sullen and pensive, when they smiled and raised their hands in greeting we smiled too and nodded back. I was amazed at how easy it was to pretend, if only for a second or two, that instead of scattering my brother's ashes among the bracken, we were simply out for an afternoon stroll on a warm summer afternoon. I was overcome with shame, and I was sure our smiles must have appeared so false and badly acted that I couldn't believe the dog-walkers didn't turn away in embarrassment. Yet they carried on blithely past us, their dogs scaring up small schools of blue tits from the brush.

Only a few minutes later we reached the trig point at Hesworth Common, where the downs could be seen rising and slipping in successive waves into the distance. The earth itself was in flight, rippling outwards from the spot where I stood, staring.

We didn't stop there long, and soon we were hurrying down a short slope on the other side of the common. We rushed and bustled as though in a hurry, though none of us had anywhere else to be. The track diverged at several points, though we ignored the pathways that led towards the wiry press of holly trees and those that skittered further down into the swaying sea of bracken, where I had no doubt that a host of sleeping adders lay coiled. Instead we followed a thin, curling trail winding through the woods.

The whole area was as labyrinthine and difficult to navigate as it had been when me and Luke were kids, with every turning branching off into several competing tracks, half of which vanished into dead ends or tangled shrubs, while many of the others doubled back upon themselves or led only in large, looping circles. Nevertheless, after twenty minutes, we finally reached a clearing at the top of a squat hill that opened upon a gradual descent of heather.

The flowers were mauve and stippled with white in the feverish heat of midsummer. From afar the low-lying shrub might easily be mistaken for a dark fire glowing on the hillside. There was a sweet fragrance rising from the slope, and I remembered reading that heather is food not only for grouse, deer and bees, but also for fairies.

In fact, there was a time when fairies were thought to be so thick upon the British Isles that much was done to guard against their malice and spite. Fairies were thought to possess the ability to assume different shapes; for though some may have been tiny, impish creatures, there were also thought to be a great number of oafish fairies who resembled trolls, as well as others of incomparable stature and grace. It was said that they were responsible for the noises heard in the bones of empty houses deep at night, and also for the flickers of movement caught in the corners of mirrors, and for the cold breath that you might feel upon the back of your neck when you venture alone through an old building.

They were also said to sneak into houses and steal newborn babies from their cribs, trading each human child for one of their own. A family might only realize that such a swap had taken place many years later, by which time it would be too late to reclaim the baby that had been stolen; there would be nothing to be done but to take care of the fairy child and hope the fairies were doing the same for the little human now living in their midst. Fairy children were said to be easy to spot: if the child developed more slowly than others of its age, if its hair was thick and easy to become matted upon the comb, if its ears pointed out and away from the head, if it preferred going barefoot to wearing shoes, if it babbled away in a language of its own invention or if it lacked a healthy appetite, then you could be certain that you had been duped and had a fairy child.

There were, I admit, many occasions when I was young that I wondered whether Luke might have been the product of some similar trick. I mean, seriously, could he really have been related to me? We were so different in almost every way. Where I was a quiet child with my mum's own tawny hair, he was wild, loud, prone to tantrums and allergic at first to almost everything. Above all, he had a mane of fiery red hair. I know that many children at some time entertain the fantasy that they are different, that they must have been secretly adopted since they cannot believe they are related to the people they call mum and dad; in my case, though, it was not *my* origin I questioned but Luke's.

Where he might have come from, however, I could not say. From somewhere close behind I caught the whoops and screams of a gaggle of children giving chase through the wallows of bracken. The summer holidays of our childhood were filled with long afternoons spent in these woods, and I can recall with perfect clarity a group of us setting off from one of the paths into the dense wilds of scrub and beech, Luke leading the way. The game was, as ever, a variation on war, with the forest providing innumerable hiding places and vantage points to aid the improvisation of manic battles, long campaigns and covert operations against some imaginary enemy lurking in the undergrowth.

Though I was two years older, Luke was bossy and loud and had, as usual, taken charge. The rest of us had long ago learnt that it wasn't worth trying to argue with him once he had assumed command. His voice was hushed and low and we moved as quietly as possible. He stopped only to listen for the muted crackle of movement in the brush that might announce an impending ambush. He was dressed in camouflage, the flack green and dull brown swirls covering both his trousers and jacket, buttoned tight to the neck. Two thick horizontal lines of battle paint stretched out from the bridge of his nose across his cheeks, blotting out his freckles.

When he posted sentries behind two trees, all of us, aware of how his mood could turn if his instructions were not followed, instantly fell in line. A chunky Swiss army knife poked out from his back pocket and several times as he leapt from one short ridge to another, or dropped to his haunches to duck beneath low-sweeping branches and fallen trunks, it looked as if it might tumble out and be lost among the soggy blanket of leaves and mulch that covered most of the woods.

Soon he was on his belly, crawling forward on his elbows beneath the pleats and hems of the bracken. The reason we would all follow his commands in these games was not that he made a good leader nor that he knew the terrain better than anyone else – indeed, it would be impossible to tally up the number of times he picked a path only to turn back and try another a few minutes later, testing out each trail regardless of how far it might take us from mum, the dog or the car. Rather it was that his never-ending monologue invested our movements with so much adventure. It really seemed that instead of making everything up from half-remembered snatches of war films, Luke was actually describing what was happening: that the bracken really had been transformed into an overgrown jungle at the end of the world, that every distant dog bark was in fact the rat-a-tat of machine guns and that the sound of trampling thicket was caused by the caterpillar tracks of stealthy tanks rolling ever closer.

He turned his head and gave a quick signal with his hand, and we all drew close, each one of us lying flat on our stomachs in the undergrowth and peering over a ridge into a small clearing set between two slopes. He referred to us as his battalion, a special squad of mercenaries on a death-dodging mission against the most villainous villains imaginable, with the fate of the world heavy upon our shoulders. We lined up side-by-side, packed so close together that I could feel my brother's chest rise and fall with every breath.

They're waiting. Between that scrawny tree over there and the crooked one next to it. It's got to be a trap. I've already picked out a couple of snipers hiding on that ridge. We're outnumbered, five to one at least, but they're probably running low on ammo and it looks like they've left the west flank of their base unguarded. If we crawl round that way we'll be out of range of the choppers and we should be able to surprise them. Have your guns ready, but don't make any noise till I tell you. Right, now follow me.

We turned to our left and followed in single file as Luke crawled forwards, head down and knees scuffing through the mud as he went. Nothing else mattered but surprising the enemy and saving the day. At the far side of the ridge we gathered once again and rose up into kneeling positions, ready to leap out, firing our pointed fingers at the clearing between the trees as soon as he gave the sign.

I remember that we froze to the spot while he whispered a countdown, before throwing ourselves forward with the loudest shrieks and cries we could summon, rolling and skidding down the slope and flinging our arms and legs out wildly to beat away the hordes of enemy soldiers trying to stop us. Though I am certain that the rest of the battle continued in much the same way, I have no memory of what occurred when we reached the bottom of the slope and made it into the clearing. No matter how hard I tried to recall what happened next, I couldn't recall a thing. The end of the game was lost to me.

The spell of my daydream was only broken when a volley of barks from nearby dogs sent a spray of jackdaws fluttering in sudden, anxious flight, launching from the trees below and sailing out across the empty reach of blue above.

My parents traipsed down the hillside on a dusty path picked between the heather, and I followed close behind. The ground at the top was patchy and worn, the chalky scrub belying the greensand packed beneath, just as the invisible world of our dreams and longings lies buried under the visible one. We walked in the shadow of a single tree stretching its branches out towards the sky. Halfway down, we spread a blanket over a patch of dry grass and settled there, looking down to the foot of the hill where the speckles of mauve and white gave out into a grove of beeches.

None of us had much to say.

Finally my mum reached for the rucksack sitting between us and unzipped the top. It took a few moments of fumbling for her to pull out the metal urn buried at the bottom of the bag and wrapped snugly in a couple of spare jumpers. She rose to her feet and, after unscrewing the lid, made her way into the heather. We watched in silence as she took deep handfuls of the ash inside and threw it up around her as though it was confetti. Unexpectedly, the summer breeze caught the first few clusters and blew them back towards her. She was soon covered with a light spray of silver powder. From where we sat it looked as though she was being attacked by a flurry of fake snow. The woods, it seemed, were reluctant to accept Luke's ashes.

Once my mum had turned so that the wind was with her, she began to walk among the low shrubs before the trees, tossing great clouds of grey into the sky and barely stopping to watch them disperse before she had thrown another. Fog was spewing from the open urn, much as a genie might appear when welling from an enchanted lamp.

I read that it was once believed that at the moment of a man's death an almost imperceptible mist would seep out from his open mouth before melting away into the air. And there are those who swear the body is lighter after death, though something similar might be said of those left behind – ever since the funeral I had felt almost weightless, as if the natural laws of gravity that had kept me tethered to the earth no longer applied. This certainly seemed true of my mum too, and she seemed almost swept up with the ashes she was scattering – though I noticed that, however far she flung her arms out to throw the dusty clouds away from her, she kept the urn cradled close to her body, tight between the crook of her elbow and her chest.

My dad strode down to meet her and take his turn, and before long he was shaking out the urn to scatter the last flecks of cinder into the leaves and over the grass. Then he returned to the backpack to dig out a bottle of champagne and several plastic cups. We drank a toast and then lapsed back into quiet. From somewhere far below the disembodied voices of walkers calling to their dogs passed over us before falling away, and if I listened closely I could also make out the snap of leaves and the crunch of bracken broken underfoot, the low rustle of the trees and a car starting up on one of the dirt roads at the edge of the woods. I set my cup against a ridge of mud and grass and lay down on my back. The sky span out above me and I realized that this was the first cloudless day since the funeral.

I listened hard for the sounds of the First Bracken Battalion making their way through the woods in some crafty and carefully planned pincher movement. In those games we were constantly about to spring upon an enemy who was always just around the next corner. Almost, nearly, not quite, soon. We'd never find them now.

Half an hour later we rose to pack away the empty urn and plastic cups, stuff the rug into the backpack and make our way back to the car park. As we left, I looked down the slope once more, hoping to see the grey patches where the ashes had fallen. I could make out nothing but shocks of wild heather and the melting sun becoming tangled in the highest branches of the trees on the slopes.

As we drove away down the dirt track, I turned back in my seat to see the summer sun low in the sky, slipping into the bracken behind us. I stared and stared at the sun, searching for something I might have missed that might make sense of everything, but it was untouched by either cloud or the beating wings of birds, and finally it burnt so strongly into my eyes that even when I turned away for a few moments, everything I looked at was hazy with light, as though fire had turned the whole world to ash.

Reflection

Eco-writing refers to literature that engages with the landscape, fauna and flora of the natural world. It encompasses nonfiction, novels, poetry and stories that explore biology, ecology and environmental sciences, and it reveals a vital fact that more and more of us are waking up to: that the natural world around us defines and shapes our lives.

In fact, many recent concepts in eco-writing shed light on issues relevant to writing about grief and loss. For instance, while most life writing focuses on relative, sequential and numerical time in short-term units such as hours, days and years, eco-writing encourages us to think about *deep time*: the history of the earth and its landscapes stretching back billions of years. This pushes us to reconsider our relation to the world around us, and the transitory nature of human experiences.

There's also the notion of *shadowtime*, which refers to the feeling that we are living in two different timescales at the same moment. For instance, the sensation we might get from drinking a coffee at our favourite café while being aware at the back of our mind that forest fires are raging and the planet is growing hotter and hotter. Meanwhile, *solastalgia* is a term that means feeling nostalgia for a way of life that is disappearing as we speak. Both shadowtime and solastalgia are expressions of a form of grieving. We do not only mourn people; we also mourn the way things used to be and the things that seem to be changing all around us. This kind of grief also causes disconnection, anxiety and disorientation.

Living in cities can often cause us to think of our lives as separate or disconnected from nature. But we don't have to go to the countryside or the beach or the forest (as I did in this chapter) to pay increased attention to the natural world. The environment – the plants and animals that share our living space, the topographies and landscapes that we interact with – is integral to every facet of our lives. Even the most miniscule details of our everyday lives (the foods we eat, the weather we struggle through, the technology we use, the transportation we choose) are intimately bound up with the environment. Pathetic fallacy isn't just a simple literary device that lets the reader know there's going to be drama coming when we hear thunder and storm: it's a reflection of the fact that our moods, emotions and experiences are deeply intertwined with our environment. In other words, if we write about our lives without engaging with the natural and ecological world around us then we are missing something vital.

The 'how'

The concept of deep time encourages us to think about how narrow our conception of time really is. Sometimes we obsess over the smallest of details while ignoring the big picture. In this chapter I wanted to explore how we perceive time: how some moments can slow down and an hour can seem to last a lifetime, how the past can sometimes seem to be just as alive as the present and how the deep history and stillness of the woods can seem to warp our own conception of passing time.

- Tip:

    Don't be afraid to slow down. There is a tendency in writing to plot out pages and plans in terms of the next big emotional moment, the next reveal, the next climactic scene. That can encourage us to rush ahead and focus only on the dramatic and the life-changing.

    Don't neglect the tiny details and little rhythms of our daily lives. Take time to step back and show the small, routine textures of life when not much happens. After all, that's one thing that makes life writing real and authentic.

The natural world is startling, immersive, occasionally even overpowering. And yet so often this fails to translate onto the page. By default many of us turn to visual description to depict a landscape, and we end up with long paragraphs lacking variety and punch. That's because so much of the power of the environment isn't actually visual at all. Its effect on us is so powerful because it is cumulative, made up of the sounds, the smells, the textures, the atmosphere itself. That's why I sought in my writing to try and include a diverse collection of sense experience when describing Hesworth Common: the specific plants and trees, textures and topographies, weather and sensation, the sound of birds and the appearance of animals and even local folklore that conjured the mood of the woods.

- Tip:

    Use texture and movement when writing place. We are rarely static: we interact with the world around us, through walking, hiking, climbing, playing, running, dawdling, swimming. This movement is part of how we experience different environments.

Think of how you feel moving through these environments: the sounds you hear and the scents in the air, the feel of the mud or mulch or tarmac or gravel or sand beneath your feet. Don't think of the landscape as something that stands apart. Try to write it as something which you are engaged and engaging with.

It is all too easy to fall back on clichés when depicting the environment. Rolling hills. Crashing waves. Shimmering skies. Then there are the colours: green grass, green hedgerows, green clearings, green hills, green groves. Green, green, endless green! This can lead to unique and exciting settings coming to seem predictable and banal.

- Tip:

  Try using paint colour charts. I've always found those colour charts used by Dulux or Craig & Rose to be a great inspiration for finding original ways to describe colour and texture.

  Flip through the charts and find the specific shade and hue you're aiming for, and see if you can either improve on the name given in the chart or run with it and explore the hue, texture and tone you want to summon on the page.

Staying with cliché, all too often we categorize nature as something comforting, peaceful and familiar. And there's no doubt that a walk in the park or along the beach can be all of those things. Yet this ignores the fact that the environment is far weirder, more startling and mercurial, than we often admit.

- Tip:

  Embrace the strange. Make it as odd as possible. Don't fall into the trap of the lazy anthropomorphic: namely, describing all animals or plants as though they are just like us. Instead, zoom in on the sounds, sights or behaviours that are unsettling, inexplicable, completely outside our own experiences.

  This 'unfamiliarity' will add a new layer to your depiction of setting and stop readers from assuming they've seen it all before.

Prep

Next time you leave the house, pay close attention to your surroundings. On your way to work or to the shops, keep a lookout for a tree or plant that catches your eye: either on the street, in a nearby park, by the road, in a neighbour's garden or even in an office. I want you to either take a picture of it with your phone or make a note of how it looks. Then do a bit of research on this tree or plant: find out its name, its defining features, its lifecycle and its ecological history. Try to find out something you didn't know before, and make a note of any surprising details. These will come in handy later on.

Write

As we've seen, place is integral to immersive writing. Without a clear sense of environment and location, the reader will get lost, confused or – worst of all – bored. All of our experiences are bound intimately to the locations where they happened: close your eyes and think of a time you had your heartbroken, and you'll likely remember exactly where you were. A bus stop being battered with rain. A whitewashed hospital corridor. The school fields where the mud has recently been churned by a rugby match against the local rivals. When we talk about ghosts, this is often what we mean: a memory so intense that it has become inseparable from the place where it once occurred.

I want you to write about a place that is important to you. It can be a place where wonderful things happened, or where heart-breaking things happened; a place of action, or a place of peace and reflection. Your task is to tell us why this place means so much to you. What is special about it? What is unique about it? Tell us why there is no other place like it in the entire universe.

- You will need a little description, but try not to just write paragraph after paragraph about what can be seen there. Utilize all the senses in order to tell us about the atmosphere there, the geography and topography, the weather and the nature.

- Try to balance between the tangible (things we can see, touch, smell, interact with) and the abstract (the emotions, sensations and reflections this place gives rise to).

- Think of place as a character. What would this place say to you? How would it sound? How might it choose to communicate with you?

- Dive into its significance. What memories are stored in this place? In the same way that as soon as I went to the woods I remembered Luke leading the bracken battalion as a kid, tell us what experiences are awoken by this place.

- Don't get mired in memory and description. Work to build in research about this area: its architecture, its local history or the natural flora or fauna there (just like we gathered in the pre-writing task).
- What is this place renowned for? Local folklore, gossip and urban myths can add colour and variety to setting.
- Make connections. Try out unusual similes and metaphors to try to make us see place in a surprising or different way.
- Imagine and experiment. We all know how humans see parks. But how are they experienced by squirrels? Try to take a leap away from your own perspective and imagine how this place is seen and experienced by others: by kids, say, or by birds, animals, even by plants, bricks, trees!
- Don't be afraid of magic. Places have a power over us: conjure, explore, bend time, show how the environment moulds people to its purpose.

In other words, I want you to write about this important place from as many angles as possible. Keep the place as the central focus, but try to look at it – and write about it – in as many different ways as you can. Some will work, and some won't. Don't let that worry you: instead, try to keep going until you've written about this place in as many different ways as you can.

Follow up

Grab a highlighter (or use the Word version if you wrote on a computer or tablet) and go back over the piece you've just written. Use one colour to highlight sentences about the environment, surroundings and nature. Use another colour to pick out writing about yourself, your experiences and your memories in this place. Are they roughly equal? If not, why might that be: What do you tend to spend more time writing about? How might you rectify this and achieve a roughly approximate balance? Do you spend more time on visual description, or on your sensations and emotions in this place? Which parts did you find easiest to write?

    This post-writing analysis is useful because it helps us identify our 'tells' – the things we tend to fall back on in our writing and do too often – so that we can work to make sure we're not always following similar patterns or relying on the same tics or tricks. By forcing ourselves out of our usual habits, we're more likely to try different things, and that's how we grow as writers.

Read

To venture further into the fascinating world of eco-writing, why not check out the interview with renowned explorer and ecologist Robert MacFarland about lost words, deep time, adventure, philosophy and 'The Worlds Beneath Our Feet' on the On Being website.

Try

Have you ever heard of the Japanese concept of *shinrin-yoku (森林浴)*? It means *forest bathing,* and refers to the benefits of immersing yourself fully in a natural landscape. Many of us take baths to relax and replenish, and that is the purpose of this activity too. So often we walk or hike through beautiful natural landscapes. But *shinrin-yoku* means to sit or stand still in a forest (or indeed a field or hill or any natural landscape) and bathe in the atmosphere, using all the senses to be in nature and close the gap between us and our environment. So that's what I want you to try: find some woods or a park or any green space that is easy to get to, and spend a decent chunk of time there. Not walking or jogging, not exploring, just staying perfectly still and soaking in the feeling of being in a different natural space, as a reset from your usual routine.

Chapter 12
The unknown

My journey

Everyone has one. A memory that bothers you, that nudges and needles, that won't let you be.

When you're sitting in traffic on the way to work, drifting in and out of daydreams or late at night when you're skimming on the surface of sleep: that place your mind circles back to. The scene that plays in the cinema on the underside of your eyelids. The one you can't blink away.

Everyone has one, and for Luke it was the whale. For a year and a half after we saw the giant skeleton on the Isle of Wight he was obsessed. *Could it swallow our car? What about our house? How about the whole school? What if it took a bite out of our ferry on the way home? How quickly would we sink? How many people had died by being gobbled up by whales? And besides Jonah and Pinocchio, had anyone been swallowed by one and lived to tell the tale?*

I must have been around seven when we saw the whale bones, since I am fairly certain that Luke was close to his fifth birthday. We had taken the ferry across from Portsmouth to the Isle of Wight and were staying in a tent on one of the many campsites that are dotted across the east coast of the island.

We can only have been ten minutes' walk from the beach, because when we dived deep into our sleeping bags in the evening it was possible to hear the low rush of the breeze sweeping in off the sea and the distant crashing of the waves – and, after that fateful day, Luke also swore he could hear the sound of whales splashing about beyond the shore and calling for their long-lost brother.

The highlight of the holiday was our trip to Blackgang Chine, a cliff-top amusement park dating back to the early Victorian era. There we travelled on a miniature railway, wandered through a giant hedge maze and played on a pirate ship. Towards the end of the day, after walking through a garden filled with fibreglass dinosaurs, we entered the main hall, and stared with mouths wide open at the giant skeleton of a huge finback whale filling the whole atrium.

Wow, was all Luke said. I think it was the size of it, the dizzying scale that lodged the whale in his brain. The spine itself, thick as a tree trunk and spiked with fat antlers of vertebrae, was close to 90 feet long and curved above our heads all the way down to the distant end of the hall. The giant ribs arched down around us on both sides, straining against every wall. *Look*! He gasped. I followed his gaze and stared up with him at the giant skull. The great eye sockets were empty and dark, and the gargantuan jaws – longer than the two of us even if Luke was standing on my head – yawned open as though ready to consume the whole of the theme park and everything else in its path.

A second later both of us were running, breathless and panicked, as far from that hall as possible. It was too claustrophobic in there: as though we were standing in the pit of the skeleton whale's stomach, snared in some bestial cemetery just beyond the limits of our comprehension. On the grass outside we panted and wheezed, then caught each other's eyes and started giggling. Only an hour later both Luke and I were begging our parents to let us go back and look more closely at the whale once again.

The questions started that night: *How much can whales eat in one sitting? What do they sing about? How do they get so big?* And they didn't stop even once we got the ferry back home at the end of the holiday and were back in the bunk bed we shared back home. *How had it ended up there, on this old-fashioned amusement park on a crumbling island? Where had it come from?*

Over the months that followed, just when it seemed he'd forgotten all about that monstrous attraction, he'd recount to me some strange fact that he seemed to have summoned up from out of nowhere. *Did you know that whales are classified as royal fish*, he told me once, *and so when a whale washes up on the beach in England the Queen is entitled to its head and tail*?

In the months after Luke's death, I got the idea into my head that I might go back to the Isle of Wight. A pilgrimage of sorts. An act of time travel back to our shared childhood. But the truth was that I had no idea whether the whale still resided in Blackgang Chine, since for many years now the outlying reaches of the cliffs have been gradually crumbling into the water below and so, with each landslide, the park has been forced to move further and further inland. With time maybe all our memories go the same way.

In fact, the steep chine from which the amusement park took its name crumbled into the sea many years ago. I remember that even when we visited twenty years ago, much of the southern edge of the park, near the shaded area where we sat at picnic benches eating our crisps and sandwiches, was marked off by fencing, and when we peered over we could see what was left of the chine sloping sharply towards the water below. An overgrown path was also visible, leading down to the sea where, close to two hundred years before, a ship was wrecked against the ravine and all on board were lost among the waves.

That was another fact Luke had latched onto: that the Isle of Wight is notorious for shipwrecks – and couldn't that be because of grouchy and badly behaved whales?

Whatever the true cause, the isle *is* well-known for shipwrecks, particularly the area surrounding the three tall chalk stacks that rise from the water at the western-most point of the island. The Needles, as they are now called, might from a distance be mistaken for the huge, jagged fins of some tremendous leviathan lurking beneath the surface. A lighthouse was first erected nearby towards the end of the eighteenth century, though it is said to have been little help to sailors in times of storm or blizzard since the light would often get lost amid the spray and drizzle. It was after one such storm in 1842 that the inhabitants of the villages nearby awoke to find a giant sea creature stranded upon the beach.

They must have been dumbfounded by the sight of a huge finback whale lying on the sand. It may well have still been alive when the first of the locals arrived at its side, its last breaths shuddering through its bulk, its tail not yet still. Shortly afterwards the beast was hauled away and sold at auction. The buyer was a man named Alexander Drabell, who had recently bought a large stretch of land on the island. Once he had sold the blubber, oil and baleen of his colossal catch, he had the bones bleached before he reassembled the skeleton and put it on display in his newly opened park of curiosities and wonders, which he christened Blackgang Chine – and which Luke and I visited 150 years later.

I cannot help but wonder if I am not a latter-day Mr Drabell, for in writing this book I can't help thinking that I have parcelled my brother up, carved his life into chapters and put the bones on display. After all, I have given Luke as little choice in the matter as the whale had when it came tumbling onto land. Whenever this worry gnaws away at me, I remind myself that, unlike the great beasts that spend their lives hiding deep beneath the waves, Luke relished attention. He wanted to be seen. No. More than that – he wanted to be talked about.

In the months after the funeral I found some comfort in researching obscure whale facts – in doing something only the two of us would really understand. Did you know that back in the second century AD, an ancient Greek text called the *Physiologus* recorded that there exists a whale so large that it resembles an island. Sailors tie their ships to its back and plant their anchors deep among its folds. They stalk out from their ships, thinking they have found land, to make camp upon its calloused hide. But – the ancient text continues – when the whale feels the heat of their campfires, it plunges deep into the ocean, and all the men upon it are lost.

Of course, distance can be difficult to fathom, especially when you are far from home. From a distance even the strangest hunch of dark might seem like a safe bet. When I was young and had my brother by my side, the future looked vast and promising, and yet with every year without him the possibilities ahead seem to shrink a little. It is no longer the case that anything is possible. I once thought my life might have some important meaning: I would achieve something significant that would have an impact upon the twists and turns of human history. I would write a book that changed the world, lead my country, invent something vital to human development. Now I have come to accept that it is enough to hold on while the whale dives and live.

Survival is no small thing.

I threw myself into facts. Did you know that during the First World War, there was a huge demand for whale oil? It was not only used to make glycerol for the manufacture of nitroglycerine for explosives, but was also used in edible fat production, while soldiers on both sides were instructed to cover the soles of their feet with grease made from whale oil in order to protect themselves from trench foot. One estimate suggests a single battalion in the mud, rain and horror of Ypres could get through 10 gallons of whale oil every day.

Did you know that, Luke? Had you found that fact yourself?

Did you know that there has recently been a huge surge in whale sightings around the northern coast of Great Britain. Only a few years ago, a Sei whale was found in the middle of a field in East Yorkshire, more than 800 yards from the coast. And that of course reminds me of what Luke told me all those years ago: that whales are classified as royal fish, and so when one dies upon the English shore the Queen or King is entitled to its head and tail.

Yet so much remains unknown. How often do whales give birth? No one really knows, because they are so difficult to get close to and study in the wild. Why are they so huge – why, indeed, did whales start growing, some 4 million years ago, from the size of elephants to something far more monstrous? There is no clear answer. Why do whales sing? Scientists have many conflicting theories. How do some of them manage to live over two hundred years? Biologists cannot agree. I have more questions than answers too. How did we not realize that Luke was clearly not well? Why didn't he tell anyone what he was going through? Where is he now, gone into some next life that I can only guess at or into nothingness? So much remains unknown.

All we can do is hold on. Hold on while the whale dives.

Did you know that there are no known reports of whales killing one another, and few of those outside captivity harming humans?

Even now I always keep my eye out for more facts about whales to offer to Luke, because I've come to learn that the conversation between the living and the dead never really ends, and there is no way of knowing when a voice will reach out from the darkness and remind you suddenly of a life once lived, but not yet given up.

Reflection

The great poet John Keats used the term *negative capability* to characterize the capacity of writers and artists to pursue their vision and to dive into emotions and ideas even when this causes rational or intellectual confusion and uncertainty. He described it as 'when a man is capable of being in uncertainties, mysteries, doubts, without any irritable reaching after fact and reason'. In other words, writing can demand suspending our usual logical way of thinking and leaping into the unknown and uncertain. Writing our own experiences and emotions, in particular, can mean letting go of our need to make sense of everything we feel or do (or write!), and instead committing to exploring it fully and without judgement on the page.

When writing about the intangible (especially our beliefs and our more complex emotions) and our inner lives, it can be helpful to focus on open-ended querying and intuitive thinking rather than reasoning and finding definitive answers. I have no idea why my brother remained obsessed with whale facts for those few years as a child, or why that skeleton got so lodged in his mind. I have no clue what he was thinking. I still do not know why he didn't share the fact he was clearly struggling and unwell with any of us, and I cannot ask him now. I remain uncertain about whether there may be any kind of 'life' after death. I am not even sure why I keep gathering whale facts when there is no one left to share them with. But nonetheless I decided to dive in and explore them in this chapter by embracing negative capability.

In fact, it was the open-ended nature of the writing that allowed me to find the emotional heart of this experience, and to explore what it meant for him and me together rather than trying to rationalize this interest in whales. I didn't have to force the whale to become a symbol that would explain or illustrate everything Luke or I felt. At the same time, the more I wrote, the more I discovered unexpected resonances in the facts about whales that informed the way I thought about myself and my brother. More importantly, this open-ended and instinctive approach also allowed me to find some healing through writing about this brief obsession. There were many paragraphs (I'm sure you can spot them) that I wrote directly to Luke, and I felt as close to him as ever as I typed. I felt close to him again, and for now that was enough.

Moreover, through exploring those ideas and experiences, I was able to identify that link between our past all those years ago at Blackgang Chine and the present, and to see that through writing I was able to keep that 'conversation' and connection – between now and then, between him and me – alive.

The 'how'

As the concept of *negative capability* reminds us, our writing doesn't always have to be logical, or make sense, or tie up every little loose end – especially as we draft and find our way! Even as we redraft and revise, it's useful to remember that we don't need to spoon-feed the reader: let them make connections and figure out links for themselves.

- Tip:

    Use paragraph breaks to switch gears. We usually start a new paragraph for each new idea, speaker or change of time or place. But that's not the only thing they can do.

    Why not experiment with using them as a leaping off point: jump into an unexpected thought, a contrasting memory or a different point of view. Use those line breaks to surprise your reader.

Writing from real life can often mean acknowledging that there are things we do not know, questions we will never learn the answers to and gaps we can never fill. As I wrote, I was often gripped by doubts and uncertainties (did Luke really say that? Wouldn't he argue with this characterization of him? Am I really remembering this right?) and sometimes these anxieties stopped me from writing altogether. That's why in this chapter I chose not only to acknowledge those worries, but to make them an explicit part of my journey.

- Tip:

    Get metatextual. Metatextuality refers to times when a text makes critical commentary on itself or on other texts. So break the fourth wall: tell the reader about your struggles in writing about certain times or events or people.

    Admit to your blocks and worries. Reveal your doubts and anxieties rather than trying to bury them in a perfect draft. It's a great way to invite your reader a little closer in.

When remembering Blackgang Chine, I recalled that we travelled on a miniature railway and wandered through a giant hedge maze. But what else did we do? I had to go back through old photos of that early holiday to find a snap of the two of us playing on a pirate ship. Only then did the description of our trip feel complete. Why? Because the sentence felt wrong without three details. In fact, both narratologists and anthropologists have suggested that people understand concepts, ideas and principles better in groups of three.

- Tip:

    Use the rule of three. This is a great way of maintaining rhythm and momentum, and can be used for sentences, as well as for actions and situations.

    Try to sprinkle in some *hendiatris* (where three words emphasize one key idea, like 'sun, sea and sand') and some *tricolons* (where three phrases or sentences are used which are parallel in structure or length, such as 'I came, I saw, I conquered') to make your descriptions memorable.

Our holiday on the Isle of Wight was fun and exciting, yet in my writing I wanted to highlight that unnerving shift from excitement to obsession. I also wanted to signify the way even joyful memories can lead to spiralling emotions and anxieties. I did this by returning again and again to unsettling images and motifs: from the whale skeleton to the metaphor of a cemetery, through to the references to the First World War and trench foot.

- Tip:

    Build atmosphere through the accumulation of tiny details. Try to include a couple of specific phrases or word choices per page to amplify the mood of your writing ('footsteps' or 'heartbeats' suggest suspense or tension, for instance, while references to huge spaces and landscapes suggest awe and wonder).

    Don't overdo it, but try to be consistent in your vocab and image choices to create a cohesive mood for each chapter or scene.

Prep

To prepare for the writing task, I want you to put down this book (wait! Not just yet! Finish reading this paragraph first!) and find a comfortable posture: you could sit, lie or stand. Set a timer for five minutes, then close your eyes and try to remain as still as possible. Focus on your breath: try to keep it steady and regular. Try not to move – but if you feel uncomfortable, you can stop at any time. The goal is to use this time to focus on breathing, and so empty out your mind of all the usual background clutter. When the timer goes off and the five minutes are up, move to your notebook or computer and spend just a couple of minutes noting down the things you are feeling and the things that come to mind in that moment. This will hopefully prepare both your brain and your body for sustained reflection and creativity.

Write

Our beliefs, our ambitions and even our doubts all have a profound influence on our lives. That's why I want you to write about something invisible. Something intangible – but vital nonetheless. Something that only you know.

Let's be clear from the outset: you might find this difficult. I know that my own first impulse as a writer, whenever I start a new chapter or section, is to invite readers into a scene through visual description: to set the scene by focusing on the sights and colours and sensory details of a particular place at a particular time. When those options are stripped away, I feel uncertain of how to begin. You might feel the same. You might struggle to scaffold your writing without a familiar structure. Try to keep going all the same and not worry about what usually works for you.

We've practised writing about our bodies, our landscapes and our homes, but now I'm asking you to dig a little deeper into beliefs, values, obsessions, ideas and write about something invisible that has, in some way, affected your life.

- Perhaps an idea came to you instantly about the belief that you want to explore. If so, leap straight in!
- On the other hand, if you're not sure where to start, consider this question: How has a particular value or belief or idea influenced a decision you made in the past?
- Don't step outside of history. Consider when this belief or obsession began, and when it had the biggest role in your life. My brother was obsessed with questions about giant whales only for a brief period as a child, and I can pinpoint exactly when it began even if I cannot identify when it began to fade.
- Avoid vagueness. It's easy to use flowery language to talk about love. But it's more interesting to talk about how we have experienced love in our lives, or how we show (or struggle to show) love to others.
- Don't judge – especially yourself! Beliefs, values and obsessions don't have to be rational or even fully explainable. If they mean something to you (or to someone you care about), then that's reason enough to write about them.
- Dive into details. Be as specific as possible.
- Beliefs and obsessions tend to evolve and adapt over time: Can you describe how yours has changed?
- Don't get too caught up in the abstract and philosophical. Big ideas are great, but link them to everyday details, actions and events.

Try to write for thirty minutes, and try to generate two pages – remember, it doesn't have to be perfect, since the aim here is to generate new and different material (we can clean it up and work on it further later on).

Follow up

Let a decent chunk of time go by (ideally a day, but at least a couple of hours) before you return to the writing you just did. Then pick one paragraph from that writing: ideally one that you're not happy with. Go through it and underline any words that seem clunky, awkward or overused. Highlight any repetition or redundant phrases. Try to identify any sentences where you're not communicating anything that develops the reader's understanding or adds anything new. Once you've done that, take those awkward or unnecessary sentences and rewrite them using completely different language: change the order, find synonyms, reach for alternative images, examples or metaphors. Then do it again – try to rewrite the sentence in two completely different ways. This will force you to write beyond your comfort zone and try new phrasings and images that you wouldn't usually consider. Finally, read all three versions back. Does one work better than the others? If so, great. If not, take any parts that work well from each and build a new version from just the best bits.

Read

If you're interested to stay in the realm of the intangible and unknown, have a look at an interview with the religious scholar Karen Armstrong, talking about how we can rekindle our spiritual bond with nature by drawing on some of the wisdom of the world's religious traditions. Search 'Sacred Nature' on YouTube to learn about some of the profound connections between humans and the natural world.

Try

'Sometimes', says the White Queen to Alice in her adventures through the looking glass, 'I've believed as many as six impossible things before breakfast'. Learning new and strange things is one way to stimulate our imagination. So pick a topic you don't know much about, and try to find out ten facts about this subject: just like I did with whales. This will broaden your mind a little and potentially feed into your writing in unexpected ways.

Chapter 13

Dreams and the subconscious

My journey

And then I woke up, and it was all a dream.

That is how every story the two of us wrote together as children ends, with the past wiped clean and the world returned to how it ought to be. In the first few weeks after the funeral, my first hope on waking was to find out that some such miracle had occurred and that Luke's death had been nothing but a hallucination. Yet I always opened my eyes to find the world unchanged from the day before.

My dreams too were stuck on a loop. Several times as the weeks became months I dreamed the same dream I'd been having on and off since I was a child: that we are all running through a crowded airport. We are panicked and frantic, sprinting past the duty-free and brightly lit food court towards our gate, the plane minutes away from taking off without us. At times I start to falter, and fall back to catch my breath a little bit, but my parents keep running madly on down the long grey hallway. From the bright windows I can see the plane moving across the runway. I try to call to my parents to wait, but my voice is little more than a croak. I have no choice but to keep running, my legs almost buckling as I try to catch up with them.

I guess as kids we'd watched *Home Alone* too many times – Luke loved the brutal slapstick violence Kevin meted out to the burglars with hastily improvised homemade contraptions and more than once tried to construct his own system of pulleys and ropes with a bucket full of water on one end and a hammer from Dad's toolbox on the other – and the idea of being left behind must have trickled into my subconscious. As a child I wanted to be first at everything. First to finish a jigsaw puzzle, a homework task, a page of a book of colouring-in. Luke too had a fierce competitive streak, and so we goaded each other into never-ending contests: who could throw the ball furthest, find the longest stick on a dog walk, build the highest tower of Lego bricks.

And of course we raced each other almost everywhere. Not only out in the woods or at the beach, but even around the house. For instance, I remember once when he was around four years old, my parents called up to us that we were going to the park, and both of us jostled to be first down the stairs, taking them two at a time until the final three, which we leaped down with the loudest whoops and hollers we could summon.

We were off to the park, that place of myth and legend whose mere mention was enough to make both of us jumpy with anticipation. If on that morning you had asked us what we thought heaven might be like, we would have answered without hesitation that it was sure to contain an adventure playground crammed with the highest slides and most precarious of rope swings. I remember that it was a Saturday morning, and this was to be the first trip the whole family had taken together since the newest baby, our younger brother, had arrived.

The journey across the three streets which separated our terrace from the park was, back then, a distance which seemed to Luke and me as immeasurable as the one that separated our house from heaven itself. Along the way the two of us argued about what we might become when we got to the giant climbing frame: Would we be pirates upon an ancient galley? Cowboys within a besieged ranch? Or astronauts scaling the sides of a space station?

As soon as we had crossed the final road, all of us holding hands in one long chain, and made it onto the green, Luke and I could contain ourselves no longer and both of us began to sprint towards the play area. Soon it was just the two of us. Nothing else mattered. In our rush, Luke and I were half-tripping over our own feet, urging each other faster as we raced towards the climbing frame, both of us eager to be the first to scramble to the top and proclaim ourselves King of the Castle.

Being two years older, I should have realized there was no way he could have beaten me. Indeed, on any other day I might have slowed down, given him a sporting chance or even fallen back and briefly let him believe he had a possibility of winning. But I was so consumed with staking claim to the climbing frame that everything else ceased to exist. I pushed my head down and tore forwards, my breath ragged as I covered the last few metres to the play area, my kingdom awaiting me. And then I was there, shoving the great metal gate open and rushing past it towards my throne.

I didn't make it to the climbing frame. Didn't even get close to the patch of wood chips that lay scattered in a circle around it – not that day nor for many weeks after. I was, though, running so fast that when I heard the scream I could not stop straight away, and I tumbled forward for a few more steps as the wails and panicked shrieks rang out behind me, until I was finally able to draw to a halt.

Even before I turned around I knew what must have happened. Time and again our parents had told us to be careful with the heavy cast-iron gate, and so by the time I spun around my legs were shaking and a nauseating feeling of guilt had made a roundabout of my stomach. Though it can only have been ten seconds before I reached them, the journey back across the playground took several lifetimes, with each footstep as slow and difficult as if I were fighting the strongest of gales.

Luke was sitting dazed on the ground, the blood running down his face like an unstoppable stream of Ribena. The heavy cast-iron gate had split open his head.

But even more terrifying than his heaving and shuddering for breath as blood dripped down onto his favourite T-shirt was the look on my parents' faces. Anger I could have coped with; it was what I expected, and at that moment I knew I deserved far worse than a slap around the ankles or the confiscation of my favourite toys. Fury, indignation, disappointment; all I would have happily accepted. What I saw instead was fear, a look I had never seen on my parents' faces before, a look that would find its way into countless bad dreams to come. Both had turned a sickly pale, and my mum's eyes were already welling with tears. I remember being struck by the shocking realization not only that my parents were as vulnerable as us but also that I alone was responsible for this sudden and traumatic change.

I felt dizzy and nauseous, and it was only then that I noticed that since returning to them I had been biting my lip, my teeth clenching down with such force that I too could taste the sour, metallic tang of blood upon my tongue.

Before I could even open my mouth to speak my dad had bundled Luke up in his arms and, together with my mum, still carrying her newborn, was running back towards the house. This time it was me who was lagging behind, though trying my best to keep up. The knot of guilt within me twisted tighter and, by the time we were all loaded in the car and hospital-bound, I felt as if I was going to be sick. I was convinced that the longer my parents went without speaking to me the greater their rage would be when they finally broke the silence. I had broken my little brother, and he might never be fixed. And what of the terrible punishment that might await me? Luke sat beside me, sobbing quietly as he held my dad's hanky to the dark gash in his head. I pressed my own head against the car window and watched the street signs blur past. What, I thought, if my parents never speak to me again?

Later that day, we brought him home from the hospital with five stitches woven across his forehead. My parents did speak to me – actually, they appeared to have no desire to punish me. Instead of calming my anxieties, however, this only added to my fear that some dreadful and unimaginable punishment would be inflicted at some unknown date in the future. This thought followed me around for many days and remained with me long after the stitches in Luke's head had been removed and the scar began to fade from plum-jam purple to salmon pink.

And with it festered the suspicion that is now reawakened – that I have let him down.

This is why I still feel a dull and queasy ache in the pit of my stomach every time I pass a playground. A reminder. And that dream too, where we are running through the terminal to reach a plane about to depart, shakes me awake with the very same fusion of anxiety and regret churning in my gut. Just a little bit too late. Already out of time. And now I can't help but wonder, as I sprinted through the airport in all those same dreams played out so many times over the decades, where was Luke? Was he lagging somewhere just behind us, and I hadn't even bothered to look back as I raced towards the gate?

And then the word catches and suddenly the dream seems like the nastiest trick that my brain has been playing on me for years. Because as I'm running through the terminal, all I can think of is that I have to get to the gate on time. It's the gate. The gate. Always the gate.

The word echoes in my head. Grief has many voices: the mad clamouring of anger and sadness; the nagging voice of doubt and disbelief; the incessant babble of longing and regret – but none is stronger than that which asks, again and again, what could I have done to stop all of this from happening?

But self-pity is exhausting. It's pointless, and boring to boot. Besides, Luke would have been adamant: I don't need *you* to look after *me*. And so I go to bed these days with no fear of an airport awaiting me. Not because those dreams have disappeared, but rather because weighed against them in the nightly lottery is the possibility of seeing my brother again. Because once in a blue moon or two, I'll close my eyes and he'll be there, waiting patiently for me, as though his death had only been some game of hide-and-seek, and I am never surprised to see him, nor he me, so we don't make a fuss, don't hug or speak of things passed between us or where he's been all this time – instead we wander into the old house or down towards the park, no words at all needed, and nowhere else to be but here.

Reflection

The founder of analytical psychology, Carl Jung, wrote that 'We also live in our dreams, we do not live only by day. Sometimes we accomplish our greatest deeds in dreams'.[1] In particular, Jung believed that dreams are a way that our unconscious mind attempts to communicate with us. In other words, sometimes our desires, fears, barriers, anxieties and even ambitions might be

---

[1] Carl Jung, *The Red Book: Liber Novus*, trans. M. Kyburz and J. Peck (London: W. W. Norton & Co., 2009), 242.

revealed to us only through our dreams. It is important, he noted, to look at dreams from different perspectives, and to remember that different symbols or images that appear in dreams will have different relevance and meaning to different dreamers.

We don't have to agree with Jung's theories about dreams to see that our unconscious mind – all the memories, urges, feelings and thoughts buried within us – often has a deep influence on our decisions and behaviours. Though often in memoir writing we might feel the urge to try and rationalize every event and action, the truth is that in the moment we don't always fully understand why we feel or act a certain way. Many times in the months after my brother died, I found myself avoiding certain places or repeating patterns of behaviour that I couldn't fully explain. So in this chapter, I wanted to explore how certain emotions and memories spill over from our unconscious and effect our daily lives.

The effect of dreams and memories on our emotions and perspectives also provides a clear reminder that we do not live solely in the present. We are time travellers, and live each day partly in the past and the world of memory, partly looking ahead (dreading, planning, worrying, anticipating), and only partly in the here and now. Each moment contains multiple times. This isn't necessarily a bad thing, and for that reason I wanted to end my journey with a turn towards the positive power and potential of dreaming: the chance to relive, to renew, to reimagine. The very same things, in fact, that we do on the page.

The 'how'

In almost every story, the narrator or protagonist needs something. This need drives the narrative forward, and the obstacles that get in the way of achieving this need form the dramatic structure of the story as it builds to a climax. This is just as true for life writing as it is for fiction. So it can be helpful, when plotting a new chapter, essay or scene, to focus on the needs that are driving the people you are discussing (particularly yourself!). For instance, in this chapter, I aimed to show how my need to revisit the past and to understand my recurring dream came to intersect and reveal something new to me. This not only provided a natural climax (the moment of realization) but also suggested the entire structure of this chapter to me.

- Tip:

    Use Maslow's Hierarchy of Needs to identify and prioritize your narrator or protagonist's motivations. Maslow's hierarchy breaks down human needs into five categories, from the physiological essentials (such as food, shelter, rest) all the way up to self-actualization (fulfilling our potential).

This provides a useful illustration of all our potential needs, and a lens to help focus your writing on how this need influences behaviour, character and choices.

Along with guilt at causing my little brother's horrible injury, I was gripped by fear that my parents would be fiercely angry with me – and might never forgive me. I waited and waited for a punishment. But it never came. The anticipation and worry that grew in my imagination, in fact, were far worse than anything my parents could have said or done.

- Tip:

    Defy expectations. People don't often behave in the way we expect, so play with that surprise. Everyone shows emotion, for instance, in different ways. Utilize that unpredictability.

    Set up an expectation in your readers about what will happen next – and then take them by surprise by showing a completely different outcome. No audience wants to read a narrative where they can predict every action, reaction and ending.

The climax of my journey in this chapter came with the realization of the hidden double-meaning of the word *gate*, which cast the airport dream in a new light and led me to reconsider my previous assumptions. This worked as a climax because I'd already set up the dream on the very first page, before looping back to the traumatic incident in the park.

- Tip:

    Make sure to seed important details early on. Sprinkle vital details like breadcrumbs throughout your draft rather than waiting to show them all at the climactic moment.

    Dropping subtle hints that will be important later on gives the reader the chance to share in an '*Ah ha!*' moment with you when their significance is finally revealed.

Dreams are often amorphous, abstract, incomplete. There are few things more frustrating than waking up just when a dream was about to reach an exciting point and you wish you could close your eyes and dive back into that moment. Although in this chapter I mainly wrote about the lingering effects of the guilt I felt for letting my brother get hurt, I also wanted to utilize the full potential of dreams to surprise and take us beyond logic into the impossible.

- Tip:

    Embrace ambiguity. You don't have to tie up every loose end. Leaving some issues unresolved and some questions unanswered can have a powerful effect and make those same questions linger in your reader's mind.

    Real life is messy and doesn't always give us all the answers, and so our life writing can reflect that.

Prep

If you Google 'What does your dream mean', one of your first search results is likely to be a short quiz with that title from Buzzfeed. I want you to focus on a vivid dream that you can still remember and take the quiz about it. Let me be clear: I'm not suggesting this is an accurate test or something you should in any way take seriously. The purpose is not to psychoanalyse your dream (I have serious reservations about a short online quiz's ability to do this), but rather to get you into the mode of thinking about your dreams from a different angle and warm you up for writing about the world of dreams.

Write

Dreams can be exciting, they can be surprising or they can be terrifying. One thing they never are is predictable. That's what makes them such a good source for descriptive writing. I want you to describe a vivid dream (ideally one you had recently so that the details are still fairly fresh in your mind). If you cannot remember any, save this exercise to do first thing in the morning when last night's dreams are more likely to still be lingering around.

For this exercise, I want you to try free writing – that's when we try not to let our fingers leave the keyboard (or our pen leave the paper). So set a timer for twenty minutes, and keep writing even when you've run out of things to say about your dream. Don't stop and think: one of the aims of free writing is to push beyond our overthinking analytical side and let our subconscious mind take over. It really doesn't matter what you write, as long as you don't stop: so jot down anything that comes into your head. Are you ready? Let's go!

- Start with the line 'I once dreamed that . . . ' and keep going. Try to follow the twists and turns of your dream, but don't worry if you find yourself going in a different direction altogether. The dream is really just the starting point.

- Ditch punctuation. Don't let full stops and paragraph breaks slow you down. Instead, keep up momentum by writing one long, continuous sentence (even if it goes on for pages and pages).
- Dreams don't follow any rules, so have fun breaking as many as you can. Let yourself be taken by surprise.
- Don't try to make sense of everything you write, or go back and correct any mistakes along the way.
- In fact, you should avoid stopping to read back through what you've written at all: the goal here is to keep going forward. We can edit later, now our only goal is to get words down on the page.
- You may feel as though you don't know what else to write. Try to ignore this feeling and keep going, even if you feel you're writing gibberish. Don't stop.
- Follow whatever idea pops into your head. No matter if it's not logical or doesn't fit with what you're describing. Throw in everything that comes to mind, even if it takes you a long way from where you began.
- Try to relax as you write, and let the writing flow from you, instead of planning or second-guessing what you should write next.
- Keep going until the alarm sounds!

Now sit back and take a deep breath. That might not have been easy, but it's useful to practice different modes of writing, and this one in particular helps us draw deeply from our subconscious mind.

Follow up

That may have felt like a strange exercise. After all, we usually only write when we have something we want to say. But this kind of unstructured writing can be useful to help us explore new avenues for our writing. So I now want you to look back through your free writing. There may be some nonsense in there, so look first for coherent sentences and keywords that leap out. Are there any words or images that recur? Did your writing seem to pull you towards any particular ideas or themes? Where did your mind take you? Note down any interesting images, ideas or phrases and see if they might be worth exploring in a more structured way in your next writing session: might they form the first building block of an essay, scene or reflection?

Read

If you want to explore the world of dreams further, a good starting point is the article from the website Very Well Mind about 'dream interpretation', which is easy to track down online. It provides a detailed explanation of the four main theories of dream interpretation (dreams as the road to the unconscious mind, dreams as a link to the collective unconscious, dreams as a unique cognitive process and dreams as a reflection of waking life) and a guide to further reading on how people have interpreted dreams throughout human history.

Try

Some researchers have suggested that keeping a dream journal encourages the kind of reflection that benefits emotional intelligence and self-awareness. So why not try keeping a journal of your dreams for a week? It's quite simple: as soon as you wake up, write down as many details as possible about what you dreamed: where it took place, what happened, who was there, what you noticed going on around you and how it ended. Don't forget to note the emotions you felt in the dream. You may begin to notice interesting patterns, symbols or images that inspire you to write more. Plus, as a form of expressive writing, it's great practice for our longer writing sessions!

Chapter 14
Talking with ghosts

My journey

When our arguments got too ferocious, first as kids warring over He-Man toys and badminton matches in the back garden and later as teenagers picking apart everything that drove us mad about each other, there were only two ways out.

The first was one of us reaching a breaking point and our anger exploding like a grenade, and then anything might happen: toys thrown straight at a face, nasty twisting pinches of any available nub of flesh, hair tugged so forcefully that a couple of times a few tangles would come loose in one of our hands. Once Luke even stabbed a pencil into my back. Luckily it hadn't been sharpened in a while, so it didn't even pierce through my T-shirt – though I certainly didn't mention those little details when I went to tell on him.

The second was one of us stomping away and giving the other *the silent treatment*. (As a child these words brought to my mind the idea of some horrible surgical procedure that had to be carried out with the utmost quiet since even a whisper might make the operation go terribly wrong.) That's how it felt a week, two weeks, three weeks after the funeral. As though he was sulking with me. Giving me the cold shoulder. Classic Luke. The silent treatment. *Again*.

The feeling lingered. Months went by – the cards and calls stopped coming, the funeral flowers wilted, the world (impossibly) kept going – and friends, colleagues, acquaintances slowly stopped talking about him as much. And that only made me yearn to hear him all the more. A single word. A mocking joke. A sarky putdown. Anything at all.

And just like when we were kids, it was me who caved first: one day I waited until there was no one else around and then I snuck down the garden and across the grass to the bottom hedge where I was hidden by the trees, and I shouted. I hollered and roared until my voice was sore.

Come on, you dickhead! I shouted. *Come back! You selfish prick!*

I felt foolish. And worse than that, I felt guilty for reasons I still cannot quite explain. But none of that was enough to stop me from doing it one more time.

All I wanted was for him to answer back. Like those arguments when we were teenagers, I wanted to goad Luke until he couldn't help but explode. Anything to make him speak.

Talk to me. Please.

When he still stayed quiet, I tracked down the next best thing. Two short videos I replayed again and again. One where he is arguing with my mum at the dinner table about Christmas crackers, of all things. He wasn't going to wear *some dumb paper crown for fuck's sake*. Another clip recorded from the news, where he's being interviewed at the construction site where he worked that last year about an old Second World War bomb – unexploded – found amid the foundations they were digging. He is sitting on a low brick wall, legs swinging and grinning with glee. His face already puffy and red.

I tried to ration myself, to stop myself from watching and rewatching the clips on a constant loop. But I craved it. I craved hearing his voice, just like an alcoholic craves a drink: in the full knowledge that getting it would only make me feel worse.

Luke. Say something.

But what would he say?

Actually, I knew perfectly well what he'd tell me. If he was peering over my shoulder and glancing at these pages, I knew exactly what words would come racing out of his mouth:

No, he'd huff. *You've got it all wrong. None of it was like that at all! No way. You've screwed up my words. Fucking twisted the past. All this fucking grief. It's a fucking joke!*

I started to protest but there was no response.

Nothing.

I was talking to myself.

Still I longed for his voice more than anything. Not to see him, or to hug him or hold him close, but to hear him. Because the logical part of my brain knew full well that seeing him again was impossible, but there was a part of me that couldn't let go of the possibility that late one night I might still receive a drunken call on my mobile. Just a quick call. Just a call to let us know that he's all right.

What galled me most was the suspicion that he might be right. All this grief, *all this fucking grief*, might be a kind of awful joke. Because the more I thought about it, the more I wondered whether this feeling that consumed me might be nothing more than a trick of evolution. Consider how animals in a pack protect the youngest, the smallest, even though these helpless creatures are useless to them. The desire for the group to survive is somehow hardwired into their instinct.

What if love, and the pain that is its twin, is nothing but a ruse to ensure the survival of our species? What if we feel for others so strongly because millions of years of evolution have programmed the human animal to put the group before the individual – or, to put it another way, because on our own we don't know who we are.

Without Luke, I don't know who I am.

So I clung onto him. The months I thought would cool my grief a little only served to make me more stubborn. Because the less frequently friends mentioned him, and the less his old mates reached out, the more I felt compelled to prove – in some strange sense, at least, if only in memory and echo – he hadn't completely disappeared.

This impulse drove me to spend half a weekend digging through the old boxes up in the loft of my parents' house. As soon as I climbed up the retractable ladder and heaved myself through the gap onto the nearest wooden beam, I found myself wondering why I hadn't come up there sooner. After all, Luke had always suggested camping out in the attic in order to get a glimpse of the strange ghouls and monsters who make their homes there amid the sea of yellow fibreglass. Sometimes at night we would trade tall tales about a race of hunched and shrivelled beings who lived in the attic and fed upon all the old possessions we left up there – our stories at least explained why the cardboard boxes in the attic grew dog-eared and torn, and why some of the old clothes stored there were later found to have been chewed to tatters.

I searched through those same dog-eared cardboard boxes until I found a couple of notebooks from Luke's schooldays. Finally, a trace of his voice again.

The reading, however, was unsettling. In one blue binder I found some brochures and certificates, such as documents about his work experience with The Princess of Wales's Royal Regiment, some cuttings from the local newspaper about hockey matches he had taken part in and his notes from the course he had taken after he finished school on Sports Medicine First Aid.

I also found a great number of worksheets and photocopies, among them the *Seven Essential Components of a Healthy Diet*, plans for *Endurance Workshops* and *Muscular Endurance Training* and a handout on *Care for Your Body* – this, I felt, he really should have read more carefully.

However, the page that caught my eye was one he had written in pencil on a piece of A4 lined paper. The words 'Lesson Plan' were underlined at the top of the page. The aim of the lesson is 'to climb a rope'. There was nothing unusual in its contents – the list of objectives, the development game, the concluding warm-down stretches, all measured out in five-minute blocks; but it made me think of the Indian Rope Trick, where some skilled mystic or trickster throws a rope into the air, then climbs up until he disappears, far above the heights the eye can follow, only for the slack rope to fall suddenly back to earth.

Meanwhile, in a crusty yellow notebook I found what must have been some of his earliest writing. It appeared to be classwork from primary school. The exercises were almost certainly answers to questions the teacher had set about the lessons that day, but I grew increasingly unnerved with each page I studied. Much of it seemed cryptic and sinister to me, as if subsequent events had worn away the original meaning and uncovered something hidden beneath.

One page contained a picture of a man riding a bright green tank done in garish felt-tip, and towards the end of the notebook there was a pencil drawing of a family (or, at least, a collection of people of mismatched sizes) walking up a hill. The more I flicked through the pages the more I felt myself sinking into some inescapable dream where nothing is quite as it seems.

Another page contained this story:

Thursday 12 January

Ozzie Watson found a note on the brick it said get out of town and don't come back Mr Grant went to the sweets shop to get sweets for his dog and his dog had gone it was in the caravan.

Who, I wondered, had thrown the brick? Did Ozzie Watson harbour some dark secret? Who was Mr Grant, and why did he feel it was ok to feed a dog sweets? And why had the dog gone to the caravan? Why? *Why?*

On the facing page were no more riddles – instead, Luke's attempt to account for what he had done in the school holidays:

At Christmas I got a boxing set and a skateboard and a boglin. I was skateboarding on my skateboard with boxing gloves.

Beneath this the teacher has written, in red pen, *Was that very difficult?* Yes, yes it was. He so often made things difficult.

Beside the school notebook was a half-finished scrapbook from one of our holidays on the Isle of Wight. It was mostly filled with pictures: a drawing of a ferry leaving the port, another of dinosaurs munching clumps of grass, one of a lizard climbing a branch and one of a tarantula building an ornate web as intricate in its crisscrossing design as a snowflake under a microscope.

But none of these fragments was enough. None of them were 'him', no more than the diary I kept for a few weeks when I was thirteen is 'me'.

I climbed down from the loft feeling unsettled and unhappy. His voice still just out of reach. I wracked my brain instead to try and dredge up conversations I might have forgotten, bands and movies we loved or hated, arguments and minor disagreements, jokes and plans, all that banal chit-chat, so that I could bring back the timbre and catch of his voice.

And before I knew it I was overwhelmed by a host of Lukes: Luke as he was just a few months before, ripped and strutting; scrawny teenage Luke, all lip and grit; Luke reclaimed from childhood, a freckled whirligig thing with his feline allies, his leather jacket and boxing gloves; bouncer Luke in his black suit and stern expression; practical-joker Luke crouched inside a cupboard waiting to leap out; Luke who would argue with me until he was blue in the face; toddler Luke who used to follow me around and copy every word I spoke; and then all the half-glimpsed Lukes of the years we spent in different cities; all the might-be could-have-been Lukes; all the possible Lukes that would be living out there still if it wasn't for that one day. And each of these Lukes spoke with a different voice, and together were so loud in their banter and mocking giggles that I could no longer hear anything else amid the din, the din, the din.

I clamped my hands around my ears.

Minutes went by, my head spinning. I'd finally got what I yearned for – and I couldn't bear it!

At last, silence.

Typical.

Just like him.

It felt as if I had finally asked him to tell his side of the story, and all he had to say was this:

And this:

And this:

Reflection

For the bereaved, memory can be both a source of great comfort and a cause of stress and anxiety. Memory, after all, is the foundation of our sense of who we are. Much about memory is still poorly understood, but we do know that the hippocampus helps us form episodic memories, which are then sent to the neocortex during sleep for us to be able to process and understand these new experiences, and also that the amygdala is the part of the brain that attaches an emotional significance to our memories. Thanks to this knowledge, research has now proved that it is possible to implant false memories (as far back as 2012, for instance, scientists at MIT managed to implant a false memory in a mouse).

More pertinently for us, neuroscientists have also noted that the act of recording, writing or telling a memory can enact a change on the memory itself. We do not remember original events so much as recall the last time we remembered them. This worry gnawed away at me when I first started drafting my journey: Was my writing in some sense replacing the 'real' Luke that I was hoping to remember and keep alive on the page? Would my brother die a second time through my writing about his life?

One solution to this concern was to return to primary sources to create a more objective and less changeable portrait of my brother. Along with the video recordings and notebooks that I mention in this chapter, I also interviewed our parents, our relatives and his friends to gather stories and sides of him that I hadn't heard, and to corroborate my memories of things he'd said and done. The other way I dealt with this anxiety was to acknowledge it directly in my writing rather than pretending it didn't exist. By drawing on what I'm fairly certain Luke would have said, I could at least show that there is always another point of view and that my memories are not definitive – or even always accurate!

Interestingly, back in 1960, Hans Loewald wrote that through investigating the interaction between the conscious and unconscious elements in our minds and dealing with our repressed fears and conflicts, we are able to transform the 'ghosts' that haunt us into ancestors: those living memories inside us that provide us with a sense of continuity with the past.[1] In other words, if we are not afraid to face them and engage with them, then each 'ghost' offers the potential of being tamed and transformed into something useful and beneficial.

The 'how'

The historian Steven Mintz has argued that 'Nothing brings the past back to life quite like primary sources. Letters, diaries, trial transcripts, and other original

---

[1] Hans W. Loewald, 'On the Therapeutic Action of Psychoanalysis', *International Journal of Psychoanalysis* 41 (1960): 18.

documents allow us to hear the living voices of the past'.[2] Primary sources can not only provide variety to your life writing, but also heighten authenticity: even a short excerpt, like I included from my brother's school notebooks, can add something startling and new to a page.

- Tip:

    Gather evidence. Find letters and emails. Re-read text messages and WhatsApp chats. Look at photos and videos. Interview friends and family members (even in an informal way). Be prepared for some of this material to wrench you open and to have a strong emotional effect, so don't start this until you feel stable enough to do so.

    Remember, the purpose here isn't to find new directions to take our writing into (though it is bound to help generate new ideas). The goal instead is to find little revealing details (in clothing, turns of phrase, little jokes) that we can sprinkle into our writing to make it more true to life and to bring out character.

Researchers don't only gather primary and secondary sources. Another thing they do is set out the scope of their research. This is vital for writers too. For me, I decided that for those parts of the memoir set in the present I would only write about the months immediately following my brother's death. I also made the choice to only include my brother's and my voices in my writing, in order to both reflect the intimacy of our relationship and the claustrophobia of grief.

- Tip:

    Set limits. In the same way that a researcher begins by formulating a methodology that defines the parameters of their work, so writers benefit from identifying the scope of their projects. Decide what you will focus on and try to stick to it.

    Just as important is what you will leave out. Consider what is necessary for achieving your goals, particularly in terms of *who* will appear and *when* you will write about. What distracts from that focus, and what adds to it?

It was important for me to give Luke a chance to 'answer back'. To remind both the reader and myself that he would almost certainly have disagreed with some of my characterizations and depictions of himself and our shared past. Without

---

[2]Steven Mintz, 'Using Primary Source Documents', *OAH Magazine of History* 17, no. 3 (2003): 41.

that, I would have felt like a sleazy used car salesman trying to hoodwink a potential customer by failing to mention the dodgy brakes.

- Tip:

    Show your doubts. Instead of trying to hide away any uncertainties and anxieties, make them part of your narrative. Writing memoir doesn't mean writing the definitive record of the past. Point out the holes and gaps. Acknowledge things you don't know.

    Life writing can be difficult. Don't be afraid to discuss these difficulties or to talk about what you struggled with. None of this will put the reader off. Instead, it will build empathy and understanding.

My own doubts and longings were the driving force of my journey in this chapter, giving it momentum and connecting the different scenes and times together. It was therefore important to show how intrusive and disruptive this voice in my head really was, and so I made an effort to show it interrupting and breaking the paragraphs on the page.

- Tip:

    Experiment with italics. Use them to show inner thoughts that disrupt or question or argue back. Brief snippets of inner monologue go a long way to reminding the reader that the narrator is also a character in their own story.

    They're not just for inner monologue. The unusual visual slant of italics really leaps off the page, and so they can function like a spotlight: consider italics for highlighting realizations, repetition or words that have a special or particular resonance.

Prep

Let's put those research skills into practice: I want you to carry out an interview with a family member or friend. The goal here is to fill the gaps in your own recollection regarding a memorable event, situation or occasion that they were present at. Pick someone you are comfortable with and are happy to chat with about this time (remembering that one or both of you may have a number of emotions stirred up by these memories). Before you sit down with them, write a list of questions you plan to ask: make these as detailed as possible so that you can elicit as much information as you can. Make sure they understand your goals at the beginning and consent to being interviewed, and consider whether you plan to record them speaking on your phone, use a transcription app or make notes the old-fashioned way. When you carry out the interview, focus on trying to elicit specific details about that time rather than letting the conversation ramble off topic or getting stuck on how their memories may contrast with your own.

Write

To write well, we have to keep challenging ourselves. Otherwise we risk growing complacent, predictable, locked into familiar patterns.

That's why I want you to go out of your way to challenge yourself in your writing task. Specifically, I want you to contrast your own memory with someone else's account of the same day or situation. The goal here is to set both accounts side-by-side on the page and explore the differences between them.

Use the material you gathered during the interview you just carried out for the Prep task. Be selective: hunt for a recollection that is markedly different from your own memory in some way.

Remember to stay focused and write about *one particular day or situation only*:

- Move back and forth. Write one paragraph on your memory and then another from theirs. Then switch back, and so on. This will help maintain equilibrium.
- Aim for balance: try not to give more space to either point of view. Avoid favouring one or the other. Instead, present both to the reader.
- Stay in the scene: don't be tempted to digress. Stick to that one time and place, and give as many setting details as possible.
- Don't be afraid to juxtapose: show those moments where the memories are markedly different or distinct in some way.
- Zoom in as far as you can. Bring small details (especially colours, sounds, shapes, people) into as much focus as you can to make the scene distinct and realistic.
- Avoid abstractions. Don't be tempted to analyse the differences or discuss the reasons why the two memories deviate. Focus solely on the scene first, then reflect at the end (if you wish).
- Keep coming back to a central moment, idea or theme to keep us anchored in that moment.
- Use dialogue and interaction to add flavour and variety to the scene and immerse the reader fully in the time you are depicting.

- Don't be afraid to use inner monologue and intrusive thoughts (from yourself or the person you interviewed) to disrupt the narrative. This can also be a good way to help you transition between different perspectives.

Write for at least thirty minutes or until you have shown both memories of this event or situation in full. You might well have found it a challenge to give equal weight to both, but it's fantastic practice for the kind of balancing acts that are vital for strong writing.

Follow up

Look back through the very first paragraphs of what you just wrote. How did you set the scene? Is there any way you can ground the reader more quickly in this time and place? I'd like you to do a little bit of research to find a fact that could add some authenticity to this scene. For instance, can you find out what news stories were happening on this day? What was the weather like? What were other things happening in the world at that exact same time? A little googling can help find one of these facts that you could add to the opening paragraphs to add an extra level of realism and credibility to the scene.

Read

We're all well-versed in using Google to find what we need, but have you ever checked out Google News Archive? It provides free access to scanned archives of newspapers, some of which date back to the eighteenth century. This is a useful archive for adding authentic historic detail to your scenes set in the past. You can choose the timeline view to help you select news by period: Why not have a look at the front-page stories from around the world on the day you were born?

Try

If you've found some of this research work useful to your writing, then keep going: write a bullet point list of research goals. For example, you may want to carry out more interviews with relatives; visit a library to look at local resources; track down old photos, maps and newspapers online and so on. Consider what extra information may help you develop your life writing in different directions or might add depth and flavour, and make a note of all your ideas in bullet point form to help guide your research.

PART IV

Writing as magic

The chapters in this section will focus on using all the techniques and tools we have discussed so far to commit to larger writing goals and bring those into fruition. Each chapter will zoom in on specific ways that experimentation can refresh and rejuvenate writing we might be stuck with, thinking about how we involve our passions, our ghosts, our innate sense of the poetic and our powers to create a new path onwards.

Chapter 15
Pleasures and passions

My journey

In 'The Red-Headed League', Sherlock Holmes reminds Watson that, as a rule, the more bizarre a thing is, the less mysterious it proves to be. It is only the commonplace that is puzzling.

'My life', Sherlock declares, 'is spent in one long effort to escape from the commonplaces of existence'.

There is, of course, nothing more commonplace than death, and nothing harder for the mind to fathom. Maybe that's why I found myself turning again and again to the stories of Sherlock Holmes, as one would to an old friend. As soon as I dived into my favourite old Conan Doyle stories I was far from that melancholy house, far from my family's deep and churning sadness, far from myself and back instead in the warm and familiar fireside room in 221B Baker Street.

I read and I read and I read. For in the world of these stories every problem, no matter how complex, turns out to have a startlingly simple explanation. (Apart from one outlier which involves a mongoose.) I craved answers. Why had Luke's heart grown to such a monstrous size without anyone realizing? And why had it happened to him and him alone? A genetic quirk of luck set him apart. Just like his red hair.

Yes, Luke was in a red-headed league all of his own. Everyone else in our family has the same mousy brown hair as me – parents and grandparents, distant uncles and aunts, cousins many times removed. Yet his hair was not the light strawberry-blond that often goes with pale skin, nor the brighter orange associated with the Celts, but a deep and fiery red closer to flame than gold. I never once heard him called ginger or carrot-top, and though this was probably in part because he would have been quick to attack anyone foolish enough to have dared, it must also have been because his hair defied such descriptions. Luke was marked out from birth as different – an exotic bird with bristling plumage. Now what would Holmes have made of that?

I decided to turn detective myself, and in my search I found that red hair is caused by a simple gene variant and is, furthermore, a recessive characteristic – which accounts for the fact that it may appear in children whose parents are not themselves redheaded. It is a sleeping trait, rarely awakened. The same is also true of the genetic mutation that helped his heart swell up. This too had slept through many previous generations, as though biding its time. A coincidence? The stories of Arthur Conan Doyle suggest there is no such thing. But I could not stop myself from wondering why both these sleepers woke in him alone.

Would Sherlock Holmes search for a connection between these two facts? The physicians of the Middle Ages believed that people with red hair had too much blood and were therefore thought to have a sanguine temperament. There we have it: the heart and the hair. Redheads were said to be spontaneous, impulsive and unpredictable, and that was certainly true of my brother.

Luke's whims and impulses were legendary. At ten years old he persuaded my parents to buy him a whole set of fishing equipment – tackle, rod, lures, floats, knives and boxes for bait; for weeks he had gone on about taking up fishing. He then carried his new kit down to the river Arun and spent the day getting more and more angry at the fish swimming past his line until he was shrieking at the river and attempting to pummel the water with his fists. He returned empty-handed, packed the equipment away and never talked of fishing again.

Another time he decided that he wanted to be a photographer when he grew older. He saved up for the most expensive camera he could find, which he wore round his neck for a few weeks as he crept around the garden looking for wild and exotic creatures to photograph. After his first reel was developed – a collection of blurry tree trunks and patches of grass – he put the camera back in its box and stashed it at the bottom of his wardrobe. Perhaps he somehow knew that his life would be short and thus felt the need to cram in as many lifetimes as he could. Perhaps once he had lived a day as an artist, a fisherman or a photographer, he felt his restless inner clock telling him to move on and become something else while he still had the chance.

Perhaps that is why his heart got used up so fast.

What would Holmes have made of all these clues? Would he have seen this coming? In the story of the Red-Headed League, Holmes and Watson are visited by Mr Jabez Wilson, who brings along a newspaper and shows them an advertisement announcing that a vacancy has opened up in *The Red-Headed League*. It states that any red-headed man wishing to apply should arrive promptly at the League's offices in Fleet Street on the following Monday. Mr Wilson goes on to recount that he was not alone in making his way to the address specified in the advertisement, for it appeared that every man with even the faintest hint of red in his hair had decided to try his luck, and he spotted men with copper hair, men with orange hair, men with hair the colour of the sun just as it touches the treetops in the evening and a hundred other shades besides. Luke would have fit right in.

Like all those characters in the story of the Red-Headed League, my brother was set apart from the rest of us since birth. As a child he saved his pocket money for bangers and firecrackers, no doubt thinking that if everyone around him was determined to force him into the stereotypical role of the flame-haired wild thing, then he may as well play up to it.

At other times his blazing hair appeared to be the outward manifestation of that inner fury which he so often had trouble bringing under control. It was easy to see when he was overcome with anger – his movements would become twitchy and his face would begin to turn as red as his hair. Yet despite the fact that he had amassed a large collection of weapons (including, somehow, a police taser), his fury was most often turned upon himself. Even if he had been working on a painting for the last two hours, should he get enraged, he would tear it into tiny pieces without a second thought. Indeed, his most prized possessions might be flung across the room or smashed mercilessly against a wall until only broken shards of metal or plastic remained. Even after he had destroyed the toys or gifts he had spent months saving for, he was careful not to display any regret or remorse.

This rage started as childish tantrums that could not be quelled, and grew over the years into the most terrifying and savage transformations. Taking my cue from the renowned Mr Holmes, I tried to analyse this anger methodically. What was the source of these rages? Did he feel infuriated that those things that came so easily to others were closed off to him? Did he feel that he was set apart, that life was not how it was supposed to be?

I had little idea of the answers back when we were kids, and I have even less now. I'm clearly no detective. I only know that his rages began to decrease in both frequency and intensity around the same time that his hair turned brown. In 'The Red-Headed League', the mystery that Sherlock Holmes must solve is prompted by a sudden and dramatic change in a routine existence when Mr Jabez Wilson is given a strange new job by the mysterious league and then, just as suddenly, one morning finds his new employers have completely disappeared. In much the same way, we were all astonished when one day Luke's hair suddenly changed colour.

The initial change was easily explained: in his late teenage years, Luke bought a bottle of black hair dye and applied it, in secret, while locked in the bathroom one evening. He was so pleased with his strange new look, his hair as jet black as a handful of crow feathers, that he retouched his hair again and again every couple of weeks until the bottle was empty. Yet that was the last time he bought any kind of dye. When his new roots grew they were, to everyone's surprise, the same shade of tawny brown as my hair. After a couple of haircuts, the last remnants of the dye were gone, and for the rest of his life his hair stayed the same colour as mine.

This dramatic alteration in appearance is a mystery suited to the annals of Sherlock Holmes, and so I turned back to the book. Holmes, too, turned to his hobbies to help him focus on the problem at hand, and in the adventure of the Red-Headed League, set during the dull autumn of 1890, he suggests a little music (noting that this stimulates the mind better even than cocaine). And there, over there, even as the sound of a sonata for a single violin spills from an open window, I could see my brother. He was leaning against a lamppost. On Baker Street.

I could see his shaven head, his mouth restless with chewing gum, his shoulders slung back and arms swung low, his skin-tight T-shirt straining against his chest and a chunky silver chain jangling around his wrist. He was the object of curious glances from men with mutton chops, frock coats and fob watches as they sauntered down the street. Not one to take such attention lightly, he gave them back his best *What-the-fuck-do-you-think-you're-looking-at?* face. He was propped against the tall black jut of a streetlight, fiddling impatiently with his mobile, then glancing up when the heavy clop and smack of horseshoes on cobblestones announced a hansom cab heading down the street, the driver's red face and greying whiskers visible beneath his cloth cap as he tugged on the reins and rounded the corner. Luke at first feigned a lack of interest, as he always did when faced with something he did not understand, and turned his gaze back to his phone, while the Baker Street Irregulars mulled slowly by.

What would it have taken to finally stir him from flicking through his text messages? The thick pea-soup fog curdling upon the street? The pale and ragged children shivering in vacant doorways? The ladies in crinolines, flat bodices and hourglass bustles? Or, would it have been the sounds – sounds such as the cries of the match-selling beggars asking for Christian charity, the cat-calls and haggling rising from the busy markets, the regular din of competing church bells, the clatter and racket of cabs and carriages and the barrow boys at street stalls hollering out their prices?

No, none of these. Whenever Luke went to an unfamiliar place, the first thing he would talk about was the smell. He would always be the first to comment on the musty smell that lingers in the houses of the elderly, the scent of damp that always hung about the inside of our family tent or the tang of chlorine that he identified as it wafted through the air whenever we drew near the local swimming pool. So within seconds he was clamping both hands over his nose, unable to believe the stink of the nineteenth century: the sickly reek of the thick and choking fog, the overpowering odour of the bubbling sewers and, more powerful still, the foul stench of the Thames – the murky waters overflowing with animal carcasses, dead strays and rotting human corpses.

I could see him stooping suddenly as his stomach heaved, his phone notifications now completely forgotten – he was, he sensed, not where he should be. And so he started moving, hurrying down the road, ignoring the dour-faced gentlemen and cockney street sweepers in his way. He had only been to the capital a couple of times in his life, but as he studied the successive street signs (Baker Street, Regent Street, Marylebone) he no doubt recalled the names from school holidays when we would spend long evenings squabbling over the Monopoly board. He soon began to nod his head, a little of his confidence restored, and whispered to himself as he increased his pace. *No problem, I've got this down*.

I pressed my eyes closed and clung on to this daydream, following my brother for as long as I could. I could not let it go, no matter how absurd the picture. He began to revel in the shocked stares and gasps he got from men and women upon their errands. It was the kind of attention he always delighted in, and his movements became more and more theatrical as he noticed people stealing glances at his skinny blue jeans, his great silver belt buckle the size of a cigarillo case and his shiny white trainers gradually being darkened by the street's endless dust and slop.

The longer I focused on the scene, the more real it felt. There was something within me that was desperate to believe that he might just be alive *somewhere*, if not in heaven then in some equally distant and unknown place. And why not in the world of Sherlock Holmes, a world in which a man might topple down a cliff and later return to his Baker Street rooms unscathed?

Yet as hard as I tried, I could not hold onto him – restless as ever, now bored of showing off to the gathered crowd, he marched down the street until all trace of him was lost amid the thick pea-souper. I tried to console myself by returning to the book propped open on my lap. However, I soon realized that I would have to turn back to the beginning of the story; on my last attempt at following the narrative I was unable to keep my mind from straying far from the words on the page. In the first weeks of shock and numbness after Luke's death, I assumed that as time went by we would slowly uncover answers to all the questions that plagued us about what had happened. Yet none arrived, and so I had finally given myself over to the idea that much of it would remain always a tangle of guesswork and conjecture. I am no Sherlock Holmes.

That is why I had to leave my brother striding down Baker Street past hansom cabs, dandies and dilettantes. Because I could not quite picture him arriving at 221B in order to have all our questions answered. Knowing him, he was bound to get distracted on the way: to run off on another of his mercurial tangents, indulge another of his legendary short-lived whims.

At least here, in the pages of this old book, he was somewhere I could meet him halfway. If I had to leave him anywhere, then I would leave him where I know I can find him, where memory meets imagination and something new is conjured between them. Yes, some books we dive into to get lost. But we also go to find that part of ourselves that is made of stories, revealed by stories, kept safe by stories – that part of us that lives, like my brother, between the pages.

Reflection

The French philosopher and theorist Roland Barthes wrote what he called 'biographemes': small fragmented memories of the past that he saw as a way of escaping the fact that the present so often imposes an overarching meaning and structure on the past. There is no denying that by writing about our lives, we often end up trying to fix one single interpretation on past events when there may be many. On the other hand, we often turn to books not only for escapism but to widen our perspectives and to see through different eyes. I wanted to investigate this tension between my desire for answers and the ambiguity and open-endedness that come with creativity. A contradiction or juxtaposition can, after all, be a great starting point for exploratory writing.

In addition, Barthes suggested that through writing 'the subject unmakes himself, like a spider dissolving in the constructive secretions of its web'[1]. Writing about our lives means not only reliving but also rethinking and reimagining. We are changed through writing, and so are the things we write about. This is the kind of magic power that we must therefore use carefully and responsibly.

This chapter was the point where I chose to dive fully into that magical potential. I took a risk on a creative leap beyond memory to the fictional, in order to set my brother in a new environment and purely speculative scene. This could have crashed and burned, and left me feeling bereft and as though I had desecrated his memory. But I felt confident that after spending all this writing time in his company, I could do him justice and summon him to the page. I had to trust in the power of the imagination to sustain and to keep alive. I knew that I succeeded by how happy writing this scene – and reading it back later – made me feel. As though Luke was with me again. In fact, my happiness with how this turned out can be seen in the structure of this chapter itself: it moves from pain at the beginning to solace at the end, from grief to laughter and from seeking after answers to accepting not knowing.

---

[1] Roland Barthes, *The Pleasure of the Text,* trans. Richard Miller (New York: Hill & Wang, 1975), 34.

The 'how'

Writing about our lives doesn't mean considering a person in isolation. Our experiences are inseparable from the world in which they happen. Our favourite bands and movies, our politics or beliefs, our clothes and 'tribes', our hobbies and interests, all add to the picture of who we are. We can't strip these away, and so it's far better to dive into that melting pot of various influences that contribute to our identity. For my brother those included Schwarzenegger movies and West Coast rap and boglins and hockey games. For me, as this chapter shows, they include the late Victorian world of Mr Sherlock Holmes.

- Tip:

    Add cultural elements. They help show character. I have a friend who quotes from *Star Wars* all the time, and I could never hope to represent him on the page without this defining character trait. Pop cultural references also help ground writing in a specific place and time.

    Moreover, passion is infectious. Show us the songs the people you care about love to sing along to, the books they love, the soaps they never miss, the shows they can quote verbatim, the stars they'd love to meet, the football teams they're devoted to. It's a great way to add energy, enthusiasm and often humour to your depictions of real people.

As soon as I started writing about the stories I turned to for comfort, the image of my brother in Victorian London nudged its way forcefully into my mind and wouldn't let me be. I knew I had to build towards that fantasy as the climax of this chapter, but then the question remained: Where could I go after that? I tried several different endings (including following Luke to have it out with Sherlock Holmes) before I found one that worked. Returning to the pleasures of books and reading allowed me to sustain that uplifting effect while also tying together the themes I'd set up at the beginning of this chapter.

- Tip:

    Aim for a punchy ending. Don't let your plot falter out or meander towards a vague finish. Equally, try to avoid coming to a sudden halt once you've finished the scene. Be deliberate: ask yourself whether ambiguity or resolution work best in each situation.

    That doesn't mean you have to resolve everything or tie up every single loose end. There's no need to sum up at the end of every chapter or scene. A good ending should thrum, like the last note of a song, echoing long after the fingers have left the piano. Try to finish on an image, feeling or idea you want to linger in the reader's mind.

Of course, this ending only worked because I'd already made sure the theme of books and reading was firmly planted in the reader's mind. Not only does this chapter start with the description of turning to favourite stories for consolation, but on every other page there are reminders of me returning to the book or diving deeper into the tale of Sherlock Holmes. With these gentle nudges, I built an expectation that paid off in the final paragraph.

- Tip:

    Sprinkle breadcrumbs throughout your writing. Once you know the theme you're focusing on and the ending you're working towards, go back through your writing and drop in hints that subtly prepare the reader for what's coming.

    The key here is finding balance. Too many references to the same image, idea or action will seem like clunky repetition. Too few and the reader will forget about the theme. A small reminder every couple of pages is a good rough guide, but it's always best to experiment until it feels like the right amount.

Sprinkling these breadcrumbs is something that can only be done properly during the revision process. Don't try to accomplish this during the first draft: that's best used for getting your ideas down and discovering what you really want to say. First drafts are often messy, baggy, all over the place. In the second (and third, and fourth . . .) draft, you can refine and zoom in.

- Tip:

    Redraft strategically. You can't focus on everything at once, so give yourself a different task for each revision. Try to be as specific as possible about what you want to achieve when you revise.

    For instance, your first revision of a new draft might focus purely on cutting preamble and digression and working on the structure. Another revision might be solely aimed at making the metaphors, descriptions and transitions as clear and crisp as possible.

Prep

Take a couple of minutes and make a bullet point list: I want you to jot down all the things you look forward to each day. The small pleasures that you take comfort in. Don't overthink: write down the first things that pop into your head. And don't try to go too big: focus instead on the little things that make you smile: a cup of tea, a hot bath, the smell of a particular candle, a dog you see on your way to work. Try to note down at least ten.

Write

It's time to zoom in: I want you to write about the unique joys and passions of the person you miss. What are the things that brought them pleasure?

The goal here is to show them in full swing. Character is always better brought to life through action than description, so I want you to show them doing, trying, playing, experiencing or rhapsodizing about something they loved to do or watch or play or take part in. What were their hobbies, what did they believe, what did they always look forward to doing at the weekend? Pick just one or two and let us see them engaged in something they loved.

Be aware: this could be triggering. You're likely to stir up a number of emotions in this task as you focus intensely on those happy times, so ask yourself before you begin if you're ready to do that – or if it would be better to wait and try this further down the line.

If you feel you're up to it, then let's go:

- Cut the preamble. Leap straight into showing the character doing what they enjoy most, and then zoom out to show us how this is situated in time and place.
- Don't forget the accessories and paraphernalia. Describe those objects that meant something to them – then follow that thread and try to show us what it meant and why this was.
- Action is rarely solitary. Show conversations, interactions, impassioned chats, even rows that may have erupted about interests and passions.
- Our hobbies and interests often make us a part of a tribe, and this in turn influences the clothes we wear, the vocabulary we use, the places we go. Invite us into this world.
- Did they ever teach you or anyone else how to take part, or explain how something related to their passion worked? If they did, then lean into this, as it's a great way to introduce the reader to their passion in their own words.

- Just because it's action, doesn't mean it has to be huge or intense: small, everyday passions (like a dog walk at the end of the day around the park down the road) can be just as engaging if you show us the details (like the spray of purple hydrangeas growing at the edge of the park by the gate).
- Check in with yourself: if you're finding it hard to immerse yourself in those memories, then step back.
- Keep going until you find a natural ending point: the end of a football match, the closing credits of a movie, returning home after a day's fishing with the catch. Aim to close with satisfaction, and a positive image.

Write until you feel the scene is complete and you've shown this passion in full detail.

You might feel a little emotionally drained after this. That's not unusual: it takes effort and energy (not to mention courage and patience) to properly immerse yourself in such moments and stay focused on them for an entire scene. Well done for getting to this point!

Follow up

Once a suitable amount of time has passed (ideally at least a day), return to that piece of writing you just did. Read through and highlight every verb you used. Do you repeat the same ones again and again? Can you switch any out for more dynamic ones? Do you settle for basic verbs (go, do, said) when there are more engaging options (hurried, attempted, muttered)? See if you can rewrite a few of them to add a little flourish and variety to your writing. This is good practice for strategic and intentional local editing.

Read

If this chapter served as a reminder that even in loss we can still find some pleasure, you may enjoy *Lost & Found* by Kathryn Schulz, a book about the intersection between these extreme emotions. Schulz describes falling in love at the same time as her father died, and she explores the complicated relationship between grief and joy in her moving and beautiful memoir.

Try

As kids, many of us had countless hobbies: playing football during breaks, collecting trading cards, learning a musical instrument and perhaps even a different afterschool club every afternoon. Then as we grow up, we narrow down our interests. Once we're adults, work and responsibilities monopolize much of our time. So I'd like you to return to the past in a more literal way: pick up again an old hobby or interest that you haven't tried in ages. Head to a skating park or practice a card trick or even dig out that recorder from the attic if you feel like it. Take just ten minutes to remind yourself of those hobbies you used to enjoy, and see if a spark of that pleasure returns.

Chapter 16
Poetic tools

My journey

We live every moment many times.

    First as anticipation
                                       [excitement]   [fear]
        Second in that fleeting
                    rush
                         of raw present.

Then finally when it is repeated
and remade, again and again, as memory
played back on the cinema-screen
lit up on the underside of our eyelids.

                                This is the moment I can't shake off.

My brother is bounding up a winding staircase that leads into a narrow gallery.

    As ever, I am following close behind.
    He is little and lithe and so fast that I am having trouble keeping up. I cannot say for certain where this strange place is, for I never returned there, and must have pushed it to the very furthest corners of my mind.
    We must have been on our way home from visiting someone (an elderly relative perhaps) because we had broken up a long drive by stopping for lunch at some bistro just off the main road.
    We trudged inside to find that the restaurant was a dark and airless place with a thick, bristling carpet that almost swallowed our shoes. The hint of disinfectant

in the air reminded me of a hospital. From the moment we walked through the door something told me that I would not like this place.

I think my parents felt much the same, but none of us had the energy to get back into the car and search for somewhere better. We settled at a table near the door and looked around.

The walls were covered with huge glass boxes filled with stuffed birds and squirrels set out in poses that suggested they had been frozen suddenly while collecting nuts or building nests and were as surprised to find themselves in this grim, stale place as we were.

Around one corner was a canteen where people were picking up wooden trays and queuing to collect plates of food before following the line around to a grumpy woman seated at a till. Luke must have been seven or eight, and it was he who spotted the sign that advertised a

Museum of Curiosities on the top floor of the building. After a little badgering, my parents agreed that he could take a look around while they got us some food – on the condition that I went with him. With that, he bolted for the staircase and I ran after him
 as quickly
  as I could.
 The stairs led up to a narrow gallery
 with many shelves   and glass cases on either side.
 There was no one up there but us.

The room was unnaturally quiet, as though it had been soundproofed to stop the noise of people in the gallery from reaching the diners below.
 Each footstep was muffled.
As soon as I stopped at the first display, I knew something was not right.

[The next few minutes were akin to one of those dreams where, though you know perfectly well that you are dreaming, it is impossible to wake.]

Inside a huge glass jar I saw a piglet with two heads sprouting from its pink puckered carcass.

At first I was sure that it had to be some kind of fake, an elaborate rubber puppet designed to scare children. But the longer I stared, the more I began to doubt my initial judgement. Both its pairs of eyes were screwed shut, and its tail was coiled behind it like the tiny, intricate spring of a pocket watch.

I stood transfixed, unable to move until I heard Luke calling in amazement further up the gallery. I turned to see him grinning wildly as he pressed his face up against another display case. Though I cannot recall what he said to me, the image is burned in my mind of his breath spilling mist across the glass in front of him. As it cleared his reflection appeared to merge with the collection of strange curiosities preserved within the jars.

There are still a few small museums hidden within pubs and inns throughout the country, yet I have never seen one as strange and ghastly as this.

The whole small gallery was crammed full of an unsettling assortment of deformations and unusual anatomical specimens.

Row upon row of curios displayed within the cabinets.
It was like some Victorian carnival. I passed countless jars
filled to the brim with formaldehyde, and bobbing amid the thick,
viscous liquid were an array of pale, malformed foetuses.

I saw a toad with an extra set of spindly legs.
    A hare with an extra eye peering back at me.
        A stillborn calf with grey, mottled hooves folded up against its chest and
        a face that was almost human.

Then there were rats and rabbits
preserved in various stages of dissection,
skinned and flayed and with rungs of muscle
unwound from their tiny skeletons.
Each of the exhibits spelled out the simplest and clearest of truths:
that the tiniest of changes is enough to transform the familiar world

into something else

                        something terrifying
    There were many more misshapen creatures on display,
        each staring at me through the glass with pleading eyes.
I hurried across the second half of the gallery with my hands up around my face,
shielding my eyes from the rest of the jars and cases.

By the time we returned downstairs I felt stunned and disorientated,
    while in contrast Luke had grown giddy with excitement.

At the table I couldn't bear to even look at my plate, let alone at the relish and enthusiasm with which my brother wolfed down his food
            – sloppy halves of grilled tomatoes,
            browned mushrooms slick in their juices,
            rashers of sunburn-pink bacon
            with curled lapels of fat,

> greasy hashbrowns and bulging sausages
> so swollen they looked ready to burst.

I managed only two mouthfuls before my stomach rebelled
and I had to make a run for the toilets, hands clutched tightly over my mouth.

Even when we left that astonishing place, I felt nauseous and perturbed. Beside me, in the back of the car, Luke was babbling on in gruesome detail about the freakish animals on display in the gallery.

> He is gone now.
> Like the curiosities in that strange museum, he is bottled in time.
> > Trapped in a moment that only I can relive.

He is always seven or eight and running
                                          up
                                              those
                                                    stairs.

    As we drove home he went on describing all the horrific things we had seen up there.

I wasn't really able to focus on what he was saying, however, as my mind was mulling over something that had been said the week before in school. For some unknown reason, in the middle of a lesson about basic arithmetic, one of the girls down the table from me had raised her hand and asked our teacher what being dead was like.

    Though this shocked the rest of the class into silence, our teacher did not seem in the least bit surprised by this uninvited question. After only a short pause, he replied that:

death was like a calm and peaceful sleep, and that we would all awake at the end of time and rise from our graves to join God in heaven.

    Then, as if there had been nothing unusual about this interruption, he returned to the blackboard.

> Each ending waiting for its second start.
> Luke   me   [waiting]
>   Something   lurking
> still behind the glass
>   rise
>   rise
>   rise

is it?

It was this deeply alarming concept that filled my head during the long drive home from that strange pub.

As Luke babbled on, I could imagine nothing more horrifying than the idea that all the creatures in the *Museum of Curiosities* might, after their own long sleep, suddenly come back to life –

> the rabbits leaping from the bottles
> trailing skin and fur and muscle behind them
> as if they were
>   the trains
>   of bloody wedding dresses
>
> the grey-tinted calf breaking free from its jar and starting to low
>
> the toad dancing on all six legs
>
> and the two-headed piglet starting to blink,
> beginning to see the end of the world in perfect double.

So . . .
Will he/won't he?
                                      Yes.
                                        Here.
                                        Now. On this page –
We live every moment many times.   We live every moment many times.
                      Many times every moment. We live
                          – inside, around, between.

> But sometimes we get caught in one alone. Entangled, ensnared, enrapt –
>   suspended out of time,
>   and helpless to do anything but watch, again
>   and again, as though from behind a wall of glass.

Reflection

The great American poet and memoirist Mark Doty said that 'Poetry is an investigation, not an expression, of what you know'. The same is true for the best memoirs: they explore, inquire, peel open, scrutinize. They take us somewhere unexpected. Often, the way they do this is to explore what is revealed through the resonance and allusions created by forging experience or emotion into language.

In my journey, I chose to use some poetic tools to create a lyric essay: a hybrid that mixes together poetry, essay and memoir. Why? Because this allowed me to explore and investigate particular images, phrases and ideas in a different and unusual way. It allowed me to create space on the page for words and concepts to fully resonate. It allowed me to experiment, to play with form and design and to heighten the power of the twists and turns of this memory and reflection. After all, one way of thinking about poetry is that it is a form of heightened language, where every word and image has a power and a purpose all its own. That's also true of the best prose. If we want to preserve our memories – and our loved ones – on the page, then we ought to use every tool in our arsenal to make our writing potent and unique.

There is so much we can learn from the world of poetry. By letting certain lines, words or phrases stand alone, we can shine a spotlight on them for the reader, helping to create a greater impact. By honing extended metaphors, motifs and symbols, we can develop memorable and thought-provoking connections. By playing with design on the page, we can speed up or slow down the narrative to build tension and anticipation. By repeating key phrases or images, we can intensify their emotional effect.

By utilizing some of the tools from the poetry playbox, I was able to balance between telling a story and reflecting the twists and turns of my thoughts and emotions. I was able to zoom in and out on different ideas and take the reader on a different kind of journey. More than anything, though, writing a lyric essay allowed me to experiment: it freed me from falling back on the usual patterns of paragraph construction that I often unthinkingly follow, and encouraged me to try different approaches to help me get to the heart of my story.

The 'how'

One useful poetic tool is the 'volta': a turning point in a poem that marks a change in tone or theme, often with the appearance of something unexpected. This turning point stops a poem or narrative from becoming predictable. My turning point was the introduction of the idea of resurrection that appears near the end of the lyric essay and connects together all the threads of the narrative.

- Tip:

    Swerve away from the predictable. If the reader can guess where your narrative is going, then something has gone wrong. Your memoir, after all, should tell a story that only you can tell. So make it unique.

    Embrace taking the reader by surprise. The 'volta' is particularly useful in the second half of a narrative, to add drama and build towards a climax.

For instance, you could introduce new and unexpected information, or show things from a different perspective.

Poems are notoriously slippery things. They do not always tell us exactly what they mean. Sometimes they demand a second read. Often they require investment, making the reader work to decipher and uncover their meaning. This is useful to remember: readers generally dislike being spoon-fed and told what to think or what the themes are.

- Tip:

    Don't be obvious. In a chapter or essay about redemption, the last thing we want to do is use the word redemption. Instead, give the reader enough hints to actively work this out for themselves.

    How might you do this? By sprinkling in a little ambiguity. By dropping in some allusions. By using euphemism rather than stating directly. Don't be afraid of leaving things a little open-ended, or setting up puzzles for the reader to keep them engaged.

One key unit of poetry is the line: the division of sentences into distinct ideas. In classical poems these might be carefully balanced (with ten syllables per line, for instance, in a Shakespearean sonnet) while in modern free verse they may vary in shape and length but are always intentional (even if they contain only one word standing alone in the spotlight).

- Tip:

    Pay attention to the line. Multiple short lines can create an abrupt, staccato effect, but too many in a row can lead to a paragraph feeling disjointed and disconnected. Long, multi-clause sentences can take the reader on a journey that builds detail and suspense. But too many of these in a row and the reader could lose track of where they started.

    An engaging paragraph should aim to have a variety of simple, compound and complex sentences to keep the reader from getting bored or getting lost. Sometimes simply altering the length of your sentences can help add momentum to your paragraphs. Experiment with this!

Poetry utilizes the power of language to not only make us think, but to make us feel on a physical and visceral level. My experience in the museum of curiosities affected me physically, long before I had a chance to process it logically or emotionally. I felt overwhelmed, nauseous, sick. I wanted to make the reader feel the same. This is why I focused on describing the food in the cafeteria downstairs in such unappealing language (the 'mushrooms greasy slick in their juices' and the 'sunburn-pink bacon'): to make something that should have been appealing and delicious seem repellent and repulsive. I hope you felt disgusted when you read it!

- Tip:

    Give the reader experiences. Don't focus solely on plot (what happened next . . .) or on reflection (what it meant . . .). Think also about what you want your reader to feel. Sensations are often the things that linger longest in a reader's mind.

    Be intentional. Do you want them to be shocked? Outraged? Sharing in a feeling of betrayal? Do you want them to feel warm and fuzzy? Pick just one and use descriptive adjectives, sense experiences and specific, detailed images to amplify that feeling.

Prep

Take a pen or pencil and a notebook (yes, we're going to do this one the old-fashioned way) and set a timer for five minutes. I want you to write a list of your favourite words. Consider the sound of these words. Include idioms or phrases if you like. If you get stuck, try to think of favourite images or descriptors. Try to jot down at least seven (my favourite number), then go back through and note down next to each one the feelings, ideas and sensations they evoke. This will help us begin to focus on greater precision in our linguistic choices for the next task.

Write

If poetry is an investigation, then it's time for us to investigate. Specifically, I want you to explore a memory that bothers you.

It could be a memory of a time when something surprising happened out of the blue and imprinted that moment onto the tissue of your brain forever. It could be one of those annoying occasions when you thought of the perfect comeback or response only afterwards, and you go over in your mind what you should have said. It could be something that happened that puzzled you, that still doesn't seem to add up. The only criteria is that it should be something that your mind has returned to many times. Something that elicits particular emotions or sensations in you – even if you aren't completely sure why. Something that you have played over and over again in your head. Something that has got stuck.

For this writing, I want you to use as many poetic tools as you feel comfortable with. In particular, try to zoom in on particular details and images. We're going for precision of description and conjuring of mood rather than quantity. Try to prioritize sensation and experience over analysis. Be open to surprise and the unexpected, and follow each new idea that your sentences open up, even when you're not completely sure where they might lead you.

- If you're not sure where to start, then begin with a question. Ask what bothers you about the memory, then lead the reader into that time and place.
- Don't be afraid to linger in certain moments. Add description that roots us in time and place.
- Consider the poetic: lean into metaphors and images. Use all five senses.
- Zoom in and show us some crisp and specific details that are unique and might catch the eye.
- Play with the other poetic tools too: use repetition for emphasis, or extend lines across the white space of the page.
- Draw from those favourite words you listed in the prep task: use vocabulary that feels particular to this memory and its theme.
- Memories are connected to emotions and sensations. Try to focus on one sensation, and be consistent with the mood and tone you are trying to create. How did you feel at the time? How do you want the reader to feel experiencing this with you?
- Make connections. Don't be afraid to reflect, question, draw parallels. Explore links between thoughts and feelings then and realizations in hindsight now.
- Don't fall back into your comfort zone: if you feel like you're following familiar habits while writing, then shift gears and do the opposite of what you were planning to do next.
- Don't shy away from ambiguity: you don't need to find answers to every question, but you have to give the reader enough information to be engaged in the investigation.
- Try to build towards a strong ending, something that will lodge in the reader's mind: a potent image, a thought-provoking question or a sudden epiphany.

Write until you have wrung every detail you can out of this memory.

Perhaps your investigation gave you a new perspective on the memory or helped you see it in a different way. Maybe you even managed to answer some of the questions you posed in your writing. That would be fantastic, but the main point is to reflect, not to solve. Most likely, even after investigating, some answers remain elusive and out of reach. That's to be expected: our goal is to explore, and anything we may find during that is a bonus. The key thing is committing to the investigation and seeing what you might uncover in the process.

Follow up

In poetry, sound is key. The earliest poems in human history employed rhyme, rhythm and musicality so that they would stick in listeners' minds and more easily be passed down from generation to generation. It's no surprise then that reading out loud is one of the best ways of testing the rhythm and tone of your writing.

Let some time pass before you return to what you wrote. Now I want you to read it aloud. Don't rush: try to focus on the sound, cadence and effects of each sentence. You are more likely to notice if the pace starts to drag when you hear it spoken out loud. You will also more easily catch any clunky phrases or awkward constructions when you hear them. Listening to our writing spoken aloud can alert us to anything that stands out: sentences, phrases or even whole paragraphs where the tone doesn't match, or parts where there are sudden jumps or shifts. Make a note of these as you go along. Listening is a key part of testing our writing to help us spot what we need to revise.

Read

If you've enjoyed dipping your toes into the world of poetry, then why not go a little further? One of my favourite poems is 'One Art' by Elizabeth Bishop, which is easy to track down on the Poetry Foundation website. A villanelle (meaning it has a strict rhyme scheme and meter, and a form that utilizes the power of repetition) about loss and recovery, it is a poem to savour and one that should definitely be read aloud!

Try

Want to engage with other writers or get feedback on your drafts but don't want to keep bugging your friends or writing group? Why not check out some online writing platforms such as Commaful (a great place to read, share and discuss stories and poems) or Wattpad (a site for reading and publishing original fiction and conversing with readers). These are useful and constructive platforms for feedback and discussion, and a good way to test the waters of sending your writing out into the world to see how readers respond. Pick one and take a look around, even if you're not ready to go all in and upload something of your own just yet.

Chapter 17
Summoning

My journey

Luke climbs out of bed, tired and unsteady after another sleepless night.

In the kitchen (how did he get down here? His body half-asleep makes the journey before his mind has fully woken) he sets a pot of water on the hob, places in four eggs and leaves them to rattle together as the water begins to bubble. While they boil he downs a glass of orange juice, then jogs back up to his room. He bounds up as quickly as possible, for though he feels his great, lumbering body to be sluggish and slow after such a shitty night, he can't resist testing himself: to confirm that, with a little effort, he can blot out any ache or pain and carry on as ever.

From a pile of creased and rumpled clothes that is spreading, like an unstoppable flood, across his bedroom floor, he digs out a pair of light blue jeans and a tight-fitting T-shirt and pulls them on. He pushes his feet into scuffed white trainers. And yawns. He passes over his collection of fake Rolexes, chunky sovereigns and silver chains, which would only get chipped and dented at the building site, and retrieves his mobile from under his gym bag – actions, all of these, from which the brain is disengaged. His mind is elsewhere.

Back in the kitchen he juggles the hot eggs between his hands. He peels them slowly, as if unwrapping a fragile gift – trailing the shell and membrane clockwise around the egg, concentrating on getting it done in one fluid movement without tearing the soft white hidden beneath. Another challenge he sets himself. He eats around the yolks, and then discards them: four doughy yellow ping-pong balls that he sweeps across the worktop and into the bin. By now his thoughts are already racing out of the door and cataloguing all the jobs that need to be done at the rundown fixer-upper he recently bought and whether to text his mates about that drink tomorrow night.

I would like to think that he stops, in the middle of his hurried morning routine, and registers something unusual about the day. Perhaps the shards of warm light breaking through the grey clouds and spilling golden puddles on the rooftops beyond the window, or the call of dogs barking coded messages to each other from distant gardens. Instead he rushes on, grabbing his lunchbox from the fridge and trying to recall where he left his car keys.

Because he knows instinctively that the best way to stop the clouds from opening is to carry an umbrella, and the most certain way to ensure grey and murky weather is to leave the house in sunglasses, he doubles back for his jacket.

Cantering back through the kitchen one last time he thwacks into a chair he does not remember being there. The world for him is never as it ought to be. He half-stumbles, cursing – but has forgotten about it by the time he is out of the door. Yet it will leave a dull green bruise, the colour of dun emeralds, on his shin. This is not unusual. Ever since he was tiny his body has been mapped with an assortment of scars, scrapes, wounds and contusions whose provenance was somehow always a mystery to him. There were a number of occasions when he was unable to recall how he sustained injuries that had been inflicted only a matter of hours before, and even when reminded he would listen to the details with his brow scrunched and his eyes half-closed, as if he was hearing the story for the first time and the events described had all happened to someone else.

Luke drives a purple, second-hand Ford Galaxy, a great hulking people-carrier that is usually cluttered with the tools and equipment he ferries to and from building sites. Today, though, it is empty save for the few hip-hop CDs scattered across the passenger seat and the tin of extra-strong mints that slides across the dashboard every time he turns a corner. Last month he forgot about the protein shake he chucked in the back to bring to work and, after seven hours in the sweltering car, it exploded all over the floor. Now the stomach-turning reek of rotten eggs and putrid milk hangs over the whole car, impossible to dispel. This forces him to drive with the windows down. But despite the cool breeze he remains sweaty and flushed.

There's something about the size of the vehicle that he relishes: being raised so high that he can look down on the rest of the traffic, peering over the roofs of the smaller cars below as though he is floating far above them and their petty concerns. So far he has written off four cars. He boasts to his mates about how much car insurance he now has to pay, and though during one crash he even managed to destroy a motorbike, each time he comes away with little more than bruises. His driving alternates between reckless arrogance and the most tentative caution. Half of him believes that he is immune to misfortune on the road, while the other half thinks that the next time he gets into an accident the guardian angel of the asphalt might finally be looking the other way.

Despite the early hour and the bass-heavy thump of the CD, he hears the building site before he turns the final corner and faces it head-on. The commotion there is overwhelming. The site is a cacophony of clanking tools and hoarse shouts. All here is noise: from the trailer and Portaloos near where he parks, across the level stretch of mud and dust, past the half-finished steel framework surrounded by pyramid-like piles of hollow metal poles, and as far as the mixture of hedgerow and traffic cones that marks the border of the plot. Noise. Noise. Noise. And once everyone has arrived and heard the foreman's few morning mumbles, the site grows even louder, until it is an orchestra of demonic percussion: the sonorous moan of the cement mixer, the purr of turning cranes, the scrape of handsaws, the high and insistent screech of drills and circular saws, the rustle and crunch of work boots wading through gravel and dirt, the scratch of steel girders being dragged upright, the cymbal crash and whip-cracks of metal sheets being whacked by the wind as they are lugged higher up the framework and, above it all, the persistent holler of jokes, orders and insults, each one affirming the ceaseless rhythm to which the universe works.

Luke currently works as a steel erector and, as ever, he moves among the other construction workers, joking and clowning. He is red-faced and dog-tired, but is grinning and happy to be here. Just the previous year he was forced to take time off work after first breaking his wrist on site and, then, after an operation on a hernia in his stomach caused by his relentless and obsessive weightlifting. During those long months of inaction he had found it impossible to rest, forever prowling around his house and garden like a captive tiger.

At lunch he eats with a few of his workmates, the group of them sitting out in the midday sun in the trailer of a shoddy work truck. The conversation follows the familiar pattern of gentle ribbing and reheated jokes, a competitive volley of friendly taunts and mild mockery spun out from mouths stuffed with sandwiches. Then back to the job, the afternoon much as the morning. He has done these same tasks a hundred times before, piecing together the metal decking as though assembling some huge industrial puzzle, welding the joints of the great steel frame reaching up towards the sky and soon his thoughts are venturing further and further into the vast hinterland of daydream and fantasy.

As soon as the last hour arrives, Luke follows the others and tosses his dented yellow hard hat on the pile. He helps load away the tools, roll up the engineering plans and set out the traffic cones. He is in pain now, his chest tight, but he hides it well. It'll pass.

Since by now almost everyone on site looks sunburnt and dappled with fat beads of sweat, no one notices that his face is unusually blushed and blotched, nor that he is struggling hard for each ragged breath. He's as heedless to that big, dumb mess of distended muscle going berserk in his chest as the rest of them, and anyway he's distracted by the hilarity of one of the lads tripping over a stack of unused girders dumped beside the trailer.

On the drive back he weighs up the choices for the evening: he's too worn out to contemplate the regular trip to the gym, and with no doorman work until the weekend, he decides to make a trip to the house he has recently made the down payment on. He has to be doing something. He can't bear to sit around doing nothing. Can't stop for a second. Because if he does, then who knows what will catch up with him?

His new house is a wreck, and he estimates that it'll be a couple of months before he can finally move in. But is there anything more exciting than the start of a new project, when all is promise and potential? Once again his mind rushes ahead: as soon as he's done with this new derelict building, he wants to build another small house on the empty plot beside it. And why not? He has the basic knowledge, access to discounted equipment, friends in the trade and a near-certain chance of getting planning permission approved. He smiles to himself as he drives, hollers along to his hip hop and slaps one hand against the steering wheel in time to the beat.

Maybe he should finally start to take up the crusty old carpet. Or should he leave that until he has stripped the last of the wallpaper from the walls? Either way, he is so wrapped up in his projects that he barely notices the high layers of thin cirrostratus spooling out in wisps around the early evening sun.

The whole sky is slowly coming unravelled at the edges.

Without warning, he changes his mind and decides to head first to mum and dad's. Why not? It's pretty much on the way.

Hey? Anyone around?

Luke lets himself in through the unlocked front door and makes his way straight to the kitchen.

He roots around in the fridge in search of something that might take his fancy, but closes it again empty-handed.

Mum comes in from the garden and chats with him about the fixer-upper, and about the tools he might need to borrow from the garden shed for working on his house.

Is he feeling alright, she asks.

He shrugs off the question. He doesn't mention the sleepless night, the trouble breathing, the spasms and numbness in his back and left side. All the family is used to him being surly and uncommunicative when he is tired or preoccupied, and they have also learnt that the more he is pressed on a subject the more likely he is to close up or grow irritable and ill-tempered.

So mum lets it drop and doesn't try to force him to speak about his obvious discomfort or the bags beneath his eyes. At any rate, he quickly changes the subject:

Can I borrow your new car? I'll bring it back after I've done a couple of jobs there. Two hours tops.

She isn't keen on the idea.

Come on mum, don't be a killjoy!

As he's done since he was small, he keeps on until she gives in and agrees to let him take her new car for a spin – again. It's a gleaming new toy, a sleek black convertible that he takes great and unashamed pleasure in driving around and even more pleasure in the possibility of being seen in.

Won't you at least have a bit of food before you go?

But he's already grabbed the keys and waved away her offer.

[I would like to imagine him now taking a few strides across the gravel drive and then turning, pausing midway between the car and the front door as though his body and mind are pulling in different directions and for once he does not know which to follow. Maybe he even does. Maybe not.]

His enormous bulk is soon wedged tightly into the compact vehicle. A colossus in a convertible. The pain in his chest is getting worse. But still he drives away without a second thought.

[And if this were a movie, maybe he would hear me calling to him from a future he cannot predict, that it is not too late, Luke: there is still time for you to return inside, to admit that you're not invincible and to tell someone about all the pains and aches and irregularities that have been plaguing you for weeks. All logic suspended, and my voice travelling across time to reach him. *It is not too late, even now*, I speak even as I type the words. *Go back inside. Or drop by the doctor's. Do anything, anything else. But just don't drive away.* He does not listen.]

Instead he heads east. The little black convertible makes its way down past Littlehampton, another rundown seaside town. He turns early to avoid looking too long at the limitless cobalt blue: it gives him the creeps.

So he takes the longer, inland road, still mulling over the jobs he needs to get done this evening. He shifts restlessly in the driving seat, unable to settle. He must think about the new house – think, think, think. His mind rushes through each room in turn, transforming it as he goes: the mildew, the dry rot, the rising damp, the cracked windows, the splintering frames, the peeling wallpaper, the stained carpet. At last, as if by the wave of a magic wand, the whole house is radiant and new. His house, his place will soon be ready. Ready for him.

Again that horrible niggle. That twinge reaching through his chest. Crackling like an electric shock. Again he pushes it away.

Tells himself he just needs a decent night's kip. Needs to get back to the gym, get in better shape.

Soon he turns left onto the narrow road that leads to the ruined building that is awaiting him. He passes a primary school and a church in quick succession. By now the sinking sun has turned as red as his hair once was and is covering the office blocks, railways station and the shorefront pubs offering deals on midweek combos of burgers and beer.

It is here that time slows down, and each second takes on an almost unbearable clarity. His left hand reaches for the gear stick, changes down into second before he flicks the indicator and takes the corner, turning right onto Poulter's Lane. He doesn't feel right at all.

As he passes a solitary red post box he struggles to draw a loud, wheezing breath, and his head is spinning – everything is wrong. His hands fumble on the wheel as he suddenly pulls over.

Onto the verge. He reaches for the seatbelt.

Beyond the short stretch of grass where he has haphazardly parked is a Day Nursery and a tiny newsagent already locked up and shuttered for the evening.

Across the road, amid the countless semi-detacheds with pristine gardens, is the Old Guard House, a family-run Bed and Breakfast.

Further up, there starts a line of lampposts each with its head bowed.

[If this were a film, at this moment the cameras would pull back and pan out from the sleek black car. We would watch the car slowly grow smaller as we ascend, rising far above until it becomes a tiny black dot on the empty residential street; until the street itself becomes lost in the interlinking web of roads, lanes, terraces and alleys that make up the town; until the town too is dwarfed by the great stretch of yellow-brown fields and churning sea that surround it; until everything is obscured by clouds and we are far above the earth with nothing to attend to but the beginning of minor piano chords, perhaps a swell of maudlin violins and then the final credits.

But this is not a film, nor is it real – for we are not there, and neither is he.]

The street is empty. The sleek black convertible is gone. The sirens have long since faded into the distance and, by this hour, the streetlamps are glowing.

It is deep into the night by the time the car finds its way to my parents' home – but every light in the house is still on. The convertible appears as if of its own will, like a migratory bird whose knowledge of the route back is written deep within. The car has made its own way back without its driver. Or almost. For wedged up against the accelerator is a single scuffed white trainer.

Reflection

The term 'catharsis' comes from Ancient Greek and literally means to *purge*, *cleanse* or *purify*. The concept was a central tenet in Greek tragedy, where at the end of a play, the protagonist comes to the realization that his terrible situation was caused by his own actions. This catharsis cleanses him and allows him to move forward; meanwhile, the audience also shares in these intense emotions and leaves the theatre feeling purged. Today, the term is most commonly used to refer to the act of releasing thoughts and emotions by expressing them, in order to find renewal.

Writing about my brother's last day was cathartic. It released wave after wave of pent-up emotions: many of which I had been avoiding. By zooming in on the day that I had kept trying to ignore and push away, I was forced to confront my own complicated feelings about how and why my brother died.

The anger, the guilt, the anxiety and the sheer profound sadness I felt at what happened that day often threatened to stop my from finishing writing about it, and many times I had the strongest urge to turn away, to somehow end the chapter without reaching that pivotal and heart-breaking moment that it was building towards.

But at the same time I felt the pull of it as though it had its own gravity. It wasn't a straightforward process. In order to recreate my brother's last day, I needed to do a lot of research: to track his movements on that day, to confirm as best I could what he ate and where he went, to understand the nature of the jobs he did at the construction site, to pinpoint the next tasks he had to complete at the derelict house he'd recently scrabbled together the down payment on. It was only once I had an exact and complete timeline of his every movement that day that I allowed myself to imagine: to move with him through each hour and to try and inhabit his thoughts and feelings. This helped me feel closer to my brother. Writing his last day also forced me to process his dying, his death, in a different way, and to release some of the feelings I had been carrying around with me about that day.

Nonetheless, it was important for me to disrupt this communion with my brother with asides and interjections that reminded both myself and the reader of the fictionality of this recreation. I could speak to him and with him this way, but it was important not to get carried away and think he could listen, or to mistake this version for the real Luke. Catharsis, after all, depended for the Ancient Greeks not only on the drama of representing intense emotions, but on accepting difficult truths. It's no surprise that I felt such a powerful emotional release after writing this chapter.

The 'how'

In the first draft of this chapter, I'd tried to get as close to the facts as possible, making sure I moved through all of his actions that day. In the second draft, I added another layer of detail, in the form of imagined thoughts, fantasies and daydreams, in order to get closer to the emotional truth of his life. Still, something was missing: so I added my own interjections and asides to create a counterbalance and a dramatic juxtaposition in order to heighten the tension and provide a greater point of connection with the present.

- Tip:

    Revise away from the obvious. Even when the ending is fixed and unavoidable, try to make the journey to get there a little more surprising.

Chronology is great for first drafts to provide structure, but when revising we can complicate and keep the reader engaged.

You can do this by disrupting the flow: cutting away to other moments, foreshadowing, adding a brief flashback, interjecting with reflection, making connections or even throwing in facts or data.

I've never liked the word 'editing' very much. People often use it to describe only that last read through of a draft to fix spelling, grammar and sentence-level issues (this is actually *copyediting*) rather than focusing on all the different types of editing that we ought to be doing. Just as 'writing' includes research, brainstorming and planning before we even write the first sentence, so 'editing' includes a range of activities and intentions. It's important not to mix these up.

- Tip:

    Carry out *strategic* edits. If you read through your draft with the intention of 'editing', you will probably waste your time. Sure, you might catch an awkward mixed metaphor here or a bit of repetition there. But you likely won't make productive revisions.

    Start with an intention. For instance, give yourself a task of only doing content editing: reading through to see if this narrative fits together and makes sense. Or do structural editing: see if there is a balance between the beginning, the middle and the ending. Or focus only on tone and imagery. Pick one task at a time only and stick to it.

Revision also offers a chance to experiment. Get the key ideas and information down in early drafts, and then let yourself play. Pick out an image and try to thread it through to make a motif. Prune away repetition and clunky transitions (first, then, next . . .) to cut down to the very essentials. Try out switching tenses, perspectives, order.

- Tip:

    Get physical with your draft. Print it out for starters – our eyes have a tendency to skim and scan when we read (or scroll) on screens. Take out some highlighters and mark down every description in red and every transition in yellow, for instance, to see how you balance between different modes of writing.

    Or better yet, get out a pair of scissors and start chopping up the paragraphs. Then shuffle them up and try putting them in a different order. How does this change the narrative? Does it create new potentials or ideas? Does it create interesting juxtapositions? Test your writing to see what happens when you do things differently.

The last edit I do is the line edit. I *only* start this when I'm satisfied that the draft is as strong as it can be: the structure fits the content, the imagery and detail serve the theme, the tone is consistent and nothing is missing or feels lopsided. It's important to do these global edits first, otherwise you'll end up wasting time doing the copyediting again and again and again. When I do this last edit, I'm looking for two things: anything clunky that stands out (including fragments, run-ons and repetition) and phrases that could be made more beautiful or powerful by a little revision.

- Tip:

    Read backwards. I don't mean literally starting with the final word of the piece and then every word before it. That wouldn't make any sense. I mean read the last sentence first. Consider it. Then read the sentence before it. And so on, until you reach the beginning.

    This will help see each sentence in isolation, instead of rushing on to the next one. By taking each sentence out of context, we're better able to judge it on its own terms: Does it add to the narrative in some way? Is it complete and well-phrased? Or is it redundant?

Prep

What do you find hardest in writing? Maybe it's crafting an ending that brings everything together? Perhaps constructing natural-sounding dialogue? Maybe integrating setting details? I want you to take three minutes to brainstorm a list of aspects of writing that you sometimes struggle with. Try to jot down around five things that can be difficult for you, or that you're not sure work in your drafts. This will focus your mind on the things to pay attention to when we dive into strategic editing.

Write

Editing, as we have seen, is far more than just that last final polish and proofread. Nonetheless editing has an unfair reputation as the most boring, slow and mind-numbing part of the writing process. This is unfair: editing can, in fact, be an immensely creative and experimental act. So what I want you to do now is to *rewrite*.

I suspect you might be a little like me. I've got three or four notebooks lying around with ideas, paragraphs, outlines and plans. But that's nothing – on my laptop I've got more than a dozen documents in various folders with narratives I either didn't quite manage to finish or that didn't turn out the way I hoped and so I decided to set aside. The abandoned, the half-finished, the messy incomplete projects that ran out of steam. Does that sound familiar?

Choose one of those. Ideally a piece of writing that has a beginning, middle and end (or at least the bare bones or plans for one). A standalone story or chapter idea, rather than plans for a different or longer work. You may have to re-investigate a few of your old drafts before you find one that you are comfortable revisiting. Our goal is to breathe new life into an old piece of writing.

Of course, there's no point in just going back to it with the same expectations: if we don't have an idea of what we'll do differently, then we may end up making exactly the same mistakes or finding ourselves with just the same kind of unsatisfactory draft that made us ditch it in the first place. The most important step then is committing to a new experiment: select how to revise it into something completely new. Perhaps you could rewrite it from a different person's perspective. Perhaps you might switch the tense and set all action in the immediacy of the present moment – or alternatively, frame the narrative as a reflection on the past from the distance of the present. Perhaps you could change the voice from first person to third person (or even second person) point of view. Perhaps you might revise the tone to focus on a joyful, celebratory mood rather than a melancholy, meditative one.

Pick one of these, or come up with your own idea for how to dramatically alter this draft. Then it's time to rewrite:

- Be intentional. This means identifying the key areas that need work before you start and making sure you pay close attention to these as you revise.
- Changing tense or perspective doesn't mean just altering the grammar of each sentence. It means rethinking priorities: What are the major themes and ideas that you want to highlight? Then edit to make sure each paragraph speaks to these themes and ideas.
- Move from summarizing to dramatizing. Early drafts often tell us what happened (*we argued, then he stormed out*), rather than show us the full scene (*his face turned beetroot. 'How could you think . . .' he stammered*).
- Aim for a balance between different modes: setting description, characterization, dialogue, interaction and reflection. If you've got two paragraphs in a row of one of these, then it's probably time to shake things up a bit to avoid monotony.

- We live in a visual age, so don't forget to work on those visual details to show us the places, people and objects that are important.

- Look for the emotional beats of your piece: the places you want the reader to feel something. What is it that you want them to feel? Try to ensure tonal consistency throughout the pages, revising anything that doesn't fit.

- Are you building towards some kind of climax? Where is the heart of this piece?

- Don't be afraid to prune. Cut away all the extraneous information or unnecessary detail. Does each sentence further the story or add to our understanding of these characters or times? If not, be brutal and delete it.

Write until you have changed each page of this draft to fit the new style, perspective or tone that you are experimenting with.

Let me be clear: this experiment might improve the draft and help you forge something entirely new. However, it's equally likely that it could make the draft worse, or move it further away from what you hoped to achieve. The fact is that there is no way to know whether drastic strategies will work or not without giving them a try. We have to commit to experimenting and playing with our work in order to see what happens, with no guarantees that each new attompt will be productive. So don't go into revision thinking it's a magical solution. It's not. So be patient. It might take two, three or even more attempts before you find a way forward that works for your piece.

Follow up

Now that we've done some strategic global editing, we can zoom in and do some copyediting. Pick one sentence-level issue to examine in your draft. It could be dialogue tags (*said, shouted, whispered*), verbs or transitional phrases – something small that we use frequently. Then skim through your draft, looking only for these. Do you tend to repeat the same words or phrases many times? Do the tenses and perspectives all match up? Are there any clunky choices that don't fit the tone or the action? Can you make any a little more dynamic and evocative? Revise accordingly for variety, consistency and effect. Next pick another sentence-level issue and repeat the process.

Read

Once editing is complete and you've tried out your piece with a beta reader or writers group and you're happy with it, then it's time to send it out into the world. It's important not to send our work anywhere and everywhere though: it's best to find the right home for it. Many websites host lists of active calls for submissions and writing contests. Some of the most popular are the *Community of Literary Magazines and Presses* website, and the *Poets & Writers* website's classified page. Look through these listings until you find a call for submissions from a magazine, anthology or contest that fits with the theme or focus of your piece.

Try

It's time to be brave. Once you've found a call for submissions that seems to be a good match for your piece, send it out. A few things to remember:

- Don't submit to a magazine or literary journal that you haven't read. You need to look through at least one issue to see if your writing fits with their ethos and style.
- Keep your cover letter professional and to the point.
- Don't fear rejection: it's a part of the writing life. If one venue rejects your piece, keep moving and try submitting it somewhere else.

Good luck!

Chapter 18
Endings

My journey

The frost has gathered upon the ferns by the time I return to the Bracken Woods, and the path between the outstretched fingertips of needle and frond has become a ragged patchwork of ice. I follow it through the forest, the crunch of frozen leaves and twigs beneath my winter boots echoing louder with every step I take.

Already close to six months have passed since my brother's death, yet it might as well have been a single day or even an hour, so fresh is the sting of it. We have gone back to our jobs, our homes and our familiar patterns, with the unspoken hope that the world might return to how it once was. Grief has gradually calcified and sunk to the pit of my stomach. Here it sits like a stone. Sometimes I can almost forget it's there.

From somewhere up ahead comes a birdcall I cannot place, and I draw my coat tighter around me. I dip my head to focus on the track. If I don't give the forest my full attention then I might lose my way. The deeper I venture between the trees, the more I'm reminded why I kept putting off returning here.

I pass the scattering of silver birches and start down a rough slope made slippery by patches of ice gilding the mud. Towards the bottom I stumble, dodging several gnarly stumps of hardened roots. I push myself faster, and keep on at such a speed that it does not take me long to reach the clearing at the top of the hill where we scattered his ashes half a year before.

Save for the frost and the grey skies, nothing has changed since my last visit. I feel oddly disappointed. I wait for something to happen. For the rustle of leaves in the woods below to turn into something more definite, or for someone to emerge into the clearing. Why have I come back? It's hard enough saying goodbye once, so why do it all over again?

Thick spools of mist spill from my lips with each breath. I'm no longer sure what I am doing. I search across the uncovered slope, wishing for the snow that has been forecast for this evening, for a great fall of sleet that will render the whole world invisible and wipe away everything.

Each winter we would pray for snowstorms, though Luke and I could never agree upon the strength of the blizzards we required. He was more particular about the amount of snow he wanted: not enough to stop the bus from taking him to school, but too much to allow the day to continue as usual. His perfect winter day was one where the fearsome weather would prevent most of the teachers from making it to school yet, somehow, would not obstruct his friends from making their way to the huge playing fields beside the classrooms, where the lot of them would spend the day engaged in one huge snow-fight. He dreamed of epic battles involving not just a few snowballs tossed at opposing armies but elaborate operations involving digging trenches, plotting out complex tactics of attack and counterattack and drawing the enemy into sudden skirmishes in which they would attempt to bury one another in missiles, bombs, rockets, grenades, cannonballs, shells, shrapnel and torpedoes, all fashioned from the greying slush covering the ground.

I make my way down amid the stretch of heather. A cold breeze stirs the needles of the evergreens at the foot of the clearing, and soon the branches also start to rustle, as if trying to shrug off their own haunted shadows.

And if they are haunted, I know who is responsible. Luke would have quite liked to be a ghost. He often pretended to be a poltergeist. As a little boy he spent countless hours chasing us with a ghostly white sheet clutched around his shoulders. Even as an adult he spent a disconcertingly large amount of time hiding in wardrobes, behind doors or under beds, waiting for friends or relatives to arrive home so that he could leap out, screaming like a banshee and watch them reel backwards in surprise. What had he been practising for?

The icy grass is patchy and worn upon the slope. I take slow, tentative steps as I work my way down over the chalky scrub, trying in vain to find the exact spots where the ashes might have fallen. I slip off one of my gloves and crouch down to run my fingertips through the heather. His ashes must have been borne off by the breeze, or devoured by the omnivorous roots of the trees and plants. Or perhaps they linger still, too small now for the eye to recognize, upon the bracken and the shrubs. Though my fingers are soon numb, I stay in this hunched position for as long as I can bear it. When I rise again I find the last evidence of daylight has been lost among the billow and brume.

Every instinct tells me to turn around and start back walking in order to get back to the car and make it home before night falls.

I remain rooted to the spot.

The wind is tugging at my clothes as urgently as a little child. Out of nowhere, I am overcome with the strangest of sensations – I'm suddenly convinced that everything that has occurred in the last six months happened to someone else and not to me at all.

I raise my gloves in front of my face and begin to flex my hands, to make sure that this body still belongs to me and is acting on my orders. It is still mine, and so are these memories. They are mine.

They are mine.

I feel a sudden kick of adrenaline, and before I know it I have started down the hill, intent on finding another way back to the car park. At the bottom of the slope I spot a rough track meandering between the trees. There is no need to retrace my steps. Not now. I follow the track around until it opens into an expanse of bracken.

As I walk down the new route, it occurs to me that this is the first outing in many months when I have picked a new path instead of automatically repeating one I have been down many times before. The feeling of being freed from my usual habits makes me almost giddy, and reminds me of the unexpected excitement of those schooldays all those years ago that Luke was always praying for. One in particular leaps to mind: a winter about fifteen years ago, when a heavy early-December snowfall had forced all the local schools to close.

I was in my final year of primary school and already dreading what might happen when the summer term finished, while Luke was a few months short of nine. He begged and begged to go out that snowy morning until finally our parents allowed the two of us to head out to a nearby hill where many of our friends were gathering.

We threw on our coats, hats, gloves, scarves and boots in record time and took from the garage the sole toboggan (its twin had been wrecked the previous winter) before rushing from the house. Since the whole village was covered with a carpet of thick, fluffy snow, we were able to walk along in the middle of the deserted road. I was stuck pulling the toboggan while Luke charged ahead. Every so often he would squeal with delight and throw himself backwards into a buttress of snow, where he would lie perfectly still until I approached, only to then leap up laughing and race on once again.

To reach the hill, we had to follow the road past the village school, the Holly Tree public house, the vicarage and the parade of small shops – newsagent, laundrette, dentist and post office. We then turned off onto a scraggy footpath that followed the border of a barren field, now hidden under a heavy layer of snow. We walked in single file, and I have the most vivid memory of turning to see the deep footprints we left being cleaned away, one by one, by the trail of the toboggan we were dragging behind us.

Halfway across the field Luke began to speak. He didn't turn his head at first, so I couldn't tell whether or not he was speaking to himself. *If things get really cold, they freeze. So if we get cold enough, we'll turn to ice too. And if we turn to ice, then we might stay frozen for a hundred years. After all that time, we'll wake up in the future – and there'll be cars flying through the sky and robots who'll wait on us hand and foot.*

He spoke as if this were all incontrovertible fact, and so I did not at any point attempt to interrupt his train of thought. *But*, and here his voice took on a note of anxiety, *what will it feel like to be frozen? Will it be like having a really long sleep, or will we be awake all that time? What if my nose itches but my icicle fingers can't move to scratch it? What if I'm stuck like a statue for years and years, looking at the world around me without being able to join it?*

I waited for him to continue, but he said nothing more. Perhaps he was thinking of some science-fiction film or story that had lodged deep in his mind. I can't recall how I responded. I can only remember that, as we started up the side of the hill, our progress was made arduous and slow by our not knowing where the dense slush ended and the firm ground beneath began. After a while we were able to make out many of our classmates sprinting to and fro upon the summit.

When we finally made it to the top we went straight into action, pelting our friends with snowballs and running to join a group rolling a lopsided head for a giant snowman. I remember that while playing upon the snow-covered hill I lost all sense of my own life and felt temporarily unloosed from time. No winter day since has ever been able to compare.

As I trudge back through the Bracken Woods, I smile as I remember those snowball fights that afternoon. I had been afraid to return to the forest, that much is true – afraid to surrender my forward motion to ghosts, to get pulled deeper into the past and find my life overturned once again. But this has not happened. The muddy track winds to the left, and as I take the corner I catch a glimpse, up ahead, of the car park between the trees. I can't help but break into a grin. I've nearly made it. I've found another path back.

And so I let myself be carried away by the memory, as my mind keeps returning to the part of the afternoon when the whole group of us decided to race down the slope. Exhausted by hours of snowball fights and war games, we all carried our sledges to the edge of the summit and arranged ourselves into a rough line.

It was at this point that Luke and I began to argue, first about which of us would race on our solitary toboggan and then, after we had finally agreed to both squeeze on together, about who would sit at the front and steer. It was a pointless discussion, since we were both well aware that the toboggan always chose its own unpredictable course, regardless of how much we leaned and swerved. In the end I agreed to sit behind him, not because of the disparity in our sizes, nor because of any lingering brotherly affection, but because of his threats to kick me off halfway down if he was stuck at the back.

Once Luke had settled at the front, I wedged myself in behind, looping my arms around his waist while we waited for the other racers to make ready. One of our friends began counting down in a shrill voice that echoed around us and carried off into the valley below. Luke and I were pressed so close together in the small tub that I could feel him draw in breath as the countdown approached zero. Then a pair of hands pushed against my back, shoving us forward onto the slope.

A few bumps and jolts shook us as we started over the ridge, but within seconds we were hurtling down at a terrifying speed. The hill was far steeper than I had thought, and it felt as though we were ploughing almost vertically towards the valley below. But then, all of a sudden, we were flying.

My stomach lurched, and I lost all track of the other sledges and toboggans carrying our friends. I remember frantically clasping onto my brother. He was gripping the handles and attempting to pull us left, then right, then left again, so that we might dodge the silvery streaks of blinding light that were reflected in the snow and rose up around us like hairline cracks in the very fabric of the air.

He urged us on *faster* and *faster*. I was not sure we could gather any more speed, but still he urged us on *faster*. On and on, down and down, into the blinding light.

What is curious is that I have no memory of us ever reaching the bottom of the hill. Luke once told me that if you dream you are falling from a great height, it is vital to wake up before you hit the ground, or else you might never wake up at all. I know only that I wished our ride together would never end, that we might go on racing through the snow forever, both past and future simply slipping away as we continued our descent.

For those few moments, as my brother whooped and bellowed on our shared toboggan, I felt as though we really were gliding through the sky, shooting straight towards a blur of billowing white cumulus through which we would soon hurtle. And as we soared towards the great expanse of endless white, I held my arms tight around his stomach, determined more than ever not to let go.

Reflection

Life writing changes the writer's life. By organizing thoughts, experiences, ideas and memories on the page, we are able to see our lives in different ways. Often this seeing provokes reflection and adaptation. Writing helps us process the things that have happened to us, as well as the things we've done. It was only through writing about my brother that I managed to draw strength from the memories we shared, and only by writing honestly and openly about my struggles with grief that I have come to accept what has happened – to him, to me, to both of us. In the darkest of times, I found that creativity was a lifeline, and through it I found resilience.

Jeffrey Berman has called the act of writing a memoir about grief a form of 'mourning sickness': a gestation period during which the bereaved adapt to the loss of a loved one by questioning and then redefining themselves.[1] He theorizes that the act of writing about the experience aids the writer to navigate the changes in identity created by loss. Documenting and exploring our trauma has an adaptive function: it helps us to work through our grief. It helps us to memorialize and remember our loved ones, yes, but it also helps us to find some meaning in loss and some way to keep going.

These chapters have documented, recorded and depicted the transformations that I went through after Luke died. It made sense, then, to end with my realization that though I had lost my brother, he would in some ways always be with me. The ending I chose, of the two of us soaring into the snow, worked for me in three important ways. (1) Because for all the trauma of those months, I didn't want to end on sadness, but instead on the joy and fun we shared. (2) Because it showed the completion of my arc, depicting how I was able at last to balance between finding strength rather than misery in that world of memory, while not becoming stuck in the past. (3) Because the only ending that made sense to me was one that remained open-ended – because there is no real ending to grief: because the pain and the sadness of it never really ends. But we learn to live with it. We learn how to carry on.

I'd be lying if I said that writing always solves everything. But nonetheless, the narrative impulse that burns inside all of us – the urge to tell stories, to document, to share our memories and also to structure, to imagine and to create – is vital for our well-being. Through writing we discover possibilities beyond getting stuck and going round and round in endless circles of regret, anger and self-doubt. Writing stopped me from getting stuck. I was able to write a path out of the labyrinth of grief. Of course, despite having written an 'ending' to my journey here, I still get lost sometimes. I take a wrong turn and find myself deep in the maze. Sometimes it's easy to turn around and get out. Other times I spend days and days wandering in maddening circles. But when I'm most lost, writing about the labyrinth helps me see more clearly where I am – and therefore choose more carefully where to go next.

The 'how'

In earlier chapters, I focused on the physical and emotional devastation of grief. In the first draft of this chapter, the ending of my journey focused on those wounds and scars – a reminder that they made me the person I now am. But on reflection that didn't feel right, because it didn't fully show the joy I had been able to find in looking back on my memories of Luke. When I rewrote, I chose instead

---

[1] Jeffrey Berman, *Writing Widowhood* (New York: State University of New York Press, 2015), 6.

to focus on my gratitude for the times we'd spent together, and the strength I was able to draw from those recollections.

- Tip:

    Manifest gratitude. I know this sounds like some wishy-washy New Age inspirational claptrap, but hear me out. By writing about things we're grateful for, we train our minds to see things from a perspective of gratitude and appreciation.

    In the same way, if we write about positive memories, we are more inclined to see the joy in remembering. This doesn't mean to edit out any negative memories or avoid writing about difficult times. But it does mean writing intentionally, rather than accidentally, and being aware that we *choose* how we want to remember.

Grief memoirs always tell two stories: a story of before and a story of after. From the start, I felt compelled to write about my brother and everything that made him special, unique, infuriating – but I soon found I couldn't write about him without writing about myself too. Our stories have always been intertwined. I am who I am because of Luke.

- Tip:

    Don't be afraid to centre yourself. You can't show how much a person meant to you without showing yourself. Writing means exploring – and exposing – who you are. Let the reader hear your voice and see you in action.

    Memoir also doesn't have to be exclusively about looking back. Write about the present, and how it has been shaped by the things that happened in the past. This isn't journalism, so we're not aiming to be neutral or objective: colour your remembrances with responses, feelings, opinions and asides and make it clear how personal they are.

I knew for a long time that my return to the woods where we scattered my brother's ashes would be a fitting ending for this journey, as it allowed me to compare the raw pain and chaos of those first weeks after his death with the way I felt later, when I had begun to process what had happened. I remembered I'd been thinking during that walk about the joyful snowy day from decades before when all the usual rules of life had been briefly suspended. What had happened on that day, though? It was so long ago, after all. To unlock more details, I drew a mind map and wrote down all the thoughts, ideas and recollections that came up when thinking about winter and snow. That's how I found my way to the memory of tobogganing, which I knew I had to write about.

- Tip:

    Unleash your subconscious. So many memories are buried a little bit below the surface. How can we dig them up? One way is through creative play. So spend a little time drawing, doodling, sketching, mind-mapping, listing, scribbling and brainstorming around words, images and ideas.

    Often when I hit a creative block or don't know where to head next, I spend five minutes with a pencil and paper sketching out a list of things that come to mind when I hear a particular word (*holiday, fear, trains*). At least half the time I stumble across a memory that I'd forgotten or an idea I'd never previously considered.

All narratives are about change. When people talk about character arcs, what they mean is that a narrative feels complete because it shows us how a character has grown, developed or learned something over the course of the story. That doesn't mean that we have to write a nice, neat happy ending for every narrative – that would not only be fake but also banal. But it does mean that we need to address the changes that have occurred within the narrative.

- Tip:

    Write forwards. Show us how you have changed, and don't be afraid of looking ahead. Use all the tools in the writing playbook to predict, imagine, invent – write about the person you are becoming and the future you see for yourself.

    Perhaps even consider a flash-forward, depicting how you picture life a few years from now. Writing about the past doesn't mean we have to get stuck there.

Prep

It's time to take stock. You've travelled with me on my journey through these chapters, and you've also been on your own journey. So I want you to reflect on what you've learned and uncovered about yourself in the process. To do that, I want you to make a mind map about yourself. *Who are you, right now?* Try to avoid long, descriptive sentences about yourself. Instead jot down words, images, thoughts, ideas and changes that come to mind. You could arrange it with your lessons learned on the left side of the page, your characteristics on the right and your current goals at the top of the page. Or you can simply start with one of these and branch out to see where it leads you by association. Take five minutes, or until you've filled a page of a notebook or a sheet of paper.

Write

We've come a long way on this journey. So now it's time to write your own ending.

Don't worry if you're not there yet, or if you've still got a lot more you want to write before you reach an ending point. That's not a problem – many writers sketch out that final scene long before they have written the rest of the project so that they know where they're heading. It's useful to have that final destination in mind so that we can strategically work towards it.

You don't need to write the whole final chapter or section of your project: I want you to focus only on a single scene. That final scene ties up any loose ends you've left dangling in your narrative, and ideally also lingers in the reader's mind after they've read the last words. Try to imagine how you want to conclude your project, and what events, images or descriptions will best sum up your themes. Remember: as always, this is only a rough draft, and there will be plenty of opportunity to change, revise or alter this ending later on.

- Tie up any narrative threads. Look back through what you've written so far: Is there any information the reader needs to connect all the scenes, ideas and events together? Are there any details the reader needs to be given to bring them up to date?
- Remind readers of important scenes and events from earlier in your writing by adding some subtle call-backs: show us some objects, images, phrases or locations that will jog their memory and thereby add a sense of cohesion to this ending.
- Avoid cliché and sentimentality. Swerve away from any ending that readers can see a mile away. Also try not to have a gushing, over-the-top final scene. This isn't a movie: it's real life.
- Happy endings are great, but they're not the only option, so don't feel the need to pretend that everything is fixed or back to normal, especially when this isn't the case!
- Stay true to the themes and the tone you have already set up in your writing. Readers respond best to consistency.
- Pick the type of ending that works best for you (I've detailed a few options below).

- An epiphany – a moment of realization, where the penny drops and the narrator sees things in a new light – is a popular ending for memoirs because it demonstrates how the narrator has changed and adapted.
- A denouement is a final summing up that helps readers see the big picture, and to understand how everything that has happened before fits together. It also allows for a little reflection on what has occurred over the course of the narrative.
- Ambiguous and open-ended final scenes leave the reader wondering. These can be powerful, but they have to be intentional. You cannot leave all questions unanswered and all narrative threads untied – pick one idea or question *only* that you want the reader to ponder.
- A final image is a powerful and poetic way of making sure one picture sticks in the reader's head after they turn that final page. Just be certain that it fits well with the themes and characters so doesn't seem out of place.
- Memoirs are concerned with memory and the past, but the final scene can be a chance to look ahead or hint at the future.
- Try to have a resolution that gives the narrative closure. This means showing how something has changed, and how the dust has now settled.
- Don't aim for a 'perfect' ending, aim for one that fits with your themes, tone and voice.
- It may take a couple of tries to find the one that works, so don't be afraid to keep experimenting with different options.

Write for however long it takes to get to the last sentence and the last full stop that finishes the final paragraph.

Follow up

The ending you just wrote may not be perfect – it's a first draft, after all, so it probably needs a decent chunk of editing and revision – but it gives you a fixed goal. So let's map out how to get there: write a bullet point list detailing what you need to do to reach that ending. What are the steps that will get you to that point? What scenes do you still need to write? What details need to be established for the ending to be as powerful and clear as possible? What epiphanies or realizations will lead your narrative towards its resolution? What changes or events do you need to show to make that journey feel complete?

What information still needs to be conveyed? Make these bullet points as specific as you can. This will help you identify what you need to work on next in order to finish your project.

Read

For a poetic, thought-provoking and heart-rending story of grief and resilience, I highly recommend Hisham Matar's haunting memoir *The Return*. The book is both a memoir, a potted history of modern Libya, and a detective story as Matar attempts to find out what happened to his father, who disappeared in one of Gaddafi's prisons. Searching and reflective, the memoir shows how the author is able to make peace with ambiguity, uncertainty and loss.

Try

Hopefully these chapters have encouraged you to not only write regularly but also to push yourself out of your comfort zone and experiment with your writing. You've nearly reached the end of this book, but your writing journey is just beginning. The single most important thing you can do now is to keep going. Find a way to build writing into your daily life if you can – just a hundred words a day would help you keep up momentum. So I want you to consider making a calendar or writing schedule that can lock in time for writing. If you can commit to the same time every day (or every few days), then that's useful for building a consistent writing practice. But if your responsibilities and routines mean that's not possible, then it's even more important to look ahead and find blocks of time when you can focus solely on your writing. You've travelled a long way on this path, investing time, emotion and effort in your journey – so don't stop now!

Conclusion

Why keep writing?

Grief changes us in many, myriad ways. But writing, as we've seen on this journey together, can help us change too. Through writing about our experiences, we can process and understand what we are going through. Writing aids reflection and offers a space to unburden ourselves of all the things whirring and spiralling in our heads. Writing helps us to record and to memorialize, to store and to share the stories that need preserving. Finally, and perhaps most importantly, writing helps build resilience by encouraging us to focus on the things that are important to us, the things that make us who we are.

That's not to say that writing fixes everything. Life is still hard, messy, painful and at times unbearable. But writing can help us, at times, to find the places where the light spills in through the cracks. It can help us keep going.

This particular journey is over. But of course we're each still on our own journey. Perhaps you've managed to gain a little perspective and healing through these writing tasks. Perhaps you still feel like you're in flux, only gradually coming out of the chaos and haze of grief and starting to find a way to carry on. Perhaps you've written memories and reflections now that have helped you build empathy for yourself. Whatever stage of the journey you've reached, I urge you to write on.

Write on. Through the good days, and the rough days, and the so-shitty-you-want-to-curl-up-and-disappear days. Write on, both for yourself, and to share your stories by sending your work out into the world. Because sharing those stories helps anyone who reads them see that though we never get over grief, we are able to forge ahead and find meaning, worth and sometimes even joy through remembering and carrying on. Because sharing these stories means sharing what it means to be human – beautifully, imperfectly, vulnerably human – in an age when more than ever we need to all be reminded of what we share in common. And because sharing these stories proves that the people we love aren't lost: they remain with us, in our hearts, and we honour them by telling the world who they were.

Share your stories with your writing groups and readers; online and in person; and send them out to magazines, journals, competitions. Keep up to date with the latest submission opportunities, calls for memoirs and writing tips and prompts at sammeekings.substack.com

Write on, and keep conjuring a little of your own unique magic and wonder on the page.

Bibliography

Ali, T. (2020, 8 June), *Powerful Recall Strategy (How To Remember & Retain Better)* [Video]. https://youtu.be/-Bl02OLAOsE?si=IUqL5gn000Ayspqw.

Armstrong, K. (2022, 10 November), *Sacred Nature with Karen Armstrong* [Video]. https://www.youtube.com/watch?v=ovfqJFkuRrg.

Babalola, B. (2021), *Love in Colour: Mythical Tales from Around the World, Retold*, London: William Morrow.

Barthes, R. (1973), *The Pleasure of the Text*, New York: Farrar, Straus & Giroux.

Berman, J. (2015), *Writing Widowhood*, New York: State University of New York Press.

Bishop, E. (1983), 'One Art', in *The Complete Poems 1926–1979*, New York: Farrar, Straus and Giroux. https://www.poetryfoundation.org/poems/47536/one-art.

Bolton, G. (1999), *The Therapeutic Potential of Creative Writing: Writing Myself*, London: Jessica Kingsley Publishers.

Bosselaar, L. (2007), 'Stillbirth', *Academy of American Poets*. https://poets.org/poem/stillbirth

'Caring For Yourself' (2024), *Option B*. https://optionb.org/supporting-self.

Cherry, K. (2023), 'How to Interpret Dreams', *Very Well Mind*. https://www.verywellmind.com/dream-interpretation-what-do-dreams-mean-2795930.

Community of Literary Magazines and Presses. (2024), https://www.clmp.org/.

Couser, G. T. (2012), *Memoir: An Introduction*, New York: Oxford University Press.

Didion, J. (2006), *The Year of Magical Thinking*, Glasgow: Harper Perennial.

Douglas, C. and Carn, I. (Hosts) (2020–present), *Good Morning Grief Podcast*. https://podcasts.apple.com/gb/podcast/good-mourning/id1529978129.

Frost, R. (2004), 'Acquainted with the Night', *Twentieth-Century American Poetry*. https://www.poetryfoundation.org/poems/47548/acquainted-with-the-night

Gilbert, S. M. (1995), *Wrongful Death: A Memoir*, New York: Norton.

Haley, E. and Williams, L. (Hosts) (2014–present), *What's Your Grief Podcast*. https://podcasts.apple.com/gb/podcast/whats-your-grief-podcast/id946757971.

Harris, J. (2012), *Signifying Pain: Constructing and Healing the Self through Writing*, New York: State University of New York Press.

Hunt, C. (2013), *Transformative Learning through Creative Life Writing: Exploring the Self in the Learning Process*, London: Routledge.

Institute of Medicine, Committee for the Study of Health Consequences of the Stress of Bereavement (1984), 'Toward a Biology of Grieving', in *Bereavement: Reactions, Consequences, and Care*, 145–78. Washington: National Academy Press.

Jung, C. G. and Shamdasani, S., ed. (2009), *The Red Book: Liber Novus*, trans. M. Kyburz and J. Peck, W W Norton & Co.

Karr, M. (2015), *The Art of Memoir*, New York: Harper.

Klass, D., Silverman, P. R. and Nickman, S., ed. (1996), *Continuing Bonds: New Understandings of Grief*, Abingdon: Taylor & Francis.

Knausgård, K. O. (2013), *A Death in the Family: My Struggle Book 1*, trans. Don Bartlett, London: Vintage.

Lewis, C. S. (1963), *A Grief Observed*, San Francisco: Harper San Francisco, Reprint.

Loewald, H. W. (1960), 'On the Therapeutic Action of Psychoanalysis', *International Journal of Psychoanalysis*, 41: 16–33.

Macdonald, H. (2014), *H is for Hawk*, London: Jonathan Cape.

MacFarland, R. (2021), 'The Worlds Beneath Our Feet', *On Being with Krista Tippett podcast*. https://onbeing.org/programs/robert-macfarlane-the-worlds-beneath-our-feet/.

Malraux, A. (1990), *Anti-Memoirs*, New York: Henry Holt & Co.

Marinella, S. (2017), *The Story You Need to Tell: Writing to Heal from Trauma, Illness, or Loss*, Novato: New World Library.

Matar, H. (2017), *The Return*, London: Penguin.

Maté, G. (2022, 7 November), *The Childhood Lie That's Ruining All Of Our Lives* [Video]. https://www.youtube.com/watch?v=uPup-1pDepY.

Miller, B. (2013), 'We Regret to Inform You', *Sun Magazine*, Issue 455.

Mintz, S. (2003), 'Using Primary Source Documents', *OAH Magazine of History*, 17 (3): 41–3.

Nabokov, V. (1969), *Speak, Memory*, London: Penguin.

Oates, J. C. (2011), *A Widow's Story*, New York: Ecco.

Rando, T. (1988), *How to Go on Living When Someone You Love Dies*, New York: Bantam.

Rentzenbrink, C. (2022), *Write It All Down: How to Put Your Life on the Page*, London: Bluebird.

Rosen, M. (2023), *Getting Better: Life Lessons on Going Under, Getting Over It, and Getting through It*, London: Ebury Press.

Schama, S. (2004), *Landscape and Memory*, London: Harper Perennial.

Schulz, K. (2022), *Lost & Found*, London: Random House.

Sebald, W. G. (1998), *The Rings of Saturn*, trans. Michael Hulse, London: The Harvill Press.

Shields, D. (2010), *Reality Hunger: A Manifesto*, London: Hamish Hamilton.

Stroebe, M. and Schut, H. (1999), 'The Dual Process Model of Coping with Bereavement: Rationale and Description', *Death Studies*, 23: 197–224.

Taylor, J. (2007), *Take Me Home*, London: Granta Books.

Vann, D. (2009), *Legend of a Suicide*, London: Penguin.

Wagner, B., C. Knaevelsrud, C. and Maercker, A. (2006), 'Internet-based Cognitive-Behavioural Therapy for Complicated Grief: A Randomized Controlled Trial', *Death Studies*, 30: 429–53.

'Writing Contests, Grants & Awards' (2024), *Poets & Writers: Contests, MFA Programs, Agents & Grants for Writers*. https://www.pw.org/grants.

Index

'Acquainted with the Night' (Frost)   26
act of remembering and preserving   46
act of revisiting   65, 94
affirmations   98, 99
'*Ah ha!*' moment   140
Ali, Tansel   48
Anderson, Rosemarie   54
animal instinct   70–9
Annual Review of Psychology   98
anxiety   12, 45, 120, 131, 132, 137, 138, 151, 153, 185, 194
Aristotle   84
Armstrong, Karen   134
authentic dialogue   76–7

Babalola, Bolu   113
Barthes, Roland   163
beginnings   20, 186, 188
   anxiety   12
   begin with yourself   12
   be vulnerable   11
   bullet points   12, 166, 200
   emotion   11, 12
   familiarity   7
   follow up   14
   interiority   11
   reflection   9–10
   show, don't tell   10–11
   writing   12–14
bereavement   10, 15, 21, 33, 43, 58, 93, 94, 100
Berman, Jeffrey   195
'Beyond the Pleasure Principle' (Freud)   32
biographemes   163
Bishop, Elizabeth   178

the body
   is a battleground   49–50
   is a clock   50–1
   is a fluke of biology   52–3
   is a pose   51
   is a receptacle for pleasure   51–2
   is a site of desire   50
   is a vessel   52–3
   is capital   50
   is memento mori   49
   is taboo   52
Bolu   114
Bosselaar, Laure-Anne   58
Bowie, David   85
brutal truth   44, 46, 78
Burroughs, William   85

Campbell, Joseph   109
catharsis   184, 185
'Changing the Story'   78–9
character arc   110, 198
character in action   47
Chekhov   11
'The Childhood Lie That's Ruining All Of Our Lives'   98
childhood traumas   98
clichés   85, 86, 122, 199
cognitive research   84
Cohen, Leonard   25
cohesive mood   132
colour charts   122
Commaful   178
consistency of tone and mood   22
cut-up technique   84–5

daydream   107, 118, 126, 162, 181, 185
death drive   32

death instinct   32
deep time   120, 121, 125
defamiliarization   13
depression   9, 11, 43, 74
dialogue   36, 46–8, 54, 76, 77, 97, 154, 188, 189
Didion, Joan   14
disruption   24–5, 45, 96, 185
Doctorow, E. L.   20
Doty, Mark   173
Doyle, Arthur Conan   158, 159
dreams   41, 72, 74, 81, 84, 91, 118, 135–43

eco-writing   120, 125
Eliot, T. S.   112
embodied writing   54–8
emotional honesty   32
emotional truth   110, 185
exposure therapy   2
expressive writing   143

fable   106–14
falling action   33
figurative imagery   85
figurative language   22
flashbacks   66–8
flow state   24
forest bathing   125
free writing   112, 141–2
Freud, Sigmund   32
Frost, Robert   26

Gogh, Van   75
Google News Archive   155
gratitude   196–7

haiku   87
hendiatris   132
hermit crab essays   87–9
The Hero with a Thousand Faces (Campbell)   109
H is for Hawk (MacDonald)   37
Hofer, Johannes   43, 44
Holmes, Sherlock   158–62, 164, 165
home/sickness   39–48
    grief stages   43
    intertwined with grief   43
homonyms   85

hook   113
hypotaxis   67

identity   9, 46, 96, 164, 196
idioms   85, 176
immersive writing   123
information dump   21
in medias res opening   10
intense memories   65
intuitive thinking   130
italics   153

Jouet, Jacques   88
Jung, Carl   138
juxtaposition   69, 75, 85, 86, 95, 163, 185

Keats, John   130

L'appel du vide (call of the void)   32
life instinct   32
life timeline   96
life writing   97, 120, 139, 152, 153, 195
live 'anchors'   66
location, form of palimpsest   60–9
Loewald, Hans   151
Lost & Found (Schulz)   167
Love in Colour (Babalola)   113
The Love Song of J. Alfred Prufrock (Eliot)   112

MacDonald, George   90
MacDonald, Helen   37
MacFarland, Robert   125
Maslow's hierarchy of needs   139–40
Matar, Hisham   201
Maté, Gabor   98
meditation   58, 69, 79
memory   1, 8, 13, 15, 17, 21, 24, 27, 33, 37, 45, 48, 55, 57, 63–6, 69, 74, 77, 79, 82, 92, 123, 124, 126, 131, 139, 151, 154, 162, 163, 174, 176, 177, 193, 194, 196–8, 200
memory of tobogganing   197
metaphors   13, 21, 25, 26, 80–9, 95, 124, 132, 134, 165, 174, 177, 186
metatextuality   131

Miller, Brenda   89
mind map   197, 198
Mintz, Steven   151
monomyth   109–10
mood board   15
mourning sickness   195
myth   20, 22, 77, 106–14, 124, 136

narrative writing   2, 20, 21, 23–5, 33, 34, 36, 37, 65, 68, 69, 75, 76, 78, 87, 110, 111, 139, 140, 153, 155, 162, 174, 186, 188, 196, 198–200
   natural starting point   12
negative capability   130, 131
nostalgia   43, 120

observation   24, 32, 38
old photographs   67–8
old 'props'   48
'One Art' (Bishop)   178
open-ended querying   130
overthinking   20, 74, 141

pantsers   85
parataxis   67
pathetic fallacy   10, 120
personal ecology   115–25
personal life writing journey   20
physical effect of writing   56
physical movement   20
physiological responses to bereavement   33
Physiologus   128
planners   85
poetic tools   169–78
Poetry Foundation   26, 178
positive thinking patterns   99
posture   132
post-writing analysis   124
The Princess and the Goblin (MacDonald)   90
prose writing   87
Proust, Marcel   64
punchline   87

'The Red-Headed League' (Holmes)   158–61
repetition/redundant phrases   34, 48, 69, 86, 134, 153, 165, 177, 186

research goals   155
The Return (Matar)   201
Richardson, Laurel   20
The Rings of Saturn (Sebald)   69
rising action   33, 37
romantic myth   20
rule of three   132

Sampson, Fiona   93
Schulz, Kathryn   167
scrapbook   15, 147
Sebald, W. G.   69
self-aspects   9
self-concept   9
self-destructive impulses   32, 76
shadowtime   120
shinrin-yoku   125
social-cognitivist theorists   9
solastalgia   120
startling imagery   86
story beats   75

Todorov, Tzvetan   24
Todorovian narrative model   53
transformational writing   13
transformations   1, 4, 76, 90–100, 160, 196
trauma   2, 3, 32, 49, 56, 74, 93, 98, 196
tricolons   132
Tzara, Tristan   84

unconscious mind   138, 139

villanelle   178
vital details   140
volta   174–6
vulnerabilities   36, 78

Wattpad   178
'We Regret to Inform You' (Miller)   89
word redemption   175
worst of times   36–7
write about something invisible   133–4
writing about grief   8, 10, 11, 21
   act of revisiting   65, 94, 188
   add cultural elements   164
   authentic dialogue   76–7
   avoid listing   68

brutal truth   44, 46, 78
build balance into the way you write   21
build intrigue   21
build your own internal safe space   45
call-backs   199
challenge yourself   154–5
cliché avoiding   85, 86, 122, 199
consistency of tone and mood   22
defy expectations   140
denouement   200
disruption   24–5
doubts and longings   153
draft creation   37
editing   187–9, 200
effects of loss   14
emotional limits   23
epiphany   200
final destination   199, 200
finding balance   165
flashbacks   66–8
follow up   25–6
forget about pleasure   22
goals   35
gratitude   196–7
happy endings   199
hypotaxis   67
immersing the reader   95
italics   153
line edit   187
live 'anchors'   66
metaphor usage   25–6
midpoint self-assessment   100–1
old photographs   67–8
overthinking   20
paragraph breaks   131
parataxis   67
paying attention to the sensations   24

paying attention to transitions   45–6
pitfall   76
play to your strengths   23
in present tense   111
primary and secondary sources gathering   152
punchy ending   164–5
quick character sketch   46
remaking   25
repetition   86
revision process   165, 186, 200
run-ons   111
selection of ending   94
sentimentality avoiding   199
set limits   152
show character through action   44
starting from an inciting incident   20, 21
start writing   20
stay on task   45
stop writing midway through a scene   23
strategic global editing   186, 189
take a walk   26
and thinking   34
tricky balancing act   21–2
uncertainty   14
uneasy truths revealing   78
worst of times   36–7
write about the present   197
write forwards   198
write from the inside out   55
write your ending   110
writing safe   35
writing schedule   201
writing the future   97–8
writing 'zone'   13

The Year of Magical Thinking (Didion)   14

www.ingramcontent.com/pod-product-compliance
Lightning Source LLC
Chambersburg PA
CBHW061300110426
42742CB00012BA/1992